THE LAST JEWS IN BERLIN

By Leonard Gross

NONFICTION

God and Freud
The Last, Best Hope
1985
The Great Wall Street Scandal
    (with Raymond L. Dirks)
The Last Jews in Berlin

FICTION

Mirror

The Last Jews in Berlin

LEONARD GROSS

CARROLL & GRAF PUBLISHERS, INC.
NEW YORK

First Carroll & Graf edition 1999

Carroll & Graf Publishers, Inc.
19 West 21st Street
New York, NY 10010-6805

Library of Congress Cataloging-in-Publication Data is available.
ISBN: 0-7867-0687-2

Manufactured in the United States of America

In memory of my father,
Benjamin Gross

AUTHOR'S NOTE

THE INTERVIEWS on which much of this book is based were actually begun a decade before I became involved. In 1967 Eric Lasher, an editor and writer, journeyed to Berlin in the hope of finding Jews who had spent the entire war in that city, for much of that time hiding from the Nazis. From reports he had read, Lasher knew such people existed. But their story had never been fully told.

Lasher advertised in a Jewish community newspaper published in Berlin. Eighteen men and women responded. He interviewed all of them, as well as other survivors to whom their stories led him. All the interviews were extensive, and all of them were taped. But Lasher was unable to continue work on the book because of personal reasons, one being that he found the material so upsetting he had developed a stammer. He reluctantly but realistically dropped the project and put the transcripts of his interviews, as well as many files of allied material, in storage.

In the early 1970s Lasher and I both moved to California with our families and settled a few miles apart on the west side of Los Angeles. We had known of one another professionally; now, as our friendship ripened, he told me of the project and of his great disappointment that it had never been completed. I wondered if I might not take on the project, and, after reading through the transcripts, volunteered to do so.

The transcripts raised more questions than they answered, but they—and corollary material I subsequently acquired— proved beyond doubt that several thousand Jews in Berlin alone had undertaken to save themselves from extinction by the Nazis.

My task, as I saw it, was to choose several representative stories from Lasher's material and develop them in great detail.

In the summer of 1978 my wife, Jacquelyn, and I flew to Berlin to try to make contact with the survivors. I was filled with foreboding. Would they still be alive, and could they be located? They had told their stories once before; would they be willing to go through that ordeal again? I proposed to lead them into emotionally charged areas that had not been developed in the initial interviews; would they agree to follow? Eleven years had passed since they had been interviewed by Eric Lasher; would their memories of those years of horror still be good, or would they be vague and distorted?

Normally, in the reconstruction of current history based primarily on eyewitness accounts, there are second and even third sources to verify the facts. But in this case, many of the events involved only the individuals themselves and were known only to them.

As I met the survivors and began to explore their stories with them, I realized that while many of the safeguards of conventional reportage might be unavailable, there were other tests of credence that could be applied. The first was plausibility: did the story I was being told ring true and did it jibe with the accounts of others who had confronted the same dangers and difficulties? The second was consistency: did the story hold together, retain its form and adhere to the same facts in the face of persistent questioning? The third was comprehensiveness: was the story large in scope and vividly recalled, and did it accord with the historical record?

As a reporter I am satisfied that I have done everything I

could possibly have done to authenticate these stories. If I have used my own reason to resolve certain inconsistencies, it has always been in accord with the canons of historical reconstruction, where there was overwhelming probability that the event occurred in the manner I recounted it. And if, in certain rare instances, I have given the benefit of the doubt to what, after all the above tests had been met, still seemed like a too miraculous account of personal survival, it was because I had learned in the course of writing this book that nothing could be more miraculous than the survival of a Jew in Berlin during the last years of World War II.

Leonard Gross

Bear Valley, California
November 1981

FOREWORD

WHEN ADOLF HITLER took power in Germany at noon on January 30, 1933, some 160,000 Jews were living in Berlin, approximately one-third of a German-Jewish population of 500,000 persons who, by and large, considered themselves at least as German as they were Jewish. During World War I there had been no more loyal German subjects than the Jews, but by September 1, 1939, when World War II began, the Jewish population had been cut in half. Mostly this was a result of the emigration of Jews fleeing the physical and economic abuses that had become endemic in the Third Reich, but to some extent it was a consequence of the suicides, disappearances and murders that were the harbingers of destruction not only for the Jews remaining in Germany but for somewhere between 4,000,000 and 5,500,000 other Jews inhabiting lands overrun by the German blitzkrieg.

Exactly how many Jews were murdered during the Holocaust may never be known, but the Nazis' genocide itself is the best documented crime in history. The manner in which they proposed to exterminate these Jews had evolved over several years through a series of orders and experiments, culminating in a conference held in January 1942, in a suburb of Berlin called Wannsee, to coordinate the efforts of the various agencies involved. The conference, convened by Hitler, was presided over by Reinhard Heydrich, chief of the Security Service and deputy chief of the Geheime Staatspolizei, or Gestapo, the Secret State Police. The minutes of the meeting, attended by second-level state and party functionaries, were written by Karl Adolf Eichmann, who served under Heydrich as supervisor of the Reich Center for Jewish Emigration. At the meeting Heydrich reviewed the essentials of Nazi policy, carefully avoiding such words as "killing" or "extermination" or "liquidation." The Jews would continue to be "resettled" in slave-labor camps in conquered lands, principally Poland, where the weak among them would be eliminated immediately and the stronger would be worked until they dropped, at which point they too would be eliminated. The only Jews to receive special treatment would be those born in Germany who were now over sixty-five, those who had received the highest honors for service in World War I, invalids, Jewish officials, and Jews so prominent that their disappearance might somehow compromise the Reich. These "privileged" Jews could be sent to Theresienstadt, an old Bohemian town, where a model ghetto had been constructed to contain them as well as demonstrate Germany's "humanity" to the outside world. As things worked out, Theresienstadt proved too small to contain all the Jews who were shipped there, and many were ultimately sent to Auschwitz and their deaths.

Numbers of extermination methods had been tried, but the one the Nazis finally settled on had been developed between December 1939 and August 1941, when some 50,000 mentally deficient or disturbed Germans were gassed to death in rooms designed as public showers. Those deaths had aroused much anguish among the public, although the only outcry was contained in bitter allusions that appeared in death notices in the press. The same men who had conducted the "mercy killings" program in Germany were sent to the east to build the mass extermination facilities, and the gassings in the east began soon after they had ended in Germany.

One feature of the "Final Solution"—the Nazis' euphemism

for extermination of the Jews—was paramount and underlay the discussions at Wannsee. The actual killing of the Jews was to be top secret, in order to avoid, or at least minimize, resistance among the victims and objections by the German people, as well as by neutral nations. One measure of the Nazis' success in disguising their intentions was the response of the Jews themselves. Many being "resettled" followed the Nazis' suggestions and brought their remaining valuables with them, which the Nazis of course confiscated after the owners had been put to death.

While the Final Solution envisioned the annihilation of Jews throughout Europe, a special, proprietary interest was reserved for the Jews of Germany. None of the German Jews were targeted with greater enthusiasm than the Jews of Berlin, whose political, economic, artistic, social and simple physical presence had for so long been anathema to the ranking Nazis.

By 1941 almost half the Jews remaining in Germany were congregated in Berlin, to some extent as a consequence of local "actions" that had ousted them from smaller communities, but principally because of their desire to seek strength in numbers and anonymity in the largest of Germany's cities. The metropolitan area of Berlin contained nearly four million people. Geographically the city was as complex as it was spacious. It contained two distinct centers, the official one at the Unter den Linden, with its government buildings, triumphal arch, museums, opera house and embassies, and the commercial one at the head of the Kurfürstendamm, where hotels, shops, cafes and theaters were clustered around the Memorial Church. Within the city's boundaries were dozens of distinctive neighborhoods and commercial areas, as well as manufacturing centers. Rivers and canals wound throughout the city, connecting with many lakes. There were parks throughout the city and forests along its edges—all in all, a promising area for anyone who wished to lose himself or herself in the terrain or the crowd.

But to the Jews who inhabited Berlin during the Nazi era the city was more than a place. It was a state of mind—more civilized and sophisticated, and less swayed by the Nazis than any other municipality. On balance, Berlin was politically liberal; since 1900 it had voted Social Democratic in every election in which it had been free to do so. Culturally, the Berliners' position in the national consciousness was akin to that of New Yorkers in the United States. They tended to view the rest of the country as a suburb of Berlin. Out-of-towners, in turn, thought the Berliners arrogant and perverse; they resented their argumentativeness and independence, their proximity to power, their tolerance of bohemian life-styles. To Hitler, Berlin was "that sinful Babel." He despised it, a fact he never tried to hide, and it made him uncomfortable as well. Whenever he visited the city in the days before he took power, he always brought his bodyguards, the Schutzstaffel, or S.S., with him. Above all, Hitler resented the city's relative lack of ardor for his cause. Joseph Goebbels was said to have been so disturbed by this that he would order storm troopers to disguise themselves as civilians and cheer his own procession through the city's streets. There was certainly no visible enthusiasm among the city's population in September 1939, when World War II began.

As for the Jews, for all of the evil that had emanated from Berlin's ruling legions, the city was not the center of their hell during the first years of the Third Reich. Persecutions—including random and quasi-official acts of violence and even murder—had begun much earlier and had been much more severe in Germany's towns than they had been in the larger cities. Partly this was due to the presence of more varied and sophisticated populations in the larger cities. Partly it was because the Nazis themselves had to be more circumspect in the large cities lest they call attention, particularly in the foreign press, to their acts against the Jews. This was especially true of Berlin, the nation's capital, where the diplomatic corps and foreign press were assembled.

But by late 1941, when only friendly observers remained, the Nazis could operate more openly. By then the Jews of Germany had been forced like cattle from the outlying regions into city tenements that were the equivalent of stock pens. The shipment of Jews to slaughterhouses in the east was the penultimate step in the extermination process.

Although there had been one instance in October of 1940 when hundreds of Berlin Jews had been arrested and sent off to Poland, full-scale systematic deportations did not occur until exactly one year later. On October 18, 1941, the first transport of 1,000 Jews from Berlin was dispatched to Auschwitz. Over the next ten weeks another twenty-five transports left the city, each carrying about 1,000 Jews. By the spring of 1942 the dispatch of Jews, conducted with the same brisk efficiency that had characterized Germany's conquest of most of Europe, had reduced Berlin's Jewish population to a quarter of its original number. The process would have gone even faster but for the army, which insisted that those Jews employed in war work should remain on their jobs until adequate replacements could be found. For one member of the Nazi hierarchy, however, the continued presence of Jews in the capital of the Third Reich was insufferable.

Dr. Joseph Goebbels, the Nazis' forty-five-year-old Minister of Propaganda, a diminutive but flamboyant man whose physical handicap—his left leg was shorter than his right—had diverted his boundless energy to intellectual pursuits, was the most fervent ideologue of the Third Reich. It has been said that Goebbels' cause was revolution itself, that had a Communist of Hitler's genius come to power in Germany, Goebbels would have taken up his cause. Whatever the case, Goebbels had become, in the course of his twenty years with Hitler, at least as impassioned an anti-Semite as his leader, embracing the objective of Jewish destruction with religious zeal and pursuing its commission in every way he could.

In addition to his other duties Goebbels was the Gauleiter of Berlin, the official in charge of that political district. As such he felt particularly humiliated. Here he was, one of the principal exponents of the Final Solution, and his own district had not yet been made *Judenfrei*. On May 11, 1942, he noted in the diary that he kept faithfully, regardless of the press of events: "There are still 40,000 Jews in Berlin and despite the heavy blows dealt them they are still insolent and aggressive. It is exceedingly difficult to shove them off to the East because a large part of them are at work in the munitions industry and because the Jews are to be evacuated only by families." Six days later he wrote: "We must try to evacuate all the Jews now in Berlin. This is a thing which is unbearable. The cause is that there are many Jewish people in armament. Their families can't be evacuated. I can try to get the order canceled, and will try to get all Jewish people not in industry to be deported."

In this one instance the Nazis' propaganda minister was as good as his word. Through the summer he pressed Hitler for permission to deport the Jews. Hitler was sympathetic, but he was meeting resistance from other ministers, most notably Albert Speer, Minister of Armaments and War Production. Speer's reservations were practical, not moral. He considered the deportations a form of national self-destruction. The electrical industry, in particular, he argued, required not just bodies but intelligent workers; the Jews were the most intelligent workers available.

As fall began, the argument ripened. Hitler had summoned armaments industry experts to a two-day conference beginning September 20, at Wolfsschanze, his underground headquarters in a somber forest outside Rastenburg, East Prussia. The conference had been called to discuss the prosecution of the war, which for the Third Reich, up to that point, could scarcely have gone better. In its quest for Lebensraum for the German people, the Reich—following bloodless conquests of Austria and Czechoslovakia—had won lightning victories in Poland, France, Belgium, Holland, Denmark, Norway and Greece. Its thunderous tanks and agile Luftwaffe had made deep inroads into the Soviet Union, seizing Estonia, Latvia and Lithuania in the process; it had swept through Tunisia and Libya, driven into Egypt, and defeated all but a handful of partisans in Yugoslavia. Italian, Hungarian, Rumanian and Bulgarian troops were fighting alongside the German forces, and in the Pacific, Germany's ally, Japan, had an unprepared United States reeling. It was a time when Hitler could well afford to turn his attention to the other great objective of his Reich, the annihilation of the Jews. As the conference at Wolfsschanze neared an end, Hitler himself brought up the question of the remaining Jews in Berlin. He asked Fritz Sauckel, the head of the Third Reich's forced-labor program, whether he could replace the Jews with qualified workers if the Jews were deported.

"Let me have access to the new supplies of laborers," Sauckel said, "and I see no problem in filling these jobs."

Hitler then turned to Speer. "What do you want more than this?" he asked. "You have nothing to complain about."

What can I do? Speer thought. The responsibility was no longer his.

On September 30 Goebbels wrote triumphantly in his diary: "The Fuehrer expressed his decision that the Jewish people under all circumstances have to be taken out of Berlin. What the industrialists say about the fine work of the Jews doesn't impress me. Now all the Jews are praised for the high quality of their work. Always arguments are raised to keep them. But the Jews are not so irreplaceable as the intellectuals say. We can get 250,000 foreign workers. The Jews can easily be replaced by foreign workers. The Jews' fine work will always be the argument of the Semitophiles."

Over the next five months deportations and deaths, many of them suicides, diminished Berlin's 40,000 surviving Jews—one-quarter of the city's pre-Nazi-era Jewish population—by a third. Rumors spread among the Jews by *Mundfunk* (literally "mouthcast," but a play on *Rundfunk,* which means "broadcast") spoke of a massive roundup, but no one knew when it would happen, and many Jews refused to believe that it would happen at all, arguing that they were indispensable to the Germans.

They were wrong.

Early on the morning of February 27, 1943, units of Hitler's elite corps, the S.S., undertook a lightning roundup of Berlin's remaining Jews. Code name for the roundup was *Fabrik Aktion*—Operation Factory.

On March 2 Goebbels entered a mixed review of the operation in his diary: "We are definitely now pushing the Jews out of Berlin. They were suddenly rounded up last Saturday, and are to be carted off to the East as quickly as possible. Unfortunately our better circles, especially the intellectuals, once again have failed to understand our policy about the Jews and in some cases have even taken their part. As a result our plans were tipped off prematurely, so that a lot of Jews slipped through our hands. But we will catch them yet. I certainly won't rest until the capital of the Reich, at least, has become free of Jews."

But by March 11 it had become apparent to Goebbels just how difficult a job that would be: "The scheduled arrest of all Jews on one day has proven a flash in the pan because of the shortsighted behavior of industrialists who warned the Jews in time. We therefore failed to lay our hands on about 4,000. They are now wandering about Berlin without homes, are not registered with police and are naturally quite a public danger. I ordered the police, Wehrmacht, and the Party to do everything possible to round these Jews up as quickly as practicable."

Goebbels was wrong on two counts. First, the Jews who had slipped through the Nazis' hands had not all done so on February 27. Many had been "underground" for months. Second, while some of the Jews were wandering homeless about the city, those who had anticipated the deportations were sequestered in rooms, apartments, homes, shacks, offices and even stores—most often by the grace of Gentile friends and even strangers, sometimes as a consequence of their own ingenuity.

In any case, the hunt for the last Jews in Berlin was on.

I

DOWN TO
DARKNESS

1

HE WAS HANDSOME: his face was full and smooth and stamped with self-acceptance. But when he was angry it could be a tough face, the mouth set, the jaw pronounced, the eyes hinting at the intractable presence waiting behind his composure. Fritz Croner had publicly cursed the Nazis when they'd first appeared in Deutsch-Krone, the small, picture-postcard German town where he'd grown up. But after the Nazis had come to power he continued his life as though they didn't exist. He was the richest young man in town, with a Fiat limousine and a BMW motorcycle, the biggest one made in Germany, and he loved nothing more than to gun the motorcycle over the rutted roads of the tiny villages, trying to get from Deutsch-Krone to Berlin, 150 miles to the southwest, in under three hours. When he traveled he paid no attention to the signs that said Jews were forbidden entry to restaurants and hotels. He ate and stayed where he pleased.

Even in 1939, when life for Germany's Jews had become all but impossible, Fritz and his wife, Marlitt, went regularly to tea dances at the fashionable Eden Hotel. Fritz had met Marlitt Gelber one day in April 1936 in Sipnow when he and some friends were touring the countryside on their motorcycles to see how other Jewish families were getting along. Marlitt happened to be leaning out of her window, a stunning young woman with blond hair and blue eyes, the typically German looks that had always attracted Fritz. She was three months Fritz's junior, and—all the more ideal—she had been reared in an Orthodox Jewish home. He had coffee in the Gelber home but did not spend time with Marlitt that day because she was in mourning for her mother. When the period of mourning ended he returned to Sipnow regularly. He found Marlitt to be a quiet and private person, which was very much to his liking. Within a few months they knew that they would eventually marry—and they did in March of 1939. The ceremony was performed by an Orthodox rabbi, with all their relatives in attendance. Fritz and Marlitt said goodbye to the wedding party at 9:00 P.M. and went to the Eden for a drink at the bar. Thereafter, no matter how difficult their circumstances, they went regularly to the theater and cinema. They were young and determined to live.

They looked German, which helped their masquerade. Marlitt, especially, had exactly the structure and coloring the Nazis extolled in their propaganda in behalf of the "master race." Fritz's appearance was not so singular; you would never suspect him of being Jewish, but once you learned that he was, you wouldn't be surprised. It was his attitude that transformed him: although he was a devout Jew who even observed the dietary laws, he felt German to his marrow. To family and friends, who were aghast at the chances he took, he would say, "Look, I'm part of this country. No one has the right to push me out. I don't allow anyone to tell me what I can't do. I'm German."

To Fritz, German identity was his not simply by right of birth but by virtue of historical fact. Deutsch-Krone, his birthplace, was in the northeast corner of Germany, not far from the Polish border. No one knew exactly how long the Croner family had lived in this flat, lush lake country, with its harsh winters and miraculous summers, but there were indications that it had been centuries. Five hundred years before, "Krone" had been spelled with a *C*, and the Croners believed that their ancestors had adopted the name of the town. Fritz's great-grandfather, born in 1804, was buried in Deutsch-Krone's Jewish cemetery, proof to the Croners that their roots descended at least to the eighteenth century. However deep they were, they supported a substantial presence. Fritz's father, Willy Croner, was Deutsch-Krone's leading merchant, as proud of the Iron Cross he had won for service in World War I as he was of his officer's post in the synagogue. A leg wound had crippled him so badly that he had to use a cane, but his limp was, if anything, further proof of his devotion to the fatherland. Fritz's maternal grandfather had also been wounded in service to his country during the Franco-Prussian War. He subsequently became the president of a disabled veterans' group as well as a city official, and when he died, several hundred townspeople, half of them Gentile, came to the Jewish cemetery, where his comrades fired a volley over his grave.

That was Fritz's real birthright: a sense that he belonged. What forces had conspired to give the Jews of Deutsch-Krone such a vivid feeling of permanence Fritz never knew. It was a fact of life he accepted, and until the coming of the Nazis it had never been challenged. As a child he had played in the homes of his Gentile friends, and they in his. He had never had troubles with his classmates, nor had he ever heard an anti-Semitic remark.

There were 300 Jews in and around Deutsch-Krone, out of a population of 12,000. Except for the time and manner of their worship, nothing set them apart from the rest of the community. They were totally comfortable, accepted without question in all aspects of community life. Anti-Semitic episodes flared from time to time among a fringe element of the population, but these activities were disavowed by the majority and had no impact on the lives of the Croners or on any other Jewish residents.

By the standards of Deutsch-Krone, the Croners were rich. Their clothing-and-textiles store was the most prosperous in the community. Willy Croner was extremely active in Deutsch-Krone's Jewish life, but he mixed as easily with non-Jews as with Jews. He was not much interested in politics, and neither was his son. They were partial to the Social Democrats but, until the coming of the National Socialists, not in the least bit active. That changed on March 31, 1931, the first day that the Nazis of Deutsch-Krone went public. Wearing their brown shirts and swastikas, they marched to the memorial to the sons of Deutsch-Krone who had fallen in World War I. While members of the other political parties hooted, the Nazis laid wreaths with swastikas attached to them at the foot of the memorial. "Death to the Jews!" they chanted.

"Death to Hitler!" someone shouted from the crowd. It was Fritz, eyes glowering and compressed to tiny apertures.

Several hours later he was picked up by the police, charged with disturbing the peace, and warned that such outbursts would not be tolerated in the future. Later that day he was released.

By the end of 1932 it had become obvious that more and more members of the community were beginning to support the Nazis. The population of Deutsch-Krone was largely Protestant, and the Protestants had a greater tendency to affiliate with the Nazis than the Catholics.

By this time Fritz had become, if not a political activist, an aggressive anti-Nazi. At night he would help the Social Democrats affix their campaign signs to walls and posts around the town and tear down the signs of the Nazis. Inevitably there were clashes with the Nazis, and Fritz did his share of the fighting, a fact that disturbed his father, who thought the Nazis should be scorned rather than fought.

Fritz and his father were in agreement on one matter as 1933 arrived. They both felt that the only way to get rid of Hitler was to let him come to power, so that he could demonstrate his incompetence. The trouble in the streets, especially for Jews, had reached serious proportions; better, they said, to have an end with terror than terror without end.

But what had gone before was as nothing compared to the persecutions that began the moment Hitler became Chancellor on January 30. What surprised Fritz so much was the resentment that underlay the acts. They were motivated not by policy but by jealousy of Willy Croner's wealth and his son's popularity with the prettiest Gentile girls. Still, these people baring their hostility were not from the society in which the Croners had moved; they were the little people now suddenly able to hit back at those in the town whose success had festered in their minds.

A favorite target of the Nazis' persecutions was a thirty-year-old Jew named Salinger, who stood six feet six inches tall; it seemed to give them special satisfaction to humble a man so big. Early in February, Salinger was sent to a concentration camp at Hammerstein, about twenty miles from Deutsch-Krone, along with a number of other Jews and several Communists. A few days later word came back that Salinger had died in the camp. His body was returned to his family; it was Willy Croner's duty, as an officer of the temple's burial society, to prepare Salinger for interment. It took only one look at the marks covering Salinger's body to know he had been beaten to death.

Even then Willy Croner would not listen to any talk of emigration. Salinger's death had shaken him badly, but he saw it as a single case and the work of hotheads just come to power. It was imperative now more than ever to see these Nazis for what they were—opportunists outside the German mainstream, hornets who would plant their stingers and die.

A national boycott of Jewish shops decreed by the Nazis on April 1 reinforced Willy Croner's conviction. It passed uneventfully in Deutsch-Krone. Party members assigned to stand in front of the stores and warn shoppers away felt awkward and embarrassed. The Jewish shop owners solved everyone's discomfort by closing their stores at noon.

For a year and a half now Fritz had been learning the textile business. But it seemed increasingly evident to him—if not to his father—that his chances of one day taking over the store were slim. He decided to learn another profession. Goldsmithing had always interested him. He began to make the simplest kind of jewelry and to learn the business end of the trade. He quickly realized that he was a better businessman than craftsman. By the end of 1933 he was making more and more trips to Berlin to trade in jewels. Within another year his time was almost equally divided between Deutsch-Krone, where he helped his parents with the business, and Berlin, developing his new contacts.

Each time he returned to Deutsch-Krone he found it more difficult to maintain his old relationships with non-Jewish friends. One day, walking on the street, he saw a friend named Hans Beckmann with whom he had gone through school. Beckmann was wearing the uniform of a Wehrmacht officer. Thinking he would spare his friend the difficulty of having to deal with him in public, Fritz looked the other way. But Beckmann hailed him.

"Aren't you asking for trouble?" Fritz said when Beckmann came up to him.

"I really don't care," Beckmann said. "I'm glad to see you. I want to talk to you. I'm doing this deliberately. It's my way of advertising that I don't accept the strictures against the Jews."

But that encounter, in 1937, was the only offer of moral support Fritz received.

Almost ten years had passed since the Nazi seizure of power had tapped a reservoir of ill will against the Jews. The family store had been taken and the family pushed from Deutsch-Krone, and no Gentile friends had come forward to protest. Fritz's father, Willy, was now making gun barrels in a Berlin munitions factory, and Fritz was working on a railroad gang at forced labor for a few pennies an hour. The malevolence of the early years of Nazi power was, in retrospect, mere practice for the horrors that had since transpired. The horror of horrors had been "Crystal Night," the night of November 9–10, when Nazis throughout Germany had arisen in retaliation against the Jews for the murder, in Paris, of a young German diplomat by a Polish-German Jew.

In Berlin, Fritz had watched the Nazis burn the synagogues, rip the Torah scrolls and plunder the Torah silver, smash windows and loot the Jewish shops, feeling completely detached from what he was witnessing, as though it was an aberration that had nothing to do with him. He was German and rational; what he was watching was not German, because it wasn't rational—Polish or Russian, perhaps, because Poland and Russia had had pogroms, but not German, because there had been no pogroms in Germany, where law and order prevailed.

Fritz's feeling that he was not part of what he was seeing held through the next day as the looting continued and police arrested thousands of Jewish men—a warning, in the wake of the shooting in Paris, that no Jew should ever again touch a German—and Fritz received word of what had transpired in Deutsch-Krone. Had he been there instead of in Berlin, he would surely be dead, because a gang of young men had marched to the Croner home, not knowing it had been confiscated, intent on seizing Fritz and stringing him up on a gallows they had constructed especially for him—the final act of retribution against the richest young man in town.

Fritz had been determined never to leave Germany, but to stand and fight instead, because Germany was his as much as it was anyone's, and if he left it to the rabble, there would be no Germany left. But this was no longer his Germany, and so, one day late in 1938, he had gone to the Aliyah office for emigration to Palestine and filed his application, along with one for Marlitt. Several times a week he would join the crowds at the Meinekestrasse office to see how his visa was coming. The signs were promising. Finally the Croners' applications were approved. Fritz had already deposited several thousand dollars in a bank in Amsterdam in anticipation of their emigration. Now he and Marlitt packed their clothes and shipped them to Palestine, along with his motorcycle and some furniture.

On March 20, 1939, the Croners received notice to be at the depot that evening to take a train to Marseilles, where they were to board an illegal transport. But two hours later another caller advised them that there was no place for them on this transport after all. They would receive word of a new passage within a few days. Fritz and Marlitt rushed to the Palestine office to protest. They pointed out that they had already shipped their possessions and were almost without funds. Each day they were told to return the following day. Finally Fritz bluffed; he said that he had no more money. The bluff didn't work; the office refunded his passage money. They were off the lists.

Fritz and Marlitt suspected that the officials at the Palestine office had been putting their own relatives and friends on the ships. Nonetheless they told each other, "It's happening for the best." In truth, they had not wanted to emigrate. In spite of everything, they still felt German. They felt that somehow they would get along.

How wrong they had been, they now knew. On September 1, 1941, the Nazis had ordered all Jews older than six to wear a Star of David over their hearts as of September 19. It was a yellow star outlined in black and embroidered with the word *Jude*. Jews had been crammed together into apartments, sometimes more than twenty to a room. They were forbidden to leave their districts without permission or to be outdoors after evening curfew hours—policies whose underlying purpose became clear once the deportations began. Not only had the Jewish cattle been branded for easy identification, they had been penned into stockades where their captors could cut them out of the herd for the trip to the slaughterhouse.

In January 1942, Jews were ordered to surrender all their winter coats, warm clothing and blankets, which were then shipped to German troops at the Russian front. By early 1942 all Jewish households were required to post Stars of David on their doors. Jews were banned from public streets on which government buildings were located, as well as from the great shopping streets such as the Kurfürstendamm. Jews could not ride public transportation, except under special circumstances, or use public rest rooms. They could not use public telephones.

They were restricted to certain yellow benches in the parks, and eventually barred from the parks altogether. On May 15, 1942, Jews were ordered to surrender their pets. Soon thereafter they were deprived of all electric appliances, cameras, typewriters, bicycles and other objects of convenience. And in July blind and deaf Jews were ordered to cease wearing armlets identifying them as handicapped. Jews had to give up their telephones and radios and could not buy newspapers or periodicals. Jewish children had long since been banned from German schools; now Jewish schools were closed and Jewish children prohibited from taking private classes. Jews were no longer permitted to purchase tobacco, nor were they permitted to buy milk, eggs, fish, smoked meats, cheese, spirits or—if by some miracle they could scrape up the money—such delicacies as cake or even white bread. The list kept expanding until all that was left for the Jews were potatoes, coarse black bread—less than one pound per week, a fifth of that allotted to non-Jews—cabbage and beets, and not a good selection at that, because they could shop only between four and five in the afternoon after the food had been well picked over.

To nourish his baby daughter, Lane, born to him and Marlitt in 1941, Fritz Croner was paying a fortune for black market food. Staying alive in Berlin had become an all-consuming, day-to-day struggle, but that was as nothing compared to the prospect of deportation. Neighbors and fellow workers had already gone; their own turn could come any day.

It was a set of circumstances that had already broken the spirit of thousands of Jews and driven many of them to suicide. But, miraculously, Fritz Croner still possessed those same qualities that in the early days had helped him stare down the Nazis: toughness, resilience, an almost sublime sense of his ability to survive. He knew that one day his family would have to go underground. "To live in the underground you have to have money, money, money—and connections," he would say. And so he had acquired both. In spite of the improbable odds, he had managed—in the few hours left to him each day after his forced labor at the railroad yard—to carry on a thriving trade in precious stones and had already accumulated cash and jewelry.

He had many clients. As German currency continued to lose its value, the value of jewelry rose. People who had never owned jewelry now bought it. Much of the buying was done in the larger stores, but those stores relied on go-betweens such as Fritz Croner to keep them supplied with merchandise. A large store would ask him if he could find a good one-karat stone. He would comb the smaller stores and the wares of private gem dealers until he found what he wanted at a good price. Then he would sell the stone to the larger store. In this manner he could earn hundreds of marks—sometimes in a single day. There were days when he walked the streets with five thousand dollars' worth of jewelry in his pockets.

Not even the order to wear Jewish stars on their clothes starting September 19, 1941, put a crimp in Fritz's business. Marlitt pinned the stars to their clothes; they would wear the stars when they walked the streets of their neighborhood, but remove them as soon as they left its boundaries. What they were doing was strictly illegal, and they knew it, but they had made plans for any challenge.

One day in December 1941 a policeman appeared at their apartment. He said that an anonymous informant had denounced both of them for failing to wear their stars.

"Your informant doesn't know what he's talking about," Fritz said. "Here, look." He showed the policeman two coats on which Marlitt had securely sewn the stars—and which they always left on hooks by the door. The policeman tugged at the stars, shrugged and departed. The Croners never saw him again.

But it was episodes like these that made Fritz realize that going underground was inevitable. He was sure that events would tell him when the day was at hand. On the morning of December 3, 1942, he went as usual to his job at the railroad yard; there two Jewish colleagues showed him notices they had received from the Jewish community headquarters ordering them to remain at home that day for "statistical reasons." The only statistical reasons Fritz could imagine would be those supplied by the Gestapo, which, periodically since October 1941, had required the Jewish community to supply a specified number of Jews for "resettlement."

Fritz said nothing to his fellow workers. He watched them present their notices to the foreman, who excused them to go home. Then he approached the foreman. "I received the same notice," he said. His bluff worked; the foreman didn't ask to see the notice. Instead, with a nod and a wave and what Fritz suspected was a knowing look, he excused him for the day.

Two hours after he had left for work Fritz was back home. Marlitt had just put Lane down for her nap. At the sight of her husband she paled.

"It's time," he said simply.

Marlitt nodded. Then she immediately began to hide clothing and provisions for Lane in the baby carriage. Their own clothing would be left behind. The only possessions they would take with them were the jewels Fritz had guarded for this moment. These too would be hidden in the baby's carriage.

The next problem to solve concerned Fritz's family. (Marlitt's father and two sisters had managed to emigrate to Shanghai several years before.) Fritz sent word to his parents and his uncle, his mother's brother, to come to his apartment at seven o'clock that evening, an hour before the curfew for Jews. Then he set out for the apartment of a Frau Kosimer, a woman of seventy he had met through a stateless Russian-born jeweler named Makarow. The distance was less than a mile, normally a pleasant ten-minute walk along tree-lined streets whose buildings had not yet been hit by the bombs. Today Fritz felt as if he could make the journey in less than half that time. But while anxiety urged him on, prudence restrained his gait. He knew that his behavior mustn't seem abnormal to anyone who observed him.

Frau Kosimer was a widow who had been living in Berlin since 1938. Her husband, a Jew, had been killed when the Germans occupied Austria in March of that year. She had moved to Berlin to be near her best friend. The authorization she brought with her noted that she was Catholic, and accordingly her resettlement was accepted without question.

For several years now Fritz and the Russian Makarow had been using Frau Kosimer's apartment as a rendezvous where they could trade jewels in private and had been paying Frau Kosimer for the privilege. Their business had always been conducted in the late afternoon or early evening, so when she saw him at her doorway at this early hour, the thin lines in her angular face, more youthful than her years, deepened into creases. Months before, when the deportations had quickened, Frau Kosimer had quietly told Fritz Croner that if he ever needed a temporary refuge her home was at his disposal.

"We're in danger," Fritz said now. "We've got to leave our apartment." He tried to mask his anxiety, but he could hear it in his voice. Frau Kosimer was his only hope. It was not simply that he and his family would be without a place to go if in the interval she had changed her mind, it was the burden he was placing on another human being. Gentiles who helped Jews in any way—the Nazis called them *Judenknechte,* lackeys of the Jews—whether they were friends of those they assisted or merchants or public officials, faced fines, imprisonment or even death.

If the thought of danger to herself crossed Frau Kosimer's mind, it did not reveal itself in her response. "Then you must come here," she said at once.

Early that evening Fritz informed his parents and uncle that he, Marlitt and the baby were going underground. They were appalled. Nothing the Germans could do to them seemed as horrible as the strain and tension of living illegally. They couldn't imagine living without the papers that, in Nazi Germany, were as necessary to life as food—identity cards, residence permits, work permits, cards that permitted them to buy food and clothing and to walk in the streets, even a postal identification card that enabled them to collect mail. Unexpressed, and yet part of their reaction, was a resistance, as well-bred Germans, to the idea of living with fraudulent papers. History and experience attached a premium to obedience; in Germany one did not walk on the grass, whether a sign proscribed it or not.

Fritz argued that their only chance for survival was in going underground, but he knew that he wasn't being persuasive. Illegality was a young person's game and his parents and uncle were too old to play it. It would demand strong nerves and physical stamina. There would be the constant need to move about; how would his father manage with his crippled leg? And being underground would also demand a meticulous attention to detail, for which none of them had demonstrated the patience. When the Nazis required all Jews to turn in their gold, silver and jewels, it was Fritz, not the others, who had gone to observe the process. Seeing that the receipts listed the items and quantity—"one watch," "two rings"—but not a description or estimate of value, Fritz had turned in only his inferior pieces and held the good ones back.

There was, finally, the expense of living underground. Whereas Fritz had been working and hoarding jewels for just this moment, neither his parents nor his uncle had any such resources.

One matter was unexpressed but weighed on all their minds. For months now Fritz had been supplying his parents and uncle with much of their food. As an "illegal" he would be hard put to support his wife and child. Most of his money would be spent on rent for hiding places.

Fritz promised his family that he would get in touch with them the moment he had relocated. As soon as they had said goodbye, he and Marlitt took a careful inventory of their clothing, selecting what they knew might have to last them for the duration of the war. Fritz chose the long leather coat, leather trousers and boots that were a holdover from his motorcycling days. Marlitt chose her most practical dress and warmest coat. As soon as they were ready, they walked from their apartment as though they were taking the baby for a stroll. It seemed to both of them that they were escaping from a prison; from this moment forward they would be hunted fugitives.

That night they slept in armchairs in Frau Kosimer's apartment. Lane, one year and four months old, slept in her carriage. The next morning Makarow, Fritz's jeweler friend, found them a flat on Prinzregentenstrasse in Wilmersdorf, a centrally located residential district. The flat had been occupied by Jews who had just been deported. It had no furniture and no cooking facilities. The caretaker, whom Fritz knew, told him he could have the apartment only until January 1, 1943, when a non-Jewish family would be moving in. It was a common enough story. The Third Reich had put far more effort into armaments than it had into housing, and the bombings, even at this point, had made an already severe housing shortage so critical that the deportation of Jews had created welcome possibilities for thousands of cramped non-Jewish families. Not only was the Croners' sanctuary a temporary one but the cost would be four hundred marks, fourteen times what Fritz had been earning per month at the railroad yard. He was staggered. Even with his black market transactions, how long could they last at these prices?

But Fritz didn't voice his doubts to Marlitt. He was determined that they would make it. This was their moment of life and no one would take it from them. No one, but no one, would send them from Berlin.

2

HANS HIRSCHEL was a scholar and author whose writing had been likened to Thomas Mann's. Before the Nazi regime he had edited and published an avant-garde literary magazine called *Three Corners,* whose format was a triangle and whose existence was attributable to the postwar explosion of German creativity that had caused Berlin to be considered the equal of Paris in the esteem of progressive intellectuals. As a member of Berlin's bohemian elite, Hirschel reveled in the discussions that questioned long-held moral assumptions in public and private life. Never a practicing Jew—he had not even been bar-mitzvahed—he nonetheless took a strong, if critical, interest in religion, and had an impressive academic background in theology as well as philosophy. His dissertation, "The Diabolic in Religion," presented at the University of Freiburg, had caused chaos among the faculty with its thesis that every religious movement inevitably created its own evil concomitant.

Hirschel's weakness in these ominous times was his excessive tolerance and good nature. Even when the faculty rejected the dissertation he refused to become bitter, and although Germany's universities were notoriously anti-Semitic, he would not attribute his rejection to prejudice. He believed uncritically in people's goodness and was forever trying to put himself in others' situations in order to understand their behavior. He refused to take what happened to him personally and treated adversity with detachment. One winter day in the late 1930s he spent twelve hours at forced labor clearing snow from the Kaiserallee. As exhausted as he was the evening, he refused to see the evil of it, saying, "The guards were quite friendly."

There were ways, however, in which Hirschel was well suited to the fugitive life he had been leading since February of 1942. He was, to begin with, extremely adaptable. Born to one of Berlin's first Jewish families, he had lived much of his life in a grand apartment on the very Kaiserallee where he would later work as a slave—an irony that was not lost on him. As an underground Jew he was living in simple circumstances in a small ground-floor flat, cooking for himself and doing his own housework. And then there was his equanimity. Whereas some Jews gave themselves away by their timid manner, looking left and right as though they were afraid of being caught, Hans, tall and thin, with chiseled features punctuated by high-set ears, always seemed calm and relaxed as he walked through the streets, a pleasant smile on his face. For months after he went illegal he would stroll his old neighborhood in daylight, despite the fact that any healthy-looking man in his early forties and out of uniform was suspect. But his self-assurance seemed to dispel the possibility that something was wrong.

Occasionally he flirted dangerously with trouble, putting much greater stock in his "disguise"—a growth of beard and dark glasses—than it warranted, given his singular physique. One day he would stroll by his old tennis club, where Nazi party members now played; another day he would get a haircut at a barber shop that was known to be a favorite hunting ground for S.S. patrols looking for "illegal" Jews. His worst transgression occurred when, sauntering into the Heidelberger Platz, he chanced upon an old family friend, Hannes Kupper, a stage manager in civilian life who was now in the army and had come to Berlin to arrange for shows for the troops. Kupper gasped when he saw him. "My God," he whispered, "what are you doing in Berlin? I figured you'd either been killed or made it to England."

"Oh, no. I'm quite okay," Hans replied. "I'm living with Marushka."

Kupper cut him off. "For God's sake, man, don't tell me where you live." The point did not need elaboration; as long as Kupper didn't have the information, no one could force it from him.

It had been a stupid indiscretion that not only compromised Kupper but jeopardized Hans and the woman who was hiding him. For a while he was too ashamed to tell her what had happened, but when his conscience forced it from him, she became enraged and demanded that he never again go out without her.

Given his dependent circumstances, it was fortunate for Hirschel that he was accustomed to strong women. He had been raised by a dominating mother; his benefactress, the Countess Maria von Maltzan, was even more overpowering. The descendant of an old, noble Swedish family that had migrated to north Germany centuries before, Maria von Maltzan—Marushka to Hans—was a striking woman whom men found irresistible. "Emancipation" was not a word that would have occurred to her; she had never recognized the supposed inferiority of women, and she was as strong as many men her size and a good deal more active. She was trained in judo, rode horses like a jockey and could swim for miles. She had slim hips and walked with a man's gait, but she was also feminine enough to enjoy wearing dresses that showed off her well shaped legs.

She had met Hirschel in 1939 at a soirée given by the proprietress of a boarding school that she had once attended, and from whom Hans had once taken English lessons. She was thirty, Hans was thirty-nine. She was more quick-witted, but he had greater experience and knowledge, and the fact that he was Jewish appealed to her immensely. The wide streak of daring in her complemented her loathing of the Nazis, so that in associating with a Jew in direct violation of the Nazis' racial laws she was demonstrating her defiance.

Whatever symbolic value the relationship had for them soon became unimportant; they fell quickly and genuinely in love. But although they were lovers, they didn't live together—partly out of prudence, partly out of deference to Hans's mother who was terrified at the prospect of her son's liaison with an "Aryan" woman. If discovered, it would cause his imprisonment.

By February 1942, however, so many of the Hirschels' friends had been deported that neither prudence nor deference was appropriate. Hans moved into Marushka's flat under a subterfuge concocted by Marushka. He gave a "suicide" note to his mother that said he couldn't stand what was happening, that he could not support himself and was a burden to her. "If you are alone, perhaps it will be easier," the note concluded.

A few days after Hans went into hiding Frau Hirschel wrote the police that Hans had been missing for several days, and enclosed his note. She asked them to drag the Wannsee, a lake within the city in which many Jews had drowned themselves. As Marushka had reckoned, the police had no interest in searching for the body of a missing Jew, and from then on he was listed as dead.

Marushka's flat, on the Detmolder Strasse in Wilmersdorf, had once been a store. Marushka had curtained off a big display window and now the front of the store served as a living room. A corridor led past a bedroom and a bath to a well-lit kitchen in which Marushka kept cages of canaries and finches. The kitchen looked onto a small fenced garden, which abutted an adjoining garden in which there was an enormous, graceful chestnut tree.

When Hans moved in he brought with him a daybed that doubled as a couch. It was a massive boxlike piece built of mahogany, with a lid, hinged on the inside, which could be opened to store bedding. "You know," Marushka said one day as she gazed at the couch, "that would make a perfect hiding place for you if we ever needed one."

"I'd suffocate," Hans said.

"No, you wouldn't. We could drill holes in the bottom."

Using a hand drill, she made the holes and then covered the

underside with a loosely woven linen fabric. Inside the top she fastened a latch, so that when Hans climbed inside he could secure the lid; the pad on top would fall back into place.

Each morning thereafter, before she went off to her classes at the university—she was working toward a degree in veterinary medicine—Marushka would put a fresh glass of water inside the couch alongside a cough suppressant.

Although Hans was now living with Marushka, Luzie Hirschel continued to maintain a formidable claim on her son's allegiance. She was an exquisite woman of medium height, who had been widowed when Hans was a child. Hans's father had been a judge in Breslau at a time when Jewish judges in Germany were rare. His mother was a Grunfeld, the daughter of a builder, who had left a small fortune to each of his thirteen children on his death. Luzie Hirschel demanded a great deal from Hans, particularly after his sister, four years younger, died of a heart attack while working in Italy. While Luzie never admitted it outright, she seemed to assume that Hans would accompany her if she were deported. The very thought infuriated Marushka, who argued to Hans that if Luzie went alone, she would go to Theresienstadt, where she had a chance of surviving, whereas if they went together, they would be sent to Poland. "Hans, Poland is death," Marushka insisted.

She spoke more from premonition than fact, because reports of extermination had not yet reached Berlin, but she knew the Nazis—Field Marshal Walter von Reichenau, an ardent party member, was her brother-in-law—and she remembered Hitler's promise in *Mein Kampf* to destroy the Jews. She chose to take him at his word.

Then Marushka became pregnant, and everything changed. Luzie Hirschel was overjoyed at the prospect of the family line continuing, and she relinquished her assumption that Hans would go with her if she was deported. Hans insisted that he should be the dutiful son and accompany his mother, but now Luzie wouldn't hear of it. "A man belongs to a wife and child," she told him.

The two women became very close. Because Hans could not visit his mother lest her neighbors see him, Marushka volunteered to go each day in his stead to make certain Luzie was all right. One day in the spring of 1942 she entered Luzie's apartment to find Luzie pale and shaken: a Gestapo agent had reported her for covering her yellow star with her fur boa.

The deportation notice came a few days later. As risky as it was for Hans to appear at his mother's flat, he was determined to say goodbye, and when he arrived at 9:00 o'clock the evening of her departure, Marushka opened the door. He walked past her to his mother, whom he had not seen in six weeks. They put their arms around each other. Neither spoke. When they separated he saw that she had dressed in black, in one of her most expensive frocks. As they began to talk he noticed a small suitcase by the door with a coat next to it. Earlier that day Marushka and two of her nieces had sewn inside the lining of the coat several pieces of jewelry which Luzie hoped she would be able to use to secure favored treatment for herself.

They talked for half an hour, mostly about her wish that Hans would survive, only briefly about her own deportation to Theresienstadt. Hanging over them all was a horrible, palpable truth—that in 1938, only four years before, Luzie might have emigrated to England, where others in her family had already settled. She had elected to remain rather than leave Hans, who had failed to secure the work permit that would have enabled him to accompany her.

It was past 9:30; Hans could not risk a further wait. They rose to say goodbye. Frau Hirschel's eyes were dry. "My life started so wonderfully," she said. "The end was pretty bitter."

Her use of the past tense undid Hans; he fought back tears. Without another word he kissed his mother and was gone.

Luzie listened to his footsteps, and when she could no longer hear them, she returned to Marushka. "How *will* it end?" she asked softly.

The women embraced. A few moments later Marushka left. The next day Marushka returned to the apartment with only the faintest hope that Luzie might still be there. But a neighbor confirmed her departure, which, she said, had been so dignified that even the Gestapo had treated her with respect.

Then the neighbor, a German officer's wife, said, "Look, I'd never give you away. Hans is with you, isn't he? Is he all right?"

"Hans is dead," Marushka said.

In the following weeks Marushka could almost feel the accumulation of Hans's sorrow. She both prayed for and feared the inevitable explosion of his emotion. Late one evening, as she was returning from a working day that had begun at five that morning, she heard the sound of boisterous singing, and realized with horror that the noise was coming from her flat. She rushed inside to find Hans and another illegal Jew, an actor friend named Willy Buschoff, singing as loudly as they could, "Sh'ma Yisroel adonoy elohenu, adonoy echod."

Days later, when they were calmer, he would translate the words of this most famous Hebrew prayer: "Hear, O Israel, the Lord our God, the Lord is One."

3

RUTH THOMAS was an extremely pretty, trim woman in her late twenties who mingled easily in the most acceptable circles, which in Nazi Germany meant that she did not have "Jewish looks." She wore stylish suits with narrow skirts—her own design—which, measured against the stolid, drab, almost institutional products of Germany's clothing manufacturers, seemed like French *haute couture*. If her own creativity enhanced her appearance, it also bespoke a fresh disposition that made hers an especially attractive presence. Ruth was a person other people liked because she always seemed able to lift their spirits. The tiny lines next to her brown eyes, engraved by a permanent smile, promised the sort of merriment that would never be associated with a hunted woman. She had an enormous capacity for gaiety and an infectious laugh.

The further the Nazi persecutions distanced Ruth from the vibrant and comfortable life for which she had seemed destined by virtue of background and talent, the more determined she became not to be dismayed. What most strengthened her psychological armor in this period of peril was her capacity to see the world not as it was but as she wished it to be. The war had frustrated her attempts at emigration and imprisoned her in Germany, so the only way she could deal with the unacceptable reality that confronted her was to pretend it didn't exist. "If I can't agree with something," she often said, "I act as if it isn't there." She avoided newspapers and news broadcasts and even conversations with friends to make certain that she didn't know what was happening. If her approach to life was clearly impractical, it nevertheless reinforced her unquenchable will to survive and her conviction that she would despite the increasing odds against her. "I not only hope that Hitler will lose the war," she repeated over and over, "I am sure he will. We are an old family. We've been here one hundred and fifty years. Hitler is a parvenu. I shall survive him."

The talk was meant to buoy her own spirits, but it was supported by her temperament and the fiercely independent streak she had inherited from her mother. Anna Rosenthal was that rarity in pre-World War II Germany, an emancipated woman, well schooled and with a hard mind. She was considered by her brothers and sisters to be the strongest member of the family, for she had determined at an early age, after the death of her mother, that she preferred to make her own way financially. When she married, in her early thirties—her spouse was a distant cousin whose name was also Rosenthal—Anna was already an established businesswoman, a buyer and seller of textiles. Her husband's early death during a flu epidemic only confirmed the wisdom of her course.

Like her mother, Ruth was strong and self-assured. In 1939, when the Gestapo charged her with hoarding stockings and ordered her to accompany investigators to Gestapo headquarters, she responded, "Why should I? What's the charge? You've found no stockings."

"You're Jewish. How come you're so insolent?" one of the Gestapo men demanded.

"There's no charge," Ruth insisted. "You have to have a charge. You've searched the house and found nothing."

At last Ruth was taken to the Gestapo headquarters on the Burgstrasse, but there she remained just as adamant in her indignation at being accused without evidence. As she was being released, a man named Draeger, who had a reputation among Jews for being helpful and who had observed her with guarded sympathy, said softly to her, "If everyone had been as courageous as you, a lot of things would not have worked for the Gestapo."

Three years had passed since that incident; relatives and friends had been deported, but Ruth, her husband, Kurt Thomas, and her mother, Anna, had all survived thanks to Ruth's talent. Her designer clothes and patterns were not only well regarded in the garment industry but earned for the Third Reich badly needed foreign currency from sales abroad. The German companies that bought her designs had received special permits to employ her, and Anna and Kurt, listed as her assistants, had been sheltered under the umbrella of her work permit.

On November 9, 1942, Ruth awakened with the first symptoms of flu and decided not to go to work. She lay in bed in the Wilmersdorf apartment building she shared with numbers of other Jews, feeling so dreadful that when she heard a knock on the door late in the afternoon, she could not bring herself to respond. When she finally rose an hour later, she found a note that had been pushed under the door. It was from the Gestapo, ordering Ruth and Anna to report the next day to the same Burgstrasse headquarters where Ruth had once defended herself.

Why? The only possibility was that someone had inadvertently brought them to the Gestapo's attention. Who? The only person who had their address as well as the capacity to incriminate them was a woman who delivered black market food. Whatever the reason, Ruth knew that the time for defiance had passed. Too much had happened by this time for her to deny reality. A number of the Jews with whom they shared this apartment had already been deported. Others, unable to bear the overcrowded conditions they'd been forced to endure since the Nazis had crammed them into Jewish houses, had committed suicide. Even Ruth had been shaken by her eviction from her own apartment and the almost public life in this Jewish house, without a radio or even a telephone. Theoretically she was still safe because of her special work permit, and her mother and Kurt were protected too. But she knew the Nazis could revoke her permit at any time; in that event they would soon be on the trains, bound for the camps. God knew what awaited them in the camps. At a minimum, heavy physical work, a punishment in itself.

That evening, when Anna and Kurt returned to the apartment, Ruth announced her decision: It was time to go underground.

"You don't think it would be better if you went to the Gestapo?" Kurt said.

Ruth shook her head emphatically. Now that she had acknowledged reality, she was prepared to deal with it. "Once we go, we'll never return."

That night they tore the Jewish stars from their clothes. Carrying money and parcels of valuables they had hidden against just such an eventuality, they set out for separate hiding places: Anna to a brother, Max Rosenthal, who, married to a Christian woman, qualified as a "privileged" Jew; Kurt to the apartment of Lea Thomas, his former wife, also a Christian; and Ruth to the apartment of a Christian woman named Lisa Krauss, who worked as a secretary for a firm that operated a chain of popular pastry shops. Until the persecutions the firm had been owned by friends of Ruth's family, three brothers named Dubrin. They had told Ruth that Lisa could be trusted and had themselves entrusted many of their valuables to her before their deportation.

But Ruth and Lisa got on each other's nerves. Lisa well knew that the penalty for hiding a Jew could mean concentration camp for herself. As for Ruth, the sight of all those valuable possessions of her Jewish friends being used to advantage by this woman deeply offended her. Before she'd been with Lisa a week she decided to leave.

Kurt Thomas had suggested another possible source of help,

a friend named Barsch, who was pro-Communist and against the regime. When Ruth arrived at the Barsches' Charlottenburg apartment she discovered an unimaginable complication. Although the Barsches were sympathetic and more than willing to hide her, their daughter, Hilde Hohn, was married to an S.S. man. Hohn was serving as the administrative officer of a work camp in Poland, but Hilde, who was spending the weekend at her in-laws' farm near the Elbe River, some fifty miles west of Berlin, would return on Monday, and the Barsches stressed that Ruth would have to be gone by then. Hilde knew her parents helped Jews, and she despaired about it because of the awkward position it put her in.

The following Monday Ruth closed the door of the Barsches' apartment behind her and for the first time felt overwhelmed by the realization that she was homeless. Her psychological armor, which had protected her for so long, was now riven by reality.

As she walked slowly from the building a taxicab stopped at the entrance. Out stepped a young woman, a few years older than Ruth, but so strikingly similar in looks that she might have passed for her sister. Her features were somewhat more pronounced, but her coloring was the same, and she was also small and trim. She paid the driver, gathered up her packages, turned and saw Ruth.

Many times thereafter Ruth would wonder what had gone through Hilde's mind in that first moment of recognition. Was she, with her frank and admiring appraisal, offering that acknowledgment one attractive woman gives to another? Did she intuitively recognize in Ruth aspects of herself? Whatever Hilde was thinking, Ruth felt herself swept up by her own wave of intuition. This woman, she knew, was her only hope for the moment; she would gamble everything with one question. "Are you Frau Doctor Hohn?" she asked.

Hilde smiled slightly before she spoke. "You must be one of father's people," she said then. Seconds passed. Hilde sighed. "Come along," she said at last. "Help me carry these packages."

4

WILHELM GLASER shrugged his shoulders at life in the manner
of a sleepy-eyed Chaplin. "I'm not outstandingly intelligent,"
he would propose. Others would say he was much too modest,
but Glaser, an average-size man, believed that he had been born
to mediocrity. His saving grace was that he didn't mind. He savored what he was able to do with the talents he could employ.
If he had one technique with which to enrich his life it was that
he could gain a sense of importance through proximity to importance.

Wilhelm Glaser was an avid and discerning spectator of the
performing arts, and in Berlin in the 1920s there were hundreds
of plays and concerts to choose from, ranging from the classics
to the extreme avant-garde. After the performances there were
cafes where lovers of the arts could congregate to review what
they had seen and heard.

Willy Glaser's knowledge of theater was encyclopedic, but it
was opera, especially, that transported him. One of his greatest
treasures was a collection of photographs autographed by the
great singers of his day. After one opera—he was twelve at the
time—he cried.

"Why are you crying?" an usher asked him.

"Because it's over," Willy replied.

It was his parents who had taught him a love of the arts. A good report card won him a ticket to an opera or a concert. And yet, in spite of such incentives, he did not do well in school. His lack of ambition was surely a factor in his scholastic failure, and that lack was the result of Glaser's harsh appraisal of reality. "We were a generation that couldn't become outstanding," he would explain years later. "There was the First World War, then the inflation—which meant that you had to learn something fast in order to survive—then Hitler. It was a time when only people with outstanding brains could accomplish something, and I couldn't include myself in that group."

He never had far-reaching plans. Had he possessed the talent, he would have preferred a career in music. Had the world been a different place, he would have liked to open a travel agency, not for the money but for the opportunity to travel. There was one period of intense excitement for him, in the years after World War I, when Marxists were preaching revolution and change was in the air. "We worked six days a week," he would recall, "even Saturdays, from eight to six. All of a sudden people were proposing that we work an eight-hour day, a five-day week. The boss had been second to God. All of a sudden people were proposing that we make committees and decide our own fate."

It was a time of intense advocacy and democracy under the protection of the Weimar Republic, established after World War I, but it was a time enjoyed only by those with a taste for change and not by the great mass of Germans. They perceived the Republic as the bastard child of the victorious allies. They recoiled from the artistic and moral experiments that seemed to be carried on in accord with an adventuresome political spirit that ruled the day. They yearned for the authoritarianism that had characterized German life for as long as they could remember, and they looked upon those who had taken command of the government and the culture as an alien minority. That some of the ruling politicians and proponents of the fervid bohemian culture were Jews only served to persuade the majority of Germans of the correctness of biases against Jews that were as much a part of the Teutonic legacy as the music of Richard Wagner—himself a fanatical anti-Semite.

Nor did economic conditions ultimately help the cause of democracy under the Weimar Republic. In the early twenties ruinous inflation had destroyed the German mark and, with it, all forms of savings. The late twenties witnessed something of a recovery; Germany actually increased production in key sectors over prewar figures, and by 1930 was in the top rank of exporting countries. Increasing employment and gains by labor, many forced on industrialists by the government, had muted the cries of the Marxists, but the shocks felt in Germany from the Wall Street crash of 1929 gave a certain credence to their arguments that Germany was controlled by cartels and vulnerable to their problems. As the twenties ended, Germany slid into a depression so bad that one-third of the nation was dependent, either partly or wholly, on some form of public support.

By the time of elections in September 1930, government, industry, agriculture and labor were all at loggerheads, and German voters responded to this disorder by increasing the representation of the Nazi party in the Reichstag from 12 deputies to 107. In the process the government lost its majority—and its power to regulate industry. Production and wages plummeted and unemployment surged. The worse economic conditions became, the greater the Nazis' gains. By the end of 1932 the Weimar Republic and its democratic principles had lost all prospects, and by 1933, when Hitler came to power, Willy Glaser had lost all faith in the egalitarian dreams that had sustained him through the twenties.

His friends told Willy not to worry: bad management would quickly ruin Hitler; he would last a few months at most. Willy didn't believe them, but not wanting to draw attention to himself, he didn't argue. Later he got no satisfaction from the knowledge that he had been right. Under the Nazis the country experienced a dramatic economic resurgence, much of it a consequence of rearmament, paid for by taxes and "voluntary" contributions. The rearmament was in violation of the Treaty of Versailles that ended World War I but that did not bother the average German a bit. Unemployment shrank—from six million in 1933 to one million in 1938. Workers' conditions improved dramatically, almost entirely as a consequence of the paternalism of the state; for a pittance they could now take vacations at lakes and spas and winter resorts. None of this helped Willy, of course. Every rise in the fortunes of "good Germans" seemed to be accompanied by added misfortunes for Jews. Jewish professors lost their positions, Jewish lawyers and doctors their practices. Jewish pupils were expelled from schools and universities. Jews were forbidden to commingle with "Aryans." Jews were commanded to sell their businesses at a fraction of their value, to register their valuables and later to give them up. They were required to change their first names—the men to Israel, the women to Sarah. Their passports were stamped with a large red *J*.

When Germany invaded Poland on September 1, 1939, Willy Glaser greeted the news with foreboding but also with relief. "This will take a bloody end," he told himself, "because Hitler is insane. He is saying that the Jews started the war, and he is insane enough to believe it."

Any hope that the German people, in whom he had once believed, would recoil from Germany's involvement in a new world war was quickly removed from Willy's mind. True, he saw no excitement or commitment to the war as he walked the streets of Berlin; if anything, he could have interpreted the look on Berliners' faces as a reluctance to be involved bordering on apprehension. But the only sign of the war, other than the many uniforms on the streets, was the constant news of its excellent progress. Berlin itself remained untouched. Its residents had no feeling for the war and felt no deprivation; to the contrary, their relative prosperity seemed supported by a sense of national purpose.

Willy could only reflect with bitterness on the increased well-being and sense of contentment that filled men with whom he'd once worked. He would have preferred to have remained a worker and not become an entrepreneur; only with the greatest reluctance had he started a small textile business in the mid-1930s, after the firm that had employed him was squeezed dry by the Nazis and he couldn't find other work. In 1941 even that small enterprise had to be abandoned when, at the age of forty-one, he was impressed into forced labor as a factory worker.

As Willy's conditions became worse and worse, a mood of increasing fatalism permeated his life. Replaying the past only deepened his conviction that his life had been charted onto some tragic course. His two brothers had emigrated in the mid-1930s, one to Israel, the other to Shanghai and then to the United States. He hadn't even tried to emigrate, because he doubted that he could interest any country in his case. What country would care to receive a middle-aged Jew with neither money nor talent? Moreover, one of the sons had to remain behind to look after their mother, who, now in her seventies, had decided to remain in Germany. He knew in his heart that he also wanted to stay, and so he had assigned himself the responsibility.

And then one morning in December 1942 Willy went to his mother's home and found her door was sealed. Whenever the Nazis emptied a house of its inhabitants prior to sending them to the east, they sealed the doors so that the furniture and other possessions could be confiscated in the name of the state and then sold at auction.

Willy's mother had been taken to a building on the Grosse Hamburger Strasse that had once been a home for elderly Jews but served now as a collecting station for those Jews about to be deported. Willy went immediately to find her, knowing he was risking his own deportation and believing that deportation meant liquidation in one form or another.

He saw his mother only briefly, the two of them speaking softly, holding hands but fighting back their tears. Neither wished to make it more difficult for the other. And then she was gone.

There comes a point when life is so unredeemed that great risks seem of no consequence. It was at this point that Wilhelm Glaser began his own small war against fate. His first act was to remove his star on his way to and from work. From his apartment house in Lichtenberg to his work in Weissensee was a distance of 6.5 kilometers. Jews were allowed to use public transportation only if the distance between home and work was at least 7.5 kilometers. His work hours were 6:00 A.M. to 6:00 P.M.; that meant he had to leave for work at 4:30 A.M., and would not return until 7:30 P.M. The practical effect was that he had no time to shop for food and other necessities. And so Willy removed his star and rode the streetcars, knowing that discovery meant his own deportation. When he got off the streetcar he would duck into a doorway near his place of work—Warnecke and Boehm, a producer of paints, lacquers and oils—and pin the star back on. At the end of the day he would remove the star again for the journey home. Even the discovery of a star that was pinned on rather than sewn on meant deportation, he knew. He had seen S.S. plainclothesmen inspecting the stars of Jews on the Alexanderplatz and arresting those who failed to pass inspection. To Willy that was just one further essential risk.

Willy's home at the time was a furnished room in the first-floor apartment of a Jewish house. There was a small spy hole in the door, with a rag pinned behind it in lieu of glass. At night he would poke a pencil through the hole, push away the rag and peer inside. If no coats were hanging on the rack near the door, he would know that the people he had been living with had been picked up, and he would have to disappear.

On the night of January 31 Willy forgot to put his pencil through the peephole. He unlocked the door, stepped inside, and found himself before two big, hefty men in plain clothes.

"Is your name Glaser?" the older one said.

"Yes."

"Pack your things and come along."

When he had finished packing they took him to an apartment on the fourth floor. The apartment's occupants were no longer there. Willy surmised that they had already been picked up, but that one of them, like himself, had been late returning from work.

They waited through the night, but no one came. By 6:00 A.M. the Gestapo men were ready to give up. "Let's go," the older man said.

As they stepped outside the apartment Willy said to himself, "If God is on my side, something has to happen now. Once I'm in the car, I have no chance."

The younger man turned to seal the door. Willy shoved the older man and bolted down the stairs. The older man raced after him, but Willy threw his suitcase at his legs. The man fell over the suitcase, bounced down the steps, banged into a wall and lay still. Panic struck Willy as he remembered that the entrance to the building might be locked, as it was from eight each evening until six the following morning. But he pulled at the door and it opened. God is with me, he thought. He raced into the street, a free man for as long as his legs could keep him ahead of his pursuers.

5

FEBRUARY 27, 1943, had not been randomly chosen by the Nazis for the *Fabrik Aktion,* in which all of the Jews still involved in war production in Berlin were to be seized at their jobs and, together with their families, deported to the east. That year February 27 fell on a Saturday, and the Nazis conjectured—correctly—that the workers' families would be in their homes in greater numbers on Saturday morning than on any other day.

Past deportations had normally been accomplished with the formality of a ritual. Lists of those to be deported were made up in advance by the Reichsvereinigung, the association of the Jews of the Reich, a government-mandated organization with which all Jews were required to be registered, and which was compelled by the Nazis to administer all anti-Jewish decrees, deportation included. Those to be deported were almost always notified in advance, then ordered to report or be taken by the Gestapo to the former old people's home on the Grosse Hamburger Strasse or other collecting points. Once the prescribed allotment of Jews had been assembled—one thousand at the outset, less as time went on and the number of Jews in the city diminished—they were taken by trucks to railroad yards, where they were crammed into freight cars for the journey to the east.

This time there were no lists, no indication of a major action other than a notice to Jewish officials of the Reichsvereinigung on February 26 to organize half a dozen processing offices and as many first-aid stations. That night, troops of Heinrich Himmler's crack Praetorian Guard, the Leibstandarte of Adolf Hitler, surrounded the factories that employed Jews. Shortly after seven o'clock the next morning S.S. trucks rolled up to the factories. Troops rushed inside and grabbed every Jew they saw. The Jews were then taken to the trucks without being able to change from their working clothes or claim their winter coats. The breakfasts most of them had brought to work were also left behind.

In the meanwhile other troops had been dispatched to the apartment buildings in which Jewish families were congregated. Old persons and children were yanked from their dwellings without time to dress or pack the one suitcase the Nazis had traditionally let deportees take along, or even inform their relatives. Many children were taken without their parents. Elderly persons who were not able to climb fast enough were literally thrown onto the trucks. Many of the elderly suffered fractures.

By mid-morning thousands of Jews had been taken. A score had been brought in dead, having jumped from windows, thrown themselves under the wheels of their captors' trucks or taken potassium cyanide or overdoses of Veronal hoarded for just this dreaded moment.

Throughout the day Gestapo agents raced through the city trying to arrest the Jews before reports from the *Mundfunk,* the Jewish "mouthcast," or warnings from friends would cause them to flee.

It would have been difficult that day for any Berliner not to notice the strange, almost frenzied tempo of official traffic through the city's streets. For a Jewish woman who had trained herself for a decade to pick up menacing signs it would have been next to impossible. Hella Riede had gone to the Kurfürstendamm that morning with a friend, as much to get away from the crowded Kaiserstrasse apartment in which she had been living as to persuade herself that she was part of the busy Saturday morning commercial life bustling all about her. Hiding her yellow star with her purse, she strolled the broad sidewalks of the tree-lined boulevard, window-shopping, then flirting with the idea of going into one of the beauty shops to get her hair done. But for her star, it was the kind of adventure she could easily get away with. She had the first line of defense in any kind of deception—an appearance that made others feel comfortable. Not only was she agreeable to look at, she seemed, with her golden hair and light skin, the prototypical "Aryan" woman. Her second line of defense was at least as formidable. She kept a lock on her emotions and could will her fears into somnolence.

But as the cars and trucks sped by and the pedestrians turned to watch and then speculate among themselves as to what the commotion was about, Hella made her own shrewd guess and immediately set out on foot for her apartment, several miles to the east, possessed by a single frantic thought: Had Kurt, her husband, already been taken?

At last she reached the Kaiserstrasse, where, to her immense relief, no Gestapo cars or S.S. trucks were parked. And inside the apartment, to her joy, was Kurt, who had come home to look for her after news of the roundup reached him. He confirmed for Hella that the factory workers had been taken from their jobs. He had been overlooked because he was the only Jew working in a wholesale leather outlet. How long before that oversight would be corrected he could only guess.

Kurt, a lean man of twenty-nine, was five years older than Hella. What had attracted Hella to him initially was his warmth and openness and his efforts to help others, but ten years of jousting with the Nazis, of having to live constantly on the defensive had slowly turned him inward. Added to that was a severe case of myopia, which made him feel physically vulnerable.

Once in 1938, during a wave of arrests of Jews, the Gestapo had come looking for Kurt, and he and Hella had had to flee. Now, they both knew, they would have to take flight again.

There was only one person who might help them, a greengrocer in their neighborhood who had been unaccountably helpful. He had smiled at Hella one afternoon and said, "How come you always shop so late in the day when the good produce is gone?"

Hella, who had been covering her star with her purse, blushed. "Because I'm Jewish," she said.

"Come in the morning. Hide your star," he said softly.

So she would shop early in the morning, covering the star, until one day a clerk who had seen her walking in the neighborhood when she wasn't covering the star said to her, "You are not allowed to shop at this time." Everyone turned to stare at Hella. She fled.

A few days later there was a knock on their apartment door. It was the greengrocer. He had brought some vegetables. "From now on, come when the store closes. I'll save you some things," he said. Even after Hella resumed her visits to the store, the greengrocer, whose name was Robert Jerneitzig, continued to bring food to their apartment and often refused to charge for it. He never explained his motives.

The Riedes didn't know it at the time, but Robert Jerneitzig's wife, to whom he was devoted, was half-Jewish. Had she not been, he might still have responded to the Riedes' plight, but he would never have voiced his feelings. Jerneitzig, a squat and stocky man, displayed a shopkeeper's disposition: he was friendly but not open. He kept both his thoughts and affairs to himself, expressing himself through his deeds. Nothing of his manner or circumstances indicated that he was well off, yet he had quietly saved enough money to buy a small house in Wittenau, an outlying district of Berlin. It was to this house that his thoughts turned once the Riedes informed him of their dire new predicament.

Jerneitzig told the Riedes that they could spend the night in his apartment, which was attached to his store. Then he telephoned Joseph Wirkus, the man who had been renting the house in Wittenau since the fall of 1941. Jerneitzig spoke with deliberate calm, telling Wirkus that he wanted to talk to him confidentially about some matters, and that they had to meet that day.

Wirkus, just past thirty, was a civilian employee of the Ober-kommando des Heeres, the Army High Command. He was the chief of correspondence of one of the divisions in a center for the design of instruments of war that would later be produced by the factories. A slim, blond man of medium height, he had been rejected for military service because of a deformed elbow. (He had broken his arm in a childhood game and it had been poorly set, allowing him only partial mobility.) He liked his job—first, because he worked with a group of engineers most of whom weren't political, and second, because it carried a draft-exempt status. Whenever the military tried to grab him he had the double protection of his injury and his job. He had no taste whatever for the army or the war.

Because Wirkus was in charge of his section, he could come and go as he pleased. After receiving Jerneitzig's call he took the S-Bahn to the center of the city, then walked to the grocery on the Kaiserstrasse. Jerneitzig led him to the apartment in the back. He did not waste time. "There's a young Jewish couple I know. They need a place to stay for a few days while they find a new apartment. They can't stay in their own place any longer. You understand?"

"I understand."

"Can they stay with you?"

Wirkus had always liked Jerneitzig because of the greengrocer's friendly ways. Moreover, they were from the same farming region, and Jerneitzig bought produce from the Wirkus family farm from time to time. But until this moment Wirkus had never trusted Jerneitzig completely. He said he would talk to his wife, but he thought he already knew the answer. They were Catholics, against the Nazis from the beginning because of the party's stand against the church. Joseph was often so openly critical of the party that had anyone denounced him he would have been arrested. Moreover, both of them took seriously their commitment to helping those in need.

But not even this charitable predisposition could keep the Wirkuses from being surprised when, returning from Mass in Wittenau the next morning, they saw Jerneitzig walking toward them, accompanied by a young couple. They were sure it was the Jewish couple—but they had not yet consented to help.

Frau Wirkus was a tender, emotional woman who easily established strong personal relationships. Her reactions to strangers were instantaneous and usually positive. Whatever ambivalence she might have felt toward the Riedes because of the potential danger was dispelled when she saw the mixture of strain and hope in their faces. Her heart went out to Hella, whom she recognized as a woman she had seen shopping in Jerneitzig's store when the Wirkuses themselves were living in an apartment over the store.

Jerneitzig had not known how much convincing he would have to do to place the Riedes. As it turned out, the four young people took to one another at once. The women were physical opposites—Frau Wirkus tall, with dark hair, Hella short and blond—but the men, they all quickly recognized, bore an amazing likeness to each other, to the point where they decided immediately to identify Kurt Riede as Joseph Wirkus' brother, who had come to Wittenau because his home in Hamburg had been bombed out. Once that decision was made, they agreed the stay would be for a week, or two weeks at most. After that the Riedes would either be able to move back to their old flat or they would have found another apartment. There was also a chance for emigration, as Kurt had been trying to arrange a bribe for a government official in exchange for emigration papers.

As the conversation swirled about him Joseph Wirkus nodded agreeably, smiling from time to time as a token of reassurance. But there were long intervals when he did not listen to the others' words. Wirkus, a man of precision by temperament and training, knew the law, and he could calibrate the dangers. Any German caught helping Jews faced automatic imprisonment, but because of his sensitive job, Wirkus knew that the penalty for him and possibly for his wife, Kadi, would be death. Life was especially precious for them at this moment; five months before, Kadi had given birth to their first child, Wilfried, an event that brought indescribable feelings of joy. Wilfried's existence raised the stakes to a level beyond life or death, for the law of the Third Reich provided that where a child was being raised in a manner inimical to the State, the child could, by court order, be removed permanently to an acceptable home. Failure to enroll one's child in the Hitler Youth was one offense that could provoke such an order. Friendship with Jews was another.

So as he voiced his own reassurances, Joseph Wirkus felt doubt. And yet with this small deed he could demonstrate, if only for himself, his aversion to the Nazis. Besides, he reminded himself, the masquerade was only for one or two weeks. When he expressed that thought to Kadi, she said she felt the same.

Had they known how long the masquerade would go on, or the danger in which it would place them, they might have been less willing to offer the Riedes a refuge.

6

HANS ROSENTHAL had large brown eyes and a disarming smile; his presence, even to strangers, bespoke friendliness and warmth. Was it some remnant of this basic disposition that had catapulted him into his strange new adventure? Or was it that he was a good worker? All he knew for certain was that on this day in the late fall of 1942 he was in an automobile beside his employer, a bulky, taciturn, bespectacled Nazi, hurtling down a highway away from Berlin and toward Pomerania. What would happen to him when he got there he hadn't the faintest idea, but for the moment this bizarre passage was putting distance between him and his nightmares.

Although he was almost eighteen he looked less than sixteen years old. This was partly due to an aura of ingenuousness and innocence about him and partly to the years of undernourishment that had stunted his frame. As a child he had had a compact body and the gift of speed, which had made him a splendid soccer player. He was a better athlete than student. He had tried hard to make good grades while his father lived, but after his father died (at the age of thirty-seven) Hans seemed to abandon all scholastic ambitions. And by that time grades no longer mattered for a Jewish schoolboy in Germany.

His father, Kurt Rosenthal, was the oldest of three sons of a

Jewish father and a Christian mother who had converted to Judaism when Kurt was twelve. Kurt had been a warm and fun-loving man whose special pleasure was playing piano in a dance band on weekends. During the week he had worked for the Deutsche Bank, the same bank that had hired him out of high school. In 1937, after twenty-one years of employment, the bank had dismissed him because he was Jewish. Prior to his dismissal Kurt had suffered a kidney ailment, which quickly worsened, and he soon died.

Four years later Hans's mother was dead of cancer, and Hans and his brother Gert, seven years his junior, were orphans. At the time of their mother's death Hans and Gert were living apart; Gert, then nine, was in an orphanage, and Hans was in Fürstenwalde, a training camp for Zionist Jews planning to emigrate to Palestine.*

The atmosphere in which Hans Rosenthal grew up had not been especially Jewish, let alone Zionist. He and his parents and his brother had lived with his father's parents, the most religious of whom was his Grandmother Agnes, the convert to Judaism. Although Hans had been bar-mitzvahed at thirteen, there was always a tree at Christmas, so that he and Gert would not feel different from their Gentile friends. When Hans first embraced Zionism, it was not out of any desire to settle in Palestine but solely to escape Germany. Only later, after working in Fürstenwalde, did he become excited and committed. But his mother's death intervened, and Hans knew then that he couldn't emigrate. Even though he was only sixteen, he was now responsible for Gert.

A few days after his mother's death Hans was given permission to leave Fürstenwalde and return to Berlin to live with Gert

---

* *Every German has his "decent Jew," Heinrich Himmler remarked to his fellow S.S. officers in 1943 in lamenting why it had often been so difficult to pry many Jews in Germany from their sanctuaries and send them to the extermination camps. In the 1930s, before the mass exterminations had begun, even the Nazis had their favorite Jews: the Zionists. Although their motives could not have been more different, the Nazis—Adolf Eichmann among them—and the Zionists were united in their desire to see the Jews leave Germany for Palestine.*

in the orphanage. Three weeks later all of the Jews at Fürstenwalde were sent to Auschwitz. For Hans it was the first of many
narrow escapes.

In April 1942 Hans turned seventeen. The director of the orphanage told him that he was now too old to remain there, and
in August, Hans was transferred to a home for young Jewish
men on the Rosenstrasse. Two months later everyone at the orphanage—Gert included—was deported.

Hans was so upset over Gert's deportation that his own second instance of good fortune scarcely registered. All that spring
he had looked in vain for someone to hide his little brother.
Even his Grandmother Agnes had refused. "It's impossible to
hide a ten-year-old," she had said. "He can't remain quiet."

Hans soon found a job working in a Berlin factory that manufactured small containers of canned heat used by soldiers in
the field to warm their meals. The factory would receive huge
shipments of old cans, recondition them, fill them with flammable hydrocarbon jelly and seal them. It was good business; the
owner, Alfred Hanne, bought the used cans for thirty marks a
carload, then sold each unit for twenty pfennigs. Hanne behaved correctly to his mostly Jewish workers but without the
slightest sentiment. Several of the Jewish employees had once
been wealthy—one had owned a department store, another a
shop on the Kurfürstendamm—but the past had long since
ceased to be of consequence. A worker's salary was based solely
on performance: for every 1,000 tins manufactured above 4,000
a day Hanne paid a bonus of five marks.

Hans was soon making 9,000 tins a day. He could not allow
himself to consider that his earnestness was in behalf of his
enemy. Life had been reduced to an exquisitely simple precept:
make yourself invaluable to someone and you'll survive.

What better proof of that than this journey with Hanne? A
week before, the owner had approached him and said, "I'm
opening a new factory in Pomerania. If you want to come with
me, you can."

"I have a star," Hans reminded him. "How can I go?"

"You'll go. You'll take the star off and you'll go."

When they arrived in Torgelow, the Pomeranian town where Hanne's new factory was located, Hans discovered he was the only Jew. He did not put his star back on. Hanne quartered him in a bunk room in a building adjoining the factory hall, where he lived much better than the other workers, a few of them Belgians, most of them captured Russians who spent their nights shivering in a nearby camp.

A few days after Hans arrived in Torgelow the Gestapo raided the Jewish youth home where he had been living before he left Berlin and sent all of its inhabitants to Auschwitz. His third close call. Had Hanne known? Hans could only wonder.

Weeks passed. Hanne's manner seemed to soften. He no longer shouted so much at the workers. He ordered extra portions of potatoes and turnips for them. The Belgian prisoners told Hans they thought the change in Hanne's manner was related to the German defeat at Stalingrad. Perhaps he had concluded that the tide of battle had turned against the Germans and the war would soon be over, in which case prisoners of war and Jews who vouched for his decent treatment would be extremely helpful.

Whatever the workers' conjecture or Hanne's actual motive, the war had definitely taken a turn against the Germans and in favor of the Allies. The turnaround had begun in Egypt in the fall of 1942, where the British Eighth Army, replenished with fresh troops and armaments—many of its new tanks and planes made in the United States—had not only fought the forces of the "Desert Fox," Field Marshal Erwin Rommel, to a standstill but then put them to rout. Stalingrad was an even more significant defeat, from both a strategic and a symbolic point of view. The city, which lay astride the Volga River, was the gateway to the oil fields of the Caucasus. Hitler's dream was to take those fields and then drive through Iran to the Persian Gulf, eventually joining forces with the Japanese in the Indian Ocean. Had he not paused at Stalingrad, dream might have become fact. But he did, not because he needed the city—German troops had reached the Volga and gained control of its traffic—but because the conquest of Stalingrad had become an obsession. And so he attacked the city.

Russian troops fought the German Sixth Army for every block and rubble pile, and then, on November 19, 1942, under cover of a blizzard, the Russians began a two-pronged counteroffensive to the west of Stalingrad, designed to cut off the Sixth Army from other Axis forces. By year's end that effort had succeeded. Hundreds of thousands of German troops had either been killed or captured, and an even larger group of survivors had been left to wonder bitterly over a leadership so fanatical that it would not permit its troops to give up any conquered ground regardless of the cost in lives and human suffering. The defeat was equally devastating on the home front. Germany's civilians found their faith in their country's ultimate victory shaken.

Hans Rosenthal had no time to speculate about Germany's ultimate fate. He was too preoccupied with the task of remaining alive. After Hanne informed him about the roundup of Jewish workers in the Berlin factories on February 27, his own among them, Hans counted up his escapes. First, Fürstenwalde. Next, the orphanage. Then the Jewish youth home. Now the factories. Four times fate had put him a step ahead of the Gestapo. How long would it be before the Gestapo discovered that Hans had not been among the Jews taken on February 27, and trace him to Torgelow?

Then came an episode that made the question all but rhetorical. One day Hanne told Hans to build a storage bin for an extra load of potatoes he had ordered. When the potatoes arrived, Hans loaded the bin and then gave the Russian workers their allotment before they returned to their camp for the night. They were so emaciated that he couldn't stand the sight. He told them that he would forget to remove the key from the storage-bin lock, so that they could come in the night and take more potatoes. They came, and were caught. The next morning two policemen accosted Hans at his workplace. "You don't give po-

tatoes to the lower race," one of them told him. Then they beat
him and threatened to shoot him.

Hanne suddenly appeared at Hans's side and led the policemen off.

Instinct told Hans that it was time for Escape Number Five.
Two days later he walked out of the factory, his knapsack on his
back, and headed for the railroad station, determined to hazard
a trip to Berlin, two hundred kilometers away. He knew he
could hide in Berlin, whereas a strange boy in a small town
wouldn't have a chance.

Half an hour after the journey began, the police control came
into his car.

"Your papers please?"

"I have none. I'm sixteen years old. I have dirty clothes in my
pack that I'm taking home to be washed. I work at Torgelow.
You can call them."

The policemen exchanged looks, nodded, and passed on. But
at Prenzlau they came into the car again and looked at him. He
could hardly keep his teeth from chattering, but he managed to
muster the disarming smile that had become his automatic response to any stranger's stare.

"He looks nervous," one of the policemen said. "We'd better
check with control." Then they walked over to him. "Please
come outside," the same policeman said.

Now it's over, Hans thought. He followed them into the railway station. Then the second policeman said to his partner,
"Look, I'm hungry as hell. If we do this checking we won't have
lunch. He's just a kid. Let's let him go."

Badly shaken, Hans went to his grandparents' home as soon
as he arrived in Berlin. Grandmother Agnes opened the door.
Her somber face registered no surprise; nothing surprised her
any longer. In addition to her eldest son, Hans's father, she had
lost her two other sons. Ernst, a half-Jew like his brothers, and
married to a Christian, had been deported to Buchenwald for
refusing to wear a Jewish star; three weeks later he died of an
illness, according to a letter from camp authorities. Heinz, the

youngest, had lived with a German woman in defiance of the Nuremberg Laws, and had been captured by the Nazis after trying to escape across rooftops. Two weeks of torture in the Gestapo's prison on the Alexanderplatz had so destroyed him that he died at home shortly after his release. So Grandmother Agnes was without illusions. She was happy that Hans was alive but not happy that a new problem had arisen. What showed on her face now was a question: What will we do with him?

II

HUNTED

7

IN THEIR HASTE to snare all of Berlin's remaining Jews during their February 27 *Fabrik Aktion,* the Nazis seized many Jewish men who were theoretically under the protection of the Third Reich's peculiar racial laws. These laws conveyed a special status on Jews of mixed origin—*Mischlinge*—as well as on Jews married to German Gentiles. Such Jews were subjected to discrimination but usually exempted from deportation because of the hardships and anguish this might cause their mates or relatives. Most Gentiles who had married Jews before 1935, when the Nazis outlawed such behavior, were severely pressured by the party to divorce them, but few did, and while there was no regulation specifically prohibiting the deportation of the Jewish member of a mixed marriage, in practice that person was safe so long as his or her partner opposed it.

Once the Jewish factory workers and their families had been collected at the various concentration points throughout the cities, the "privileged" Jews, as they were known, were segregated from the larger bodies and reassembled at a detention center on the Rosenstrasse, not far from Gestapo headquarters in the center of the city. But they were not released—a strong indication that despite previous custom the Gestapo had every intention of deporting them, along with the other Jews taken in the raid, to the death camps in the east.

And there they might have gone, save for the intervention of the Gentile wives of the Jewish workers. By early the following morning these women finally learned where their husbands had been taken. First tens, then hundreds of the wives assembled on the Rosenstrasse, outside the building in which their husbands were being held. They were soon joined by a crowd of sympathetic bystanders. Attempts to scatter them were unavailing. The women pressed forward, shouting demands that their husbands be released. Each morning for several days the demonstration continued. "We want our men!" the women chorused. Their cries could be heard many blocks away. Finally the Gestapo relented and set the husbands free.

It was not the rightness of their demands so much as the shock of their demonstration that acted in the women's favor. Since 1933, when the Nazis took power, there had never been a mass demonstration against the government or party, at least not in anyone's memory, and none had ever been recorded. Certainly there had never been a public protest of any kind with regard to the Nazis' treatment of the Jews.

Privately, many Germans had helped Jews from the time the persecutions began. Survivors' reports are filled with stories of Germans slipping food or ration stamps into their pockets under cover of a crowd. For every report of a merchant who refused to serve Jews, there is another of a merchant who befriended them. None of the Jews who went underground in Berlin or elsewhere in Germany could have survived without the help of at least one Gentile benefactor. And yet the indifference of the overwhelming number of Germans to the fate of the Jews was as much a danger to those Jews who had gone underground as were the S.S. patrols sent to find them. If their identity became known, they could expect absolutely no help from strangers; to the contrary, strangers were much more likely to report them to the authorities on the grounds that the underground Jews were in violation of the law.

Anti-Semitism aside, the most formidable problem faced by the renegade Jews was the slavish penchant for obedience to authority that seemed to exist within the mind of every German. In *Berlin Diary*, his eyewitness account of Nazi Germany between 1934 and 1941, William L. Shirer writes of "the highest state of being the Germanic man knows; the shedding of their individual souls and minds—with the personal responsibilities and doubts and problems—until under the mystic lights and at the sound of the magic words of the Austrian they were merged completely in the Germanic herd." To compound matters, Shirer points out, the Germans' sense of judgment derived from narrow provincial concerns. Their preoccupation with their own point of view to the exclusion of others' interests was at the very heart of Hitler's appeal. He told them that Germans, by virtue of their superiority over other Europeans, were entitled to more Lebensraum, or living space. He did not need to convince them. They believed that they had proved their superiority by virtue of their courage and their enterprise.

Hitler's attacks against the Jews fitted neatly into the Germans' propensity for self-absorption. Had there been a plebiscite on what to do with the Jews, Germans would have overwhelmingly opposed genocide, but they condoned and even accepted the visible anti-Semitic policies of the Third Reich. Most Germans agreed, if only tacitly, that Jews had played too great a part in national life. While Hitler's allegations about Jewish dominance were wildly overstated, Jews had been prominent in commerce, dominated a number of banks, owned important newspapers, and played a disproportionate role in Berlin's spectacular cultural explosion of the late 1920s. So the Germans were not displeased that the so-called "Jewish influence" was being removed. For some Germans there were practical gains as well. They could default on their debts to Jews, buy Jewish businesses and possessions at distressed prices, secure dominant positions in markets where Jews had once been their competitors, profit from what, in effect, was slave labor, and take over dwellings once owned or occupied by Jews. Finally, as

Richard Grunberger points out in *The Twelve-Year Reich,* the Jew served a necessary psychological function. "Just as primitive man's concept of God supposed the existence of the Devil, so the German's progressive self-deification during the Third Reich depended upon the demonization of the Jew. The white outline of the Germans' image of themselves—in terms of character no less than of color—acquired definition only via the moral and physical darkness of its Jewish anti-type. Metaphysically as well as materially, the roots of the German heaven were deeply embedded in the Jewish hell."

An even more sinister enemy for the Jewish fugitives than the loyal Germans were the turncoats in their midst, fellow Jews embarked on a tragic enterprise. "Catchers" they were called—men and women either without conviction even in normal times or normally moral persons frightened out of their wits by the threat of deportation. They worked directly for the Gestapo, operating out of a so-called "Jewish Bureau of Investigation" located on the Iranische Strasse. Their pay was their freedom; as long as they could find and present "illegal" Jews to the Gestapo for deportation, they could avoid deportation themselves.

The catchers would walk through the city each day without their stars, on the lookout for underground Jews. If their prey was an old acquaintance, they would feign joy at seeing him or her and confide that they too were "illegals." If the prey was simply someone they suspected of being Jewish, they would confide their "secret" in the hope of eliciting a similar confession. Once they had their information, they would make a discreet telephone call, and the Gestapo would soon show up.

The Gestapo had been employing catchers for some time now to find Jews who were not wearing their stars or were living with false papers, but the operation intensified after the February 27 *Fabrik Aktion.* Joseph Goebbels had vowed that he would not rest until Berlin was free of Jews; he had called on the police, the Wehrmacht and the party for assistance, but searching for Jews required extraordinary measures. Who could better ferret out these illegals than their own kind?

Months before he took his wife, Marlitt, and baby daughter, Lane, for an evening stroll into the underground, Fritz Croner, the resourceful young jeweler with the forbidding countenance and the iron determination to survive, had already had his first frightening, and bitter, experience with a fellow Jew.

The Croners' steadiest contact for black market food at that time was Fedor Friedlander, a tall, extremely handsome young man of Russian descent who was exactly Fritz's age. Fritz and Fedor had gotten to know one another while working on the same railroad gang. Fedor told Fritz that if he ever needed anything he, Fedor, had the contacts. At the time Fritz was buying on the black market to feed his own family, his parents and uncle. Several times a month Fedor would show up at the Croners' apartment with the food, and the Croners would dig into a sack of rice in which they hid their money and jewels.

One evening, after returning from work, Fritz went to the rice sack to retrieve the jewels. They were gone—50,000 Reichsmarks' worth. For a moment he was struck dumb. Without his resources, not only his own family but his parents and uncle could not survive. "Who?" he said at last to Marlitt.

"Only Fedor," she answered.

From that moment on, all of Fritz's thoughts were directed toward getting back his valuables. Going to the police was out of the question; not only would they refuse to help a Jew but since March 31, 1939, it had been illegal for Jews to own gold, silver and jewels. All such valuables were to have been relinquished to the city pawnbroker by that date.

In despair Fritz turned to his friend, the stateless Russian jeweler Makarow, with whom he frequently did business.

"Why don't you try to get Friedlander to sell your things?" Makarow suggested.

"What do you mean?"

"Let it be known that you know someone who's in the market

for jewelry. The word will get back to Friedlander soon enough."

Several days later Fritz encountered a man he knew to be friendly with Friedlander. He told the man, whose name was Gorka, that he knew of a foreigner who wanted to buy jewels.

"I know someone who's got a lot of jewelry," Gorka said.

"What's his name?"

"Fedor Friedlander."

"You get Friedlander to sell to the foreign buyer and I'll give you a thousand marks," Fritz offered. His one stipulation was that his own name be kept out of the transaction.

Within another few days a meeting had been arranged between Friedlander and the "foreign buyer"—Makarow. It was to take place at the apartment of Frau Kosimer. To protect her they gave her an alias, and just before the meeting placed a card with her false name on the door of the flat. Fritz hid in a bedroom next to the living room.

Friedlander arrived. He and Makarow took seats at a table. Friedlander put two pieces of jewelry on the table.

Makarow recognized them at once as Fritz's. "I'm not interested in small stuff," he scoffed. "I want big stones."

More and more jewelry emerged from Friedlander's pockets, until the table was virtually covered. Makarow nodded agreeably. "Now you're talking," he said. "Do you mind if I have a look at the pieces over by the window?"

"Of course not," Friedlander replied.

Makarow wrapped the jewels in a cloth and carried them over to the window. Then he shouted, "Herr Croner! You can come out now."

Fritz emerged. Seeing him, Friedlander turned white.

Fritz took an inventory. Two-thirds of the missing jewels were there.

"What's still missing we will write down," Makarow said to Friedlander. "These pieces are not Herr Croner's, they are mine. Do you understand me?" The meaning was clear enough.

Where Fritz was without legal recourse, Makarow could report Friedlander to the police.

Trembling, Friedlander swore that he would return with the rest of the jewels. Then he left. But he didn't return, and Makarow did not want to risk further pursuit.

Fritz now had the bulk of his valuables back and could continue with his trading and thereby sustain his family. But he could not shake the episode. A Jew stealing from a Jew, he reminded himself over and over again. Bad enough that they were struggling to survive in a nation that had lost its mind; what chance did any of them have if they fought among themselves?

The episode had occurred in the spring of 1942, and by December, with the cold as penetrating as it can be only in the damp and overcast regions of northern Europe, Friedlander and people like him were no longer in the forefront of Fritz Croner's mind. He was learning what so many Jews had learned or would learn in their first weeks in the underground—that the greatest adversary he faced in his fight to stay alive was not the Nazis or the average Germans or even other Jews. It was himself. His key to survival lay in his determination to go on. Now, as difficulty piled upon difficulty, he could sense the shriveling of his resolve.

He was staggered by the amount of money he would need to remain alive as an illegal. Whereas before, he, Marlitt and Lane had partly existed on food purchased legally, now all of their provisions would have to come from the black market. On that market, an egg cost 20 marks—about $1.50—a liter of good milk 60 marks, a pound of butter 500 marks.

Then there was the rent. Fritz spent his days scouring the city for some out-of-the-way apartment they could move into after January 1, when they would have to give up their barren sanctuary. The prices were appalling—hundreds of marks just for a room.

But it wasn't only the cost of his illegal life that was ultimately getting to Fritz. What bothered him most was what his parents and other relatives had warned him of—the monumental uncertainty. Each day he and Marlitt lived in fear of discovery. Each day required a new explanation or improvisation. Assuming he could find a place to rent, what would he say to the landlord? How would he explain that he had no police registration, required of all residents of Berlin? Neither he nor Marlitt had any identification papers at all.

There were the constant looks from strangers. What was a healthy man of thirty-odd years doing out of uniform? So Fritz bought a cane and imitated the limp of his father, the wounded World War I veteran. But would that subterfuge fool the Gestapo?

And then there was Lane, now sixteen months old. She was a quiet child. They told one another that she felt she had to be quiet, that she had a sense of what was going on. But one day, inevitably, she would cry in some sanctuary where the existence of a child would be questioned, and then her sobbing could give them away.

The final weight on their minds was the knowledge that they were, in fact, being hunted. That had been confirmed on Christmas Eve, when they returned to their old apartment to find the door sealed, which meant that the Gestapo had come to pick them up. Fritz broke the seal and they went inside. The apartment hadn't been touched. They packed shirts, underwear, linens and other household goods and carried them down to the street, where a non-Jewish friend named Bahn awaited them with a three-wheeled motorized bike. Then they moved slowly down the street, to the accompaniment of carols being sung in apartments on both sides.

Each evening, just before the eight o'clock curfew, Fritz would meet his mother on a side street many blocks from her apartment, and she would give him cooked potatoes. He and Marlitt needed cooked potatoes because their own hotplate was so defective it would split if used for more than the few minutes it would take her to fry their *Bratkartoffeln.* But Fritz would be so nervous that he often couldn't eat. Without a flat of their own, without adequate food, without enough money to support them through their illegality, he could only wonder how they would survive. What was there about him, he wondered, that made him think he could succeed where others had failed?

During Fritz's first years in Berlin, in the mid-1930s, he had become friendly with the best known diamond merchant in the city. Laser Oppenheimer was unlike anyone Fritz had ever known before. He was a good-looking man, tall and dark, with fine features and an impressive mustache. He did not look Jewish. He spoke perfect French and had the manner of a Frenchman. When they met, Oppenheimer was fifty-five and alone. He and his wife were divorced, and he had no family in Berlin that Fritz knew about.

Oppenheimer liked Fritz at once. He recognized in Fritz a quality he would have liked to have had in children of his own. "You won't inherit wealth from me because I no longer have any, but you will inherit my knowledge," he told Fritz one day. He was as good as his word. He taught Fritz how to approximate the value of a stone on sight—to establish what kind of stone it was and evaluate its purity and weight. For these evaluations, Oppenheimer told his rapt pupil, one must depend on his sensibilities, the same sensibilities one uses to appraise a painting. It is experience that develops one's esthetic sense, in the same way that repeated tastings develop one's knowledge of fine wines.

In the years before Jews were barred from such places Laser Oppenheimer took Fritz Croner to museums and galleries on every occasion he could. He helped Fritz to distinguish great paintings from those that were merely good. He helped him develop an appreciation for antiques, fine China, and, of course, diamonds, pearls, emeralds, rubies and other precious stones. Patiently he explained why the dimensions of this cut were more pleasing esthetically than that one, when to assign a flawless rating to a diamond for its color. Slowly he built in Fritz the most important strength a dealer in precious stones can possess—a belief in his own judgment. One day Fritz purchased a brooch with an eight-karat emerald that other dealers had said was glass. To the jubilation of both teacher and pupil, the stone turned out to be genuine.

As their father-and-son friendship deepened, the two men began more and more to buy and sell jewels together. Then calamity struck Oppenheimer. He had given his valuables for safekeeping to Russian acquaintances. The men were Jews but had not been molested because they were Russian citizens. On the day in June 1941 that Germany invaded Russia, these men were arrested and Oppenheimer's possessions were seized. Part of the seized jewels had been Fritz's. When Oppenheimer came to tell him of the calamity, Fritz responded by giving Oppenheimer enough money to get back into business.

Each day after work, from then on, Oppenheimer would bring whatever he had bought during the day to Fritz to keep for him overnight. As the seasons passed and more and more Jews were picked up for deportation, Oppenheimer became more and more resolute. "They'll never get me," he told Fritz. Fritz thought Oppenheimer meant that he would go illegal.

Then, one day in July 1942, Oppenheimer did not show up for their meeting. The next day Fritz went to his apartment and rang the bell, but no one answered. Nor did Oppenheimer respond when Fritz returned the following day. That afternoon Fritz went to the Jewish community headquarters to inquire whether anyone knew of Oppenheimer's whereabouts. He learned that Oppenheimer had been found the day before on the Wannsee in a rowboat that contained a cognac bottle and a sleeping pill vial, both empty.

Now, scant weeks after going underground, Fritz Croner knew he was feeling the same depths of despair that had led Laser Oppenheimer to take his own life. It was a feeling unlike any Fritz had ever felt before; nothing before, no matter how terrible, had caused him to think about giving up. But one evening he and Marlitt discussed that very possibility. They would find a woman who would raise Lane in exchange for all their remaining money, and then they would turn themselves in to the Gestapo.

8

COUNTESS MARIA VON MALTZAN had a Swedish friend, Eric Svensson, who had lived in Berlin for years. One day in July of 1942, five months after Hans Hirschel, the avant-garde intellectual, had moved into her flat on the Detmolder Strasse and three months after his mother, Luzie Hirschel, had been deported to Theresienstadt, the countess went to see Svensson. "Eric, I've got something awful to ask of you," she began.

"Go ahead and ask."

"I'm having a baby . . ."

Eric's eyes went to her stomach, which appeared to him to be all but flat. "Where have you got it?" he asked.

"Never mind. I've got it." She drew a breath. "You know who the father is," she said. It was not a question.

"It's quite clear, yes."

"I can't go to the Registry and say Hans is the father. Will you be the father?"

Eric frowned. A nervous laugh escaped him. "For heaven's sake, I've got a wife in Sweden."

"Whom you haven't seen in twenty years," Marushka countered at once. She had thought it all out. "Look, what could happen better to you? It would be marvelous for your reputation."

Eric smiled in spite of himself. For years he had tried hard to play down his homosexuality. He was concerned about his reputation and worried about the effect on his daughter if the truth got out. For these reasons he had remained married. Now Marushka's request began to make a certain ribald sense. "It's true my wife wouldn't find out," he said aloud.

Suddenly they were laughing together.

The charade began at once. Early each evening Eric would come to Marushka's apartment and take her for a walk. They would deliberately choose crowded streets and give a firm greeting to anyone they knew. Marushka saved her shopping for that time of day. "This is my boyfriend," she would tell the shopkeepers. On at least one occasion in every shop she would become disagreeable with the owners. Eric would calm her down. It had all been rehearsed. She wanted to be certain that the shopkeepers remembered Eric. Later, sitting in her apartment, she would roll cigarettes for Eric, who was a heavy smoker. "Imagine what people think we're doing," she said, laughing. Eric and Hans laughed with her.

On September 6 Marushka felt the first contractions. A friend took her to a hospital run by the nuns of the Order of St. Vincent. "To which department have you been ordered?" the tired, cold-faced nun at the reception desk asked her.

"I'm having a baby," Marushka replied, and watched the same incredulous look she had seen so many times before.

The slim hips that had served her so well in sports and won so many admiring glances now caused her hours of labor. The pain was agonizing, but Marushka refused to cry out. Finally she told the midwife who was attending her that she was from the S.S. and asked to be drugged. As a doctor administered an injection the midwife squeezed Marushka's arm. "Women who have babies in this way don't get fat behinds when they get older," she said. To Marushka it seemed like poor consolation.

The delivery on September 7, 1942, was just as tough. A doctor put her under with ether and extracted the baby with forceps. It was a boy, frightfully small, but in the moments before he was placed in an incubator, Marushka noted that he had high ears like his father.

That night the air raids were especially heavy. Marushka was sick to her stomach. She would slip into sleep as though she was being carried off in the ebb of a wave, then crash into wakefulness with the next burst of a bomb or fit of nausea.

In the morning an old nun with a kindly face came to her bed and took her hand but said nothing.

"Why aren't you speaking of the child? What's the matter?" Marushka said.

"He's dead," the old nun said. A bomb had destroyed the generators that supplied electricity to the quarter. The incubators had shut down. All of the incubator babies had died.

For a moment Marushka closed her eyes. She wanted to cry, but she couldn't. Then she looked at the nun. "I'd like to ask you a favor. If you can't do it, just say so. Would it be possible for the child's real father to see him?"

"I'll have it arranged."

At two in the morning on September 9 Hans walked softly into a small chapel on the ground floor of the hospital. He sat for half an hour at the side of the coffin as shadows from the candles played across his son's face, imparting, eerily, the quality of life. Somewhere the nuns had found masses of flowers, and their scent filled the room. Toward three o'clock the night guard took him to Marushka's room. "I've got a visitor here," he whispered. "Just ring the bell when he wants to leave."

Hans took Marushka's hand and held it without speaking. His face was dark with grief. Finally he said to Marushka, "The only thing I'm grateful for is that mother doesn't know—and won't." He could scarcely speak the last words.

Marushka held him. "Better times will come," she promised. "Better times will come."

9

SAVED BY an S.S. officer's wife! Over and over again Ruth Thomas pondered that unimaginable irony in those first tentative days after her fate had passed into the hands of Hilde Hohn. Hilde, trim and young and pretty like Ruth herself, had taken her in on a whim and against her better judgment because she recognized in Ruth, and responded to, some aspect of herself. Was it that each of them was determined to fix a happy face on life despite the wretched time in which they lived? For the moment Ruth couldn't know, because the relationship was too fragile to be tested, and the consequences of a strain in that relationship—be it from a poorly received question or a premature attempt to be familiar—were too horrible to even contemplate. More than that: Ruth's energies were preempted by concern for her mother and Kurt. Especially Kurt. She had waited too long for marriage, and it was still too new for her not to miss his presence.

Kurt had come to her at the end of a series of events that would have broken any woman without her extraordinary mechanism for dealing with adversity. Everything that had happened to Ruth had to be measured against the riches with which she had begun life. It was not so much a matter of money—her mother was comfortably off, but not wealthy—as it was the circumstances in which she grew up and the talent she brought to life. She was a child of the twenties, a time when open, malicious anti-Semitism pervaded German society. And yet such swirls of malice scarcely touched her. Ruth grew up in the midst of a culturally abundant environment that was as German as it was Jewish, embodying a devotion to high values—a life of concerts and plays and operas and lectures that generated a constant barrage of ideas in a vibrant and free-thinking city. To be part of that society—as the most successful Jews considered themselves—was to experience a life as good as life could be. For these Jews it was an affluent life as well, in splendid neighborhoods of stately homes on large wooded lots, some of the homes nestled next to shimmering lakes, with a cozy inn here and there where one took a gigantic Sunday meal. There were poor Jews in Berlin in the late twenties—one in four was receiving charity—but Jews were well represented in remu-nerative areas of business, and if they had not yet made it to the most desirable neighborhoods near the Grunewald, Berlin's giant park on the southwest side of the city, there were those Jews who *had* made it to inspire them.

Ruth was reared in a large family of uncles, aunts and cous-ins. Going to the synagogue was a family affair. She loved it. She thought of herself as a Jewish girl for whom religion was not just a matter of faith but an expression of character.

Ruth's mother, Anna Rosenthal, made certain Ruth received the best education private schools could provide. Ruth had the mind for it. She was interested in music, archaeology and archi-tecture, and would have happily studied in any of those fields, but by the time she was ready, higher study had been proscribed for Jews. It was 1933; Ruth was nineteen. The only way she could have continued her education was to go abroad, but she didn't want to leave her mother. Besides, her mother needed her help.

Anna Rosenthal owned a designer dress shop in the best shopping district of Berlin, a few blocks from the Unter den Linden. Her manager took Ruth under her wing and taught her the business. Ruth had a flair for adapting the designs of European couturiers, and the store was soon selling her creations. If she was underemployed—if she had regrets about her lost opportunities in a more suitable field—she never revealed it. Rather, what she showed to others was her keenness, her warmth and her zest for life. She loved a good story, she loved the deep well of culture that was her heritage on both the Jewish and German sides. She was aroused by her surroundings and experiences. And she was ambitious to grow as far as possible, to be involved artistically and culturally.

And then it all began to change.

The first change involved Ruth's relationship with Aunt Martha, who was not really a blood relative but a close Gentile friend—dear Aunt Martha, who loved to eat and drink and kept getting bigger and bigger until a tape measure would scarcely reach around her. She lived with her husband and three children in Mecklenburg, a two-hour drive from Berlin. They ran an inn, which was the social center of a rich agricultural province. There the locals ate and drank beer. The restaurant had private dining rooms and a garden that overflowed with blooms and fragrance in the summer. In addition to her thriving restaurant Aunt Martha owned a great deal of land. She was a very wealthy woman and a generous one. Whenever a get-together was arranged, she would have her cook prepare abundant quantities of the most delicious food, almost all of it richer by far than anything her guests were used to in Berlin.

Ruth's mother liked nothing more than long weekends in the country, so the family would travel to Mecklenburg every holiday and almost every weekend. They would leave after lunch on Saturday and arrive in time for afternoon cakes and coffee. Ruth loved to go as much as Mother. Aunt Martha's three children—Heinz, Käthe and Ilza—were older than she was, but they treated her like a beloved younger sister. Heinz, in particular, always had presents for her and told her wonderful stories. And there was a castle to play in nearby that had belonged to Aunt Martha's grandmother.

One Saturday when they arrived they noticed a new picture on the living room wall. It was a picture of a man with a small trim mustache who wore a brown shirt and a Sam Brown belt. "Who's that?" Mother asked.

"That's our Hitler," Aunt Martha said.

"And who is Hitler?"

"He's going to make Germany great."

As the years passed and Hitler's power grew, the anti-Semitic utterances that might once have been dismissed as a lunatic's ravings had to be regarded more and more seriously. Yet Aunt Martha scoffed at the idea that Hitler meant to harm the Jews. "Just politics," she said.

And then came Saturday, April 1, 1933, and the boycott of all Jewish enterprises in Germany. Hitler had been sworn in as Chancellor two months earlier by Paul von Hindenburg, President of the German Republic, on the supposition that only he and his National Socialists—by then the largest party in the country, with one-third the popular vote—could deal with the paralysis that had immobilized the government for months. Hitler took power legally; there followed immediately a series of illegal acts designed to consolidate his power and intimidate the opposition. A fire set in the Reichstag, blamed on a Dutch pyromaniac, who may have been used by the National Socialists, gave Hitler his excuse to begin a pseudolegal process of abolishing all constitutional guarantees of individual freedom. The party's infamous storm troopers assaulted the political opposition, trade union leaders and Jews. Sheer terror purged the Reichstag of so many opposition deputies that Hitler had no trouble in pushing through the Enabling Act that gave him dictatorial powers. The boycott of Jewish businesses on April 1, 1933, which simply institutionalized storm trooper violence against Jewish professionals and businesses, was Hitler's first formal effort against the people he believed to be at the heart of a Bolshevik conspiracy to destroy Germany.

That day the bell rang in the new, more comfortable apartment Ruth and Anna had recently moved into in the Bavarian

Quarter, a neighborhood comprised mostly of Jewish families. Ruth opened the door. There stood Aunt Martha. At her side was her chauffeur, carrying a huge basket of food. Aunt Martha was confused and distraught. She and her husband had been party members since the early twenties. Their circumstances had improved even more since Hitler had come to power. But it's not easy to disavow old friendships, she told them, and she had no intention of doing so. "Hitler must not harm you," she said.

She confessed that she hadn't expected anything like the boycott. She had feared that they were starving. She feared the future. "You are such beautiful people," she kept saying over and over again. And then she made an astonishing proposal. Anna and Ruth should come and live with her. She was sure she could protect them.

Anna turned the offer down. When they parted she said, "We probably won't see each other again. Our roads will separate now."

"No," Aunt Martha protested.

"You'll see," Mother said.

But then Ruth and Anna received letters from all three of Aunt Martha's children. They were all grown now, they were all in good positions because of their political involvement, but all of them wrote that they could not imagine a holiday without Ruth and Anna, and they begged them to come. Käthe, one of Aunt Martha's daughters, had married an important Nazi, a gauleiter, the leader of a political district. Now Käthe wrote them that nothing would happen to them. "Our ambitions are only against academic people, officials, civil servants, not the people in production."

The letter reassured Anna somewhat. Then, too, they still had numbers of Christian friends, most of whom went out of their way to express their disapproval of Hitler's attacks against the Jews. And although Ruth and Anna were acutely conscious that physical aggression against Jews was increasing, not once were they themselves harmed.

One of the assets that helped the family through this time was Ruth's ability to perceive the comic aspects of life, however dour it became. The so-called Nuremberg Laws, passed by the Nazis at a party rally on September 15, 1935, held in the central Bavarian city that was known as the spiritual home of National Socialism, were a good example. These laws "for the protection of German blood and German honor" forbade marriages between Jews and "citizens of German or kindred blood" as well as "extramarital intercourse between Jews and citizens of German or kindred blood." Hard labor, fines and imprisonment awaited violators, Jews or non-Jews alike. Ruth found the laws so ludicrous she refused to take them seriously. And how could people who passed such inane decrees be taken seriously? she argued. The Nazis were so ridiculous, how could there be any danger? She couldn't see how Hitler could remain in power very long. It was just the kind of talk Mother needed to stiffen her own sagging spirits.

But it wasn't long before Ruth and her mother both had to acknowledge the threat and the danger inherent in the Nuremberg Laws, because they indirectly caused a break with Aunt Martha.

It happened unexpectedly. A young Gentile woman Anna knew was married to a Jew. The couple owned a small, well-kept hotel in Berlin. One day the woman came to ask Anna's advice. The party had demanded that she dissolve her marriage; if she didn't, she was told, she'd be forced to give up her hotel. What should she do? Anna decided to consult Aunt Martha. Several days later they met in the Bavarian Quarter apartment. Aunt Martha listened to the story. Then she said, "Divorce your husband and send him abroad." She made it clear that the issue was not so much one of keeping a property as it was safeguarding a human life. If he was out of the country, no harm could come to him.

Aunt Martha's answer stunned Anna. It might be sensible, but it wasn't ethical. Then and there she decided that the differences between them were now too great for the relationship to continue. A few days later she wrote Aunt Martha: "A woman belongs to her husband. She should stay at his side." She could not accept the manner in which Aunt Martha had viewed the problem.

Ruth and Anna would never return to Mecklenburg.

In 1937 Ruth met a Spanish Jew in his early thirties named Bernd Hertz. He fell in love with her and urged her to emigrate with him to the United States. Ruth cared for Bernd and thought that she might even love him, but she could not even consider the prospect of leaving her mother alone in Berlin, where life for a Jew had become too dangerous. Ruth told him that she and her mother would join him in America as soon as they could.

By now they were more than ready to emigrate; two relatives had already been sent to concentration camps. They applied for visas to the United States, and deposited money in banks in Switzerland and Czechoslovakia while on their holidays. Their sponsor in the United States was a young cousin who was teaching school. In the spring of 1938 they received their affidavits of support. Their papers were now in order; as soon as their number came up, their visa would be issued.

But the quota of Germans allowed entrance into the United States each year was 27,000, and several times this number of Germans, most of them Jews, had applied for visas before them.

And then came *Kristallnacht*, the night of the broken glass, November 9–10, 1938.

In Paris, two days earlier, a young German Jewish refugee named Herschel Grynszpan had entered the German Embassy intending to assassinate the ambassador, Count Johannes von Welczeck. Grynszpan's parents, Polish Jews who had lived in Hannover nearly twenty-five years, had recently been expelled from Germany along with some 50,000 Jews who had originally come from Poland. Anguished by this event as well as by the persecutions against the Jews in general, Grynszpan had shot and mortally wounded Ernst vom Rath, a third secretary of the embassy, who had come out to determine his business. Ironically, Vom Rath's own sentiments had been sufficiently anti-Nazi to prompt his surveillance by the Gestapo. When Vom Rath died of his wounds two days later, it was an excuse for the National Socialists to go on a rampage. No spontaneous riot, it was carefully orchestrated, with Hitler's blessings, by Joseph Goebbels and Reinhard Heydrich, who, as Heinrich Himmler's second in command in the S.S., ran the Gestapo and the Security Service.

The rampage laid waste to at least 7,500 shops throughout Germany. Preliminary figures from Heydrich in a confidential report to Hermann Goering on November 11 indicated that 119 synagogues had been set on fire and another 76 completely destroyed. The human toll was far worse. The number of Jews murdered that night was never accurately established, but one hundred would be conservative. Hundreds of Jews were injured and many women were raped—to the consternation of party purists, who abhorred any mingling of Jew and Gentile. Twenty thousand Jews were arrested, many of them, not coincidentally, well-to-do; it had been the intention from the outset to incarcerate Jews who could be ransomed later for a high price.

As the marauders set the torch to Jewish property throughout Germany and crashed their clubs against store-front windows, the Jews themselves, lacking specific information, could only surmise that some form of retribution was being exacted for the death of Vom Rath. Anna had already sold her shop for a pittance to a member of the Nazi party, so it was spared when the buyer intervened. But later that night the marauders reached the Bavarian Quarter. When the doorbell to their apartment rang, Ruth instinctively responded. But before she had reached the door she felt herself seized from behind and pushed roughly away. A hand went over her mouth, muffling her startled cry. It was Frieda, their housekeeper, a young woman just a few years older than Ruth—Frieda, her friend, who had worked for them for ten years, Frieda who, on her days and evenings off, had enough contact with young pro-Nazis to know how readily they could be incited to acts against the Jews. Frieda motioned to

Ruth to be quiet. The two women lay on the floor until whoever was at the door went away and there was no more sound of crashing glass.

The next year brought another calamity. Ruth had grown up with a cousin named Werner, the son of Aunt Paula, her mother's sister. Werner was five years older than Ruth and, like her, an only child. He lived close by. Ruth and Werner spent so much time together that they felt like brother and sister. They were kindred spirits too. Werner refused to be demolished by the Nazis' constraints. He adjusted his life to reality. He was a pianist. In other times he might have become a concert pianist; now he contented himself with playing cocktail music in bars. He was gifted and, until circumstances became too difficult, in great demand. After the Nazis came to power he frequently accepted bookings in foreign countries, where he would be free to play the American jazz the Nazis so abominated because of its Negro idioms. He especially liked to work on the Riviera, where single women were abundant. Werner was a lady's man who had left the proverbial trail of broken hearts. It was this propensity that eventually undid him. One day, en route with his mother to a relative's birthday party in Berlin, Werner chanced upon an old girl friend, a Gentile woman, who had not taken their parting lightly. To their horror the young woman walked up to a policeman and denounced Werner—who was having an affair with another Christian woman—for violation of the Nuremberg Laws. He was arrested, tried and sentenced to several years in prison.

Not even Ruth could come to terms with the reality of Werner's fate. For weeks she anguished over the prospect that Werner might be beaten to death by prison guards, as the Gestapo had beaten another cousin.

And then, just as she felt herself slipping for the first time in her life into an abyss of depression, Ruth met Kurt Thomas, and promptly fell in love.

Thomas, a radiologist, was in his late fifties, more than thirty years Ruth's senior, yet young in his appearance and ways.

They had been introduced by his stepdaughter, who was a customer of Ruth's. Kurt's age was simply not a problem for Ruth.
In fact, had she been an "Aryan," her affair would have been
very much à la mode; given the absence of young men called up
to military service, liaisons with older men were so common by
now among German women that the subject had already been
treated in contemporary literature.

Kurt agreed at once to emigrate and made his own visa application. But the realities were against them, for the waiting list
for visas to the United States contained the names of about
200,000 persons, almost all of them Jews. In 1939, for the first
time, the American consulate would issue the full quota of visas,
27,370. But only 5,524 German-born persons would actually
enter the United States—one-fifth as many as had qualified to
go—because of obstructions imposed by the Nazis. It would be
even worse in 1940, when only 3,556 German-born persons
would be admitted to the United States, despite the fact that
27,355 visas had been issued.

As they waited, Ruth, Anna and Kurt depended on Ruth's
dress-designing skills, which they recognized as their ticket to
salvation. Their everyday experiences reinforced their feelings
that, in spite of the worsening conditions, they themselves were
safe.

The most distressing event of 1941 for Ruth did not directly
affect her. A few months after the United States entered the
war, her cousin Werner, still in jail for having violated the
Nuremberg Laws, learned that he would be among the first
Jews to be "resettled in the East," as the Nazis put it. Despite
the uncertainty, Werner found the prospect appealing. It would
get him out of jail, for one thing. And it would at last distance
him from the madness that Berlin had come to represent. How
hard could the life in Poland be, compared to his present reality? A final consideration was the prospect of heavy bombings
by the Allies; that day might be a long way off, but Werner was
certain it was inevitable. In leaving Berlin for Poland, he would
at least be eliminating the bombings as a possible cause of

death. Werner wrote to his mother suggesting that she volunteer to come along, so that they could be resettled together. Aunt Paula took Werner's advice. Other family members could do nothing to dissuade her. The Gestapo gladly obliged.

Kurt and Ruth had postponed marriage pending resolution of their emigrant status. Now, despairing of their chances of getting to the United States, determined to grab what happiness they could, they were married. Then, suddenly, the American consulate, which had stopped issuing visas when the quota was filled, began to issue them again after the new year. Once Anna had bought their passages, they packed their trunks and suitcases and sent most of them off to American Express. The American consulate summoned them to complete the formalities for immigration. But exit visas from the German government never materialized, and soon the German government suspended all but special emigration visas.

And so they had lived, their situation constantly deteriorating, their friends and relatives disappearing, until the night in November 1942 when Ruth received the Gestapo summons.

In the weeks following their flight into illegality Kurt came often to the Barsches', where Ruth was living with Hilde Hohn, the S.S. officer's wife, and Ruth would visit him at the Kaiserallee apartment of Lea, Kurt's former wife. When Lea was in Munich visiting her daughter, Ruth would stay overnight. Soon she began to spend some nights with Kurt even when Lea was there. Ruth was not worried about Kurt's proximity to Lea; she was a woman past sixty, and Ruth was twenty-six.

Lea lived in an old Berlin apartment that had three large rooms in the front. A long hallway led from these rooms to the kitchen; several bedrooms were off the hallway. At the end of the hallway was a back door. This was to be Kurt's escape route if anyone came for him. The door that separated the front rooms from the hallway was always to remain closed.

On February 19, 1943, Ruth had two appointments. First she was to meet Hilde late that afternoon at the railway station to help her with the packages of food Hilde was bringing from her in-laws' estate in the country. Then Ruth was to meet her husband, bringing him some of the food. But Hilde's train was late. Ruth called Kurt to tell him and said that she would call again after she had deposited Hilde and the packages at the Barsches' apartment.

A short while later there was a knock on the door of the Kaiserallee apartment. Lea answered. It was the Gestapo, come to investigate a report that a Jew was living with her. In a loud, angry voice she denied the charge—just as Kurt came rushing in to investigate the commotion. He knocked one of them down, but then they subdued him and led him off.

When Ruth called from Hilde's to say she was on her way she was told what had happened. Frantic, she begged Lea to offer money to the Gestapo in exchange for Kurt's passage to Switzerland. But Lea, who herself had been spared by the Gestapo only because Kurt had once been her husband, was afraid to risk herself further, and her son by a previous marriage prevailed on her not to try.

So Kurt was gone, and Ruth could only wonder when, if ever, she would see him again.

10

THE HOUSE in Wittenau owned by Robert Jerneitzig, the green-grocer, was solidly built, with two rooms and a kitchen on the ground floor, plus a bathroom which was entered from the out-side—and a closed-in terrace. Upstairs were two bedrooms, one large, one small, with a connecting door. Above the bedrooms was an attic. Finally, there was the basement, which had been fitted out as a bomb shelter by Jerneitzig's tenants, Joseph and Kadi Wirkus, to be used in the event that they did not have time to get to the community shelter a few blocks away.

Kurt and Hella Riede, the young Jewish couple Jerneitzig had brought to Wittenau on the morning after the massive February 27 roundup of Jews in Berlin, moved into the smaller of the two upstairs bedrooms. To enter and leave their own bed-room the Wirkuses had to pass through the one occupied by the Riedes. Within a few days what at first had seemed awkward became completely natural. The Wirkuses simply didn't mind the inconvenience and even found it amusing. For their part, the Riedes were quickly convinced that they had stumbled into heaven.

They could not imagine more generous hosts. From the first the Wirkuses shared their ration cards with the Riedes without asking for recompense. The Riedes, who had managed to guard several thousand marks they had been given by their parents, contributed whatever the Wirkuses would accept. There was no problem with food. Kadi could get whatever she needed from her parents' farm in Pomerania to supplement the food they got with their ration cards.

There was a coziness to the house, due in part to the small scale of the rooms but much more to the outgoing nature of the Wirkuses. In the evenings especially, when Beppo—as Joseph Wirkus was known—was home from work, the air was filled with conversation as the couples made their first tentative appraisals of one another. The chemistry between them remained as remarkable in their first week together as it had in their first moments. The special and dangerous circumstances in which they found themselves seemed to augment and compress their responses, so that they quickly progressed to the kind of feelings that in normal times might have taken them months to approach. The men, who looked so much alike, actually began to act like brothers. Kadi, so quick to respond to people she liked, took to Hella as a sister. There were no arguments; although Kurt was still on edge from his abrupt flight, he was an easygoing man at heart and tried hard to be agreeable. Hella was even more accommodating; she was a quiet person, comfortable to be with. When Kadi went shopping Hella minded the baby, Wilfried. It quickly began to seem to Kadi that she was leaving Wilfried with his aunt. For her part, Hella felt like the child's second mother.

But what the Riedes received from the Wirkuses was far more important than food and shelter and the confirmation of friendship. It was the knowledge that there were German Gentiles who cared for them to the point of risking their lives.

A week after the Riedes moved in, Beppo conceived an audacious plan to obtain a fake identification card for Kurt. The plan hung on the uncanny resemblance between them. They had the same coloring and facial contours, and both of them wore heavy glasses. The plan was to obtain a postal identification card using Beppo's name and address and Kurt's photograph. As I.D. cards went, a postal card wasn't much; it was issued by the post office as a means of identifying recipients of money orders and registered mail. But to a Jew with no papers whatever save those that marked him as a Jew, a postal I.D. card might one day be a passport to life.

Beppo was well known at the post office because he supervised all correspondence in his division. He also had a fair idea of who at the post office would work according to the book and who would be more casual. He chose his mark with care, a quiet-mannered clerk in his fifties with whom he had had frequent dealings.

As accustomed as he was to doing business with the clerk, however, Beppo could not quiet his nerves as he approached him on February 12. His hands were damp and shaking ever so slightly, and his armpits felt wet. "I've lost my postal I.D.," he said in a voice he fought to control.

"Das macht nichts," the clerk said with a small, reassuring smile.

Beppo gave his name, address and date of birth as the clerk typed out a new card.

"Picture?" the clerk said.

Beppo handed him Kurt Riede's picture. What Beppo had prayed would happen did happen. The clerk scarcely glanced at it. He simply affixed it to the identity card, stamped the card and handed it to Beppo without comment.

When Beppo got home that evening he said to Kurt as casually as he could. "Here's your I.D. card." Kurt took the card and stared at it. Then, unable to speak, he laughed.

Next came the problem of an identity card for Hella Riede. They solved this problem in a manner that was only slightly less audacious—and every bit as dangerous.

Kadi—short for Leokadia—Wirkus had an old pregnancy priority card she had been issued by the Amt für Volkswohlfahrt, the Bureau of Social Welfare, on May 6, 1942. The card had permitted her to get priority service in stores and to go to the head of lines. Carefully Beppo steamed off the old photograph of Kadi and put a photo of Hella in its place. Had the official stamp been on Kadi's photograph they could not have managed, but luckily the stamp was on the card.

So now the Wirkuses' chances of exposure had multiplied, as had the risk of imprisonment and death, but in sheltering the Riedes and providing them with false identities, it seemed to Beppo and Kadi that they were giving their own small answer to the Nazis. It was an answer they had long wanted to give, because they believed that life for Catholics in Germany would eventually be as bad as it currently was for the Jews. Their information was fourth-hand—a friend of theirs had heard it from a friend of hers, who had heard it from a priest—but they believed it nonetheless. The priest was said to be well connected to one of the ministries; he had photocopies of official documents that described what was in store for both Jews and Catholics. The Jews were to be exterminated, and Catholicism was to be abolished. There was to be no more Communion. Baptism would be replaced with a Hitler Youth ceremony. Churches were to be preserved, but religious services would be banned. Instead of Sunday worship, there would be Saturday readings of *Mein Kampf,* complete with interpretations by the readers followed by group discussions.

The rumors that the Wirkuses had set store by might not have been accurate in their specifics, but they were solidly undergirded by fact. Catholics had always been a minority in Protestant Germany, often an uncomfortable one, but the period since the assumption of power by the Nazis in January 1933 had been particularly difficult. At first the Nazis had seemed to reinforce the position of all Christian denominations by making religious education in the schools mandatory. But as the party consolidated its power it began to phase religion out of the schools, first by eliminating the subject from graduation examinations, then by making attendance at school prayers optional, finally by scheduling religious classes at the beginning or the end of the morning, so that students who wished to cut those classes might more easily do so. In Bavaria, a region heavily populated by Catholics, the party mounted an effective propaganda campaign against Church schools, a great majority of which were soon converted to interdenominational schools.

Among storm troopers, Hitler's vanguard of roughnecks, who had frightened and beaten his opponents into submission, anti-Catholicism was so pervasive that it seemed at times to be almost as fervid as anti-Semitism. "Storm trooper comrades," they sang in one popular song, "hang the Jews and put the priests against the wall." This same scathing bias was displayed in a 1934 Hitler Youth song: "No evil priest can prevent us from feeling that we are the children of Hitler / We follow not Christ but Horst Wessel / Away with incense and holy water / The Church can go hang for all we care." By 1936, Church leaders were warning parents to try to counteract the anti-Catholic biases their children might find among the Hitler Youth, particularly its leaders. In that year the party began a smear campaign against monks and nuns, dragging hundreds of them to court on charges impugning their morality; and by 1939 the party's anti-Catholic biases had matured into an all-out Church Secession Campaign, which managed to persuade hundreds of thousands of Catholics, many of them civil servants and party members, to renounce their faith. After the war began, the party banned radio transmissions of religious broadcasts, seized church bells for scrap and, pleading shortage of newsprint, shut down the Catholic press.

The Church's ambivalent response to the Nazis had scarcely given such Catholics as Beppo and Kadi guidance. Certainly it opposed all measures designed to weaken its authority, but in many ways and on many occasions the Church acted as though it was trying to find a way to live with the Nazis. It professed its patriotism at all turns and its concurrence with Nazi policy wherever the interests and attitudes of Church and State coincided. The Church was at one with the Nazis in their opposition to communism and its manifest atheism. With regard to the Nazis' official policy of anti-Semitism, the Church's position was less formally stated. Individual priests, some of high rank, expressed their agreement that Jews had for too long exercised too great an influence on German life, thereby lending support to the Nazis' economic persecutions of the Jews. While no priests openly supported the physical persecutions that subsequently transpired, almost none of them voiced objections. The truth was that anti-Semitism pervaded Germany's Catholic Church—a fact that neither Beppo nor Kadi liked to think about. Beppo had once lived with a Jewish family; Kadi had dealt with Jewish merchants. Their memories were good ones. In their opinion, any German Catholic who did not see in the experience of the Jews a portent of the fate of Catholics was not seeing clearly. And if the story the Riedes unfolded as they sat in the kitchen after dinner each evening was any indication, their own worst fears were justified.

Their troubles with the Gestapo, the Riedes said, had begun in 1938. Prior to then, life had been difficult but not impossible. Kurt had grown up in Stendal, a pleasant community near the Elbe River, seventy miles west of Berlin. His father had died when he was very young, and he had lived with his mother in her parents' home. When Hitler came to power, all of his classmates joined the Hitler Youth. "We're not after you," one of them reassured Kurt. "You're a German Jew. It's those Jews who came to Germany from the East. They've got to get out." What small comfort Kurt took from the solicitude of his friends was quickly dissipated. He had wanted to study dentistry, but when his time to matriculate came, neither he nor the two other Jews in his class were permitted to take the *Abitur,* the examination that qualified them for entrance to a university. And so Kurt had moved to Brandenburg, just outside Berlin, to become an apprentice at the department store of Konitzer & Sons. There he joined the Maccabees, an organization of young Jews preparing themselves for emigration to Palestine, a prospect whose popularity had soared even among previously assimilationist German Jews after the advent of Hitler. One of the young Maccabees was Hella.

Kurt quickly became a force in the Maccabees, and just as

quickly won Hella's heart. She was not quite eighteen—five years his junior. To her he seemed a natural leader, completely absorbed in the affairs of the group. He made frequent trips to the Palestine office in Berlin, coordinating the group's studies with requirements for emigration and trying to arrange commitments for passage. The commitments never came, but Kurt tried his best to keep up the spirits of his colleagues.

By 1938, however, that had become an almost hopeless task. Not only was passage not forthcoming but the situation at home was deteriorating. It was a time when the smaller cities and towns of Germany seemed to be vying with one another for the distinction of being first to be *Judenfrei,* or free of Jews. Often on their own, without benefit of enabling edicts from Berlin, the local governments enacted measures designed to make Jewish residents increasingly uncomfortable. Public facilities were put off limits. Jews were tried by people's courts for violation of regulations imposed by such quasi-legal bodies as chambers of commerce or boards of trade. Jews arrested for traffic violations, real or imaginary, soon found themselves in concentration camps. But the worst pressures were economic. It was a time when Jews throughout Germany were being forced to abandon their businesses. Sometimes money was exchanged, but in amounts so small in relation to value that even in these instances the takeovers, usually by favored party members, amounted to outright confiscation. Hella's parents—her father, a Christian, had converted to Judaism—had owned a linens shop, but the store was suddenly seized. In the process they also lost their living quarters, which had been attached to the shop. To compound their misfortunes, Konitzer & Sons was taken over by non-Jews, and Kurt was suddenly out of a job.

Despite their misfortunes, Kurt and Hella went ahead with their wedding plans. On October 25 they were married and went off on a brief honeymoon. One morning after they returned to Brandenburg, Kurt took an early train to Berlin on Maccabee business. It was November 10. The newspapers were filled with accounts of the shooting in Paris of Ernst vom Rath, the young German diplomat, by the Jew, Herschel Grynszpan. As he walked the streets of Berlin, Kurt cautiously studied the faces of the people he passed. Were they studying him? Were they marking him as a Jew? Kurt's features were hard to type; other Jews might identify him at once as a Jew, but the fact wouldn't automatically register on Gentiles. Seeing the Berliners clustered at newsstands, many of them shaking their heads, Kurt wondered whether his safety in the next days would depend on his ability to pass as an "Aryan."

As he walked apprehensively to Unter den Linden he saw young men brandishing clubs and racing to the boulevard. One of them looked his way, and for a moment Kurt felt his heart had stopped. "Come on," the young man said then, "we're going to break the windows of the Jew shops."

Kurt pointed to his suit. "I'm not dressed for that kind of thing. I'm on official business. You go on."

The young man ran off. Kurt went to Kranzler's cafe, ordered a cup of coffee and tried to calm down. At three that afternoon he returned to Brandenburg, where his worst fears were confirmed. Hella, who had been waiting anxiously for him, rushed from her parents' new quarters and led him down the street. "You can't come in," she said. "The Gestapo's been here four times already to get you." She told him that dozens of Jews from Brandenburg had already been arrested and were being transported to the concentration camp at Sachsenhausen.

While Kurt waited on the street for Hella, nervously watching for the Gestapo, she packed a bag. They left at once for Hannover, to stay with an aunt of Kurt's who had married a non-Jew. A few days later Kurt's mother informed them that his stepfather had been picked up by the Gestapo, along with other Jews from Stendal, and taken to Sachsenhausen.

Kurt and Hella remained in Hannover until January 1939, when they went back to Stendal and moved in with his mother's parents. Without work, all but bereft of hope, Kurt set to the task of trying to emigrate. His application for Palestine had been turned down because of his poor eyesight. He tried the United States, but the U.S. wanted affidavits that guaranteed financial support. By that time Hella had relatives in America, but the U.S. immigration quotas meant a delay of three or four years.

Kurt tried to arrange emigration to Colombia, Ecuador, the Dominican Republic, England, Shanghai. Everywhere he went it was the same story: skills were wanted, and émigrés were required to have resident relatives or friends who would support them if necessary. Their German money was useless; if and when they left, it would be with just ten marks apiece. The State would confiscate the rest.

When the war began in September 1939 Kurt and his stepfather—who had been released from Sachsenhausen—were drafted into a forced-labor brigade. They worked first at a forestry office, and then in a sugar factory, and then were told they were to work on the construction of a dam near Saalfeld, 300 kilometers from Stendal.

Kurt was certain that once he and Hella were separated he would never see her again. In desperation he took the train to Berlin, walked into the Palestine immigration office and asked to be accepted for some agricultural or artisan courses, as though he were being trained for emigration. He was given an application. On the train back to Stendal he filled in the form and approved it himself. He showed the "approved" form at the labor office. "Okay," he was told, "emigration comes first. Go to Berlin."

Somehow Kurt managed to talk the labor office official into letting his stepfather come along. Before he and Hella and his parents could leave, however, there was another obstacle to overcome. Jews were not permitted to transport their furniture or household effects by train, and trucks could not transport goods more than 60 kilometers, except by special permit. Stendal was 120 kilometers from Berlin. Kurt went to the office of a furniture mover for whom he had once worked and explained his plight. "I'll help you," the mover said. He sent the shipment to Brandenburg, 60 kilometers away, held it there for several days, then sent the shipment to Berlin.

Kurt, Hella and Kurt's parents moved into two rooms in a large flat on the Kaiserstrasse, near the center of the city. They shared the kitchen and bathroom with several other families. Kurt registered with the labor office and was assigned to construction work on the railroad. Work began at 6:00 A.M. The early hour was no problem for him during the long summer days, but as winter came it became insurmountable. One morning his exasperated foreman demanded to know why he was always late.

"I'm night-blind," Kurt explained. "I can't see in the dark. You'll have to excuse me."

"To hell with you," the foreman said. He discharged him on the spot.

Only then did Kurt fully understand the terror of being absolutely cut off from normal life. For a Jew in Germany in these times a "normal" life was spent at forced labor. As long as he was doing something, he blended in, but once he was severed from the routines of wartime Germany, anything could happen—the most likely being deportation.

But then came a stroke of luck.

Shortly after his discharge Kurt was placed in a ten-man work gang assigned to a wholesale leather warehouse, unloading goods that had been shipped in from occupied France. After fourteen days half the group was discharged, and then, eight days later, three others were let go, until only Kurt and another man were left. Kurt was determined to keep the job as long as he could. The pay was 50 percent better than work on the railroad, and the job was indoors. He worked hard and thus caught the eye of his employer, Baron Freiherr Dr. von Neuber zu Neuber.

Neuber was a small gray-haired man with the erect bearing of an army officer and the punctuality to match. One day the baron told Kurt that his three regular male employees would all soon be drafted. The baron asked if Kurt would like to stay on if he could arrange it with the labor office. When the last remaining Jew was dismissed and Kurt stayed on, he could scarcely believe his luck.

In the months that followed, Kurt went out of his way to justify the baron's trust. He worked long hours, offered suggestions for improving the organization of supplies and volunteered for extra assignments. After the order for Jews to wear yellow stars on their clothing went into effect on September 19, 1941, Kurt would arrive at work with his star on his coat, but on the baron's instructions, would cover it with his apron. Many party members would come in to select their leather goods at wholesale prices, and the baron wanted no problems. The work went well; many party members would tip Kurt for his help. The baron's trust in Kurt grew to such a point that he would leave Kurt in charge when he went off to Paris on his buying trips.

The baron took his noble rank seriously. Unlike other titled Germans he knew, who gave mere lip service to the concept of noblesse oblige, he sincerely believed that with the privileges of nobility came obligations. For him Kurt personified the plight of the Jews, and while he could not go against official government policy, he went out of his way to let Kurt know that he didn't agree with it. "For me all people are human beings," he said one day. He insisted that Kurt pick out shoes for himself, and for Hella as well. "You have to have shoes," he said. From time to time he also gave them food.

In addition to selling shoes the baron sold leather to the larger shoe factories. His operation did not appear to Kurt to be especially impressive, but somehow the baron seemed to be well connected at the economics ministry. Whatever the reason for the baron's importance, whatever the reason for his attachment to Kurt Riede, both his attachment and his importance were soon to save Kurt's and Hella's lives.

The deportations of Jews from Berlin to the east had begun on October 19, 1941, one month following the effective date of the order to wear Jewish stars. That winter Kurt's mother and

stepfather received their deportation order. In vain Kurt and
Hella searched for a place for them to live illegally. After their
departure to a work camp in Lublin, Kurt sent them packages,
which they acknowledged by postcard. Then he sent a package
that wasn't acknowledged. He was devastated.

One by one, or in small groups, the families in the Kaiserstrasse apartment building disappeared. One evening in October 1942 two Gestapo officers fetched Kurt from his apartment
to carry the luggage of two elderly Jews who were being deported. When Kurt explained that he was night-blind, the Gestapo officers told him that Hella could go along to guide him.

The luggage—two small suitcases—was not heavy. But the
silence was oppressive as the Riedes accompanied the Jews and
the Gestapo officers to what had been a synagogue on the Le-
vetzowstrasse. Now it was a collecting point for Jewish deportees. When they arrived, one of the officers handed Kurt a
package he'd been carrying since they left the apartment building. "Here, hold this while we're inside," he said. "When we
come out we'll take you back to your home."

The Riedes were mystified but grateful. They could not ride
the public transportation alone, and it was three miles back to
their apartment building.

Minutes passed. Suddenly a flashlight was shining in their
eyes and two S.S. men were in front of them demanding to
know what they were doing out after curfew. Kurt explained
that the Gestapo officers had instructed them to wait and to
mind a package for them. The S.S. officers took the package
from Kurt and strode off. The Riedes could scarcely protest.
Then out came the Gestapo officers. Kurt told them what had
happened. "Damn!" exclaimed the one who had given Kurt the
package. He and his partner hurried away.

It took the Riedes almost an hour to walk home. Late that
night they went gratefully to bed, only to be aroused by the Gestapo and driven swiftly back to the building on the Levetzow-
strasse. There Kurt was brought before a senior Gestapo officer.
The man was in a rage.

"Did you know what was in the package?" he demanded.

"No."

"Didn't you feel something in it?"

"It was heavy and felt hard."

When the officer had finished questioning Kurt he said, "I must tell you. These men were not Gestapo officers."

Evidently the two officers had been caught taking a bribe, and the Gestapo was aghast. The elderly couple had tried to buy their freedom with some sort of valuable object, possibly a piece of sculpture.

The Riedes waited through the night in the converted synagogue. At seven in the morning Kurt went to the officer in charge and pointed out that he had to be at work in half an hour. The officer shrugged.

Half an hour later the Riedes and four others were placed in a police van and driven to the former Jewish home for the aged on the Grosse Hamburger Strasse. The fifteen-by-fifteen-foot room to which they were taken had bars on the windows and the door; inside was the elderly Jewish couple from their apartment building. The four of them remained in the room for weeks while the Gestapo investigated the episode. Soon after their arrival other Jews joined them.

Within another few weeks the room that had held four persons initially had become the living quarters of fourteen Jews being gathered for the transports. At the beginning they had all been confined to their room, just like the Jews in other rooms, leaving only to fetch their food and bring it back. Later, when they could scarcely move about, they were permitted out of the rooms to walk in the hallways.

Kurt kept thinking of ways for them to escape. He was sure that if they could get their heads through the bars on the windows, the rest of their bodies would follow. Then, using bed sheets tied together, they could let themselves down to the ground. But Hella discouraged all his ideas. "If we leave, the others will suffer," she said.

Hella did her best to keep her husband calm and prevent him

from slipping into a depression. For three months the investigation dragged on. Twice during their stay, quotas were filled and transports departed.

"Our turn is coming," Kurt predicted mournfully. "As soon as the investigation is ended, as soon as enough people are collected, we'll be among them."

Then, one evening in mid-December, the door to their room opened and a clerk entered. "Riede?"

"Yes?" Kurt answered.

"Get dressed and go downstairs. Your wife too."

Kurt turned to Hella, a stricken look on his face. "It's our turn," he said. The others in the room wouldn't look at them.

They went downstairs and presented themselves to the officer in charge.

"Go home," he said.

For a moment the Riedes were too stupefied either to speak or to move. "What?" Kurt managed finally.

"Out! Out of the building. You are free."

Without another word the Riedes left the building. They did not even speak to each other until they had walked several blocks. They walked quickly until they were back at their apartment. It had been sealed in their absence.

Kurt went to the nearest police station, explained that they had been released and asked that the seals be removed.

"They never release anybody there. You escaped," an officer said.

"Excuse me. Do you think that if I had fled I would come back to the police? I'm not that stupid. Call them."

A telephone call confirmed Kurt's story, and a police officer returned with them to their apartment and removed the seals from the door. The next day Kurt returned to work at the wholesale leather warehouse. The baron never said anything, and Kurt could never prove it, but he was sure it was the baron who had arranged for their freedom. It couldn't have been anyone else.

One month after their release from the Gestapo prison the

factory workers and their families were seized in the massive roundup of February 27, 1943. The Riedes were certain that Kurt had been overlooked and that their arrest was only a matter of time. They did not know whether the baron could help them again if they found themselves back in the prison. It was a chance they were unwilling to take. And so they had fled.

As the Riedes told the Wirkuses their story Beppo and Kadi were thankful destiny had chosen them to provide a way station for the Jewish couple. And yet the story only underscored what a dangerous service that was. Alone in their bedroom, they lay awake into the early morning hours wondering what to do. Had they not done enough already? On the other hand, how could they turn the Riedes out?

In the end it was the Riedes who resolved the dilemma. As much as they might have liked to remain, they did not want to expose the Wirkuses to further danger. Besides, they reasoned, if the Gestapo hadn't come for them, it was proof that they were still under the baron's protection.

Prior to their departure on February 27 the Riedes had arranged an all-clear signal with their old landlady. If it was safe for them to come back to their apartment she would place a white rag on her balcony. A week after the Riedes arrived in Wittenau, Beppo went to the Kaiserstrasse to check for the signal. There was nothing hanging from the balcony. He went again several days later. This time there was a white rag. He went to the landlady's apartment. She confirmed that the Gestapo had not appeared. When the rag was still in place after another several days, Kurt and Hella concluded that it was safe for them to return to their apartment.

When the time came to say goodbye, the two couples could scarcely speak. Hella hugged the baby, and seeing this, Kadi burst into tears. The two women embraced. Kurt and Beppo looked at each other awkwardly.

"There's an S.S. man I know," Kurt began. "I think he can be bribed. . . ."

"Don't throw your money away," Beppo said.

They walked through the garden to the gate. Beppo addressed both Riedes. "If there's danger and you have nowhere else to go, come back to Wittenau."

11

THE JEWS who went underground in Germany in the 1940s to escape the Nazis called themselves "U-boats," a self-mocking reference to the country's efficient and effective fleet of submarines. But the comparison was as apt as it was sardonic, because to remain underground required much the same degree of wile, stealth and courage as that employed by the crews of the submarines. Some of the Jews who had gone underground were able to remain sequestered until the end of the war. But the majority, like the submarines, had constantly to surface and prowl about. They worried about whether the Gestapo and the S.S. were on their trail or whether neighbors had reported their presence. The Germans who sheltered them became nervous as well. Either or both circumstances required them to find new hiding places every few days or weeks; only infrequently were the majority of Jewish "U-boats" able to remain in their safe harbors for months. Then there was the matter of money for food; it was up to the Jews to find it somehow. They had to secure the ration cards that would enable them to buy food, or develop black market contacts.

Every Jew not permanently hidden had to leave his residence each day as though going to work, and return home each night. During the day he had no alternative but to walk the streets, ever on the alert for Wehrmacht patrols and S.S. plainclothes-men demanding to know why he wasn't in uniform, or for for-mer friends, neighbors, and business and professional associates who might wittingly or unwittingly give him away. He had to constantly remind himself to stay away from old haunts and neighborhoods, lest he unconsciously drift toward them. Prowl-ing the streets of Berlin in this manner for twelve hours each weekday took its toll not just on the body but on clothes and shoes, which had to be repaired or replaced, a process requiring as much stealth, at times, as the daily purchase of food. Even personal hygiene was as necessary as it was desirable, for an un-washed pedestrian would surely attract attention. But soap too was rationed, and even after it was acquired it was difficult for those Jews constantly on the move to use it. If they washed themselves or their clothing in public rest rooms they increased their visibility.

Like the submariners, many Jewish "U-boats" were efficient and effective. They went underground only after elaborate planning, the hoarding of resources, the identification of safe houses and the acquisition of false papers. But Willy Glaser, the middle-aged enthusiast of the arts, had failed to make such preparations. Where more efficient Jews had slipped carefully under the surface of life in Berlin, Willy's descent into hiding had been a sudden plunge down a flight of tenement stairs. He hadn't thought about resources because he had none to hoard. False papers were luxuries for others than the likes of him; even if he had had the money for bribes, he wouldn't have known how to go about acquiring the papers. As to a safe house, he'd had no promises, only hopes.

But for once in Willy's life the hopes had been realized.

Fortunate people in fortunate times had known nothing but happiness in the garden house in which he now found himself, Willy reckoned. It was a wooden house situated on a huge piece of land in the middle of a forest a mile from Müggelheim, a vil-lage near Köpenick, on the southeast fringe of Berlin. The house had once belonged to a Jewish family named Schwerin that had had the good sense to emigrate in time to England. It was a summer house, without electricity or inside plumbing, and Willy was occupying it during a miserable winter. Yet it had been his salvation, that house, exactly the place he had had in mind as he ran away from the Gestapo on the morning of January 31, 1943. He knew the house, because it now belonged to a Christian friend, George Meier. It was to Meier's home in Berlin that Willy had gone on his first night as a fugitive.

Meier had sent him to the country house the following night. He had given Willy the keys, a small petroleum lamp and a supply of food and water. But Willy wasn't supposed to light the lamp except in a dire emergency, because the neighbors might see the light. Willy had risked the S-Bahn to Köpenick and then a bus to Müggelheim and then walked through the forest in the middle of the night until he found the house. The bed was damp, the water pump wasn't working, and the cold permeated his bones. But he couldn't light a fire, lest the neighbors see the smoke.

For three days he lived in the house without light or heat; when his supplies ran out he did without food and water. He tried desperately to control his urges until nightfall, when he could make the trip to the privy under cover of darkness. By the fourth day, when Meier came with a fresh supply of food and water, Willy was near despair. "It's like living in a dungeon," he said. And yet they both knew that there was no alternative.

For weeks the isolation continued. One day, at last, Willy opened the door a crack. Outside the sun was shining. He crept out and walked around the property. The next day he repeated the excursion, and the day after that, each time venturing a little farther from the house. With success came boldness. One day he went out the garden gate and walked for twenty-five minutes until he was in the small village of Müggelheim. There he sat in a cafe and drank a cup of coffee. The next day he walked to Müggelheim and took a bus to Köpenick, a suburb-size community. Finally the day came when he ventured into Berlin itself. It was foolish, and he knew it, but he preferred the risk to the isolation.

His greatest fear was being caught in an air raid and having to go a shelter. Berlin was like a ghost town during air raids. Everyone was required to be off the streets; there was no vehicular traffic. It was the best of all times for the police patrols to tour the shelters in their constant search for criminals, deserters and underground Jews. Thus far, however, his luck had held; he hadn't been caught in a raid, no one had questioned him, and he was beginning to believe divine Providence was guarding him.

And then one day, just as the weather was warming up and the cottage was beginning to seem hospitable, Meier came to tell Willy that it was time for him to leave. The neighbors would be coming soon to use their country homes, and there was no way that he could be explained, particularly since many of them had known him from another time and knew that he was Jewish.

It was a bitter moment for Willy Glaser, but since he had already survived for three months as an illegal, he couldn't help but believe that he could survive still longer. All he needed was another place to go.

The trouble was that there was no other place to go.

12

THE QUESTION of what to do with the orphan Hans Rosenthal when he suddenly reappeared in Berlin in March 1943 was not long in being answered. His Grandmother Agnes, to whom he appealed for help, found a refuge for him with a woman named Jauch, a small, delicate, middle-aged spinster who ran a tiny dress shop in a workers' neighborhood called Lichtenberg, on the east side of Berlin. She had bought dresses from Hans's mother. The dresses came originally from Frau Rosenthal's Christian aunt, a sister of Grandmother Agnes, who had a big job in a department store and always had extra dresses made when she ordered, so that she could give some to her niece for resale.

Frau Jauch's sole activity when she wasn't selling dresses was studying the Bible. The Bible, she said, had prophesied the evil incarnation of Hitler. The Bible also told her that the war would end in July of 1944, fourteen months hence. She lived in a tiny cottage behind her store in a neighborhood of cottages that had neither electricity nor indoor plumbing. Her cottage consisted of a combination bedroom-sitting room, a kitchen, and a five-by-six-foot shed beyond the kitchen. It was in this tiny annex that Hans had been living since his grandmother had brought him to Frau Jauch in March. Frau Jauch, who had mourned the passing of Hans's mother, had agreed at once to hide him.

His room contained a couch, a small table and a chair. It had no heat. The only time he was warm was in the evening, when Frau Jauch would pull aside the drapery that covered the door, open the door and let Hans out. It was then that she would also empty the chamber pot Hans had used during the day. He never went outside. He had remained indoors for three months.

Frau Jauch would give Hans portions of the Bible and the Psalms to read. She tried to persuade him that the Jews were the chosen people, an idea he found uncomfortable; all people, he believed, were equal.

When they spoke, which was rarely, they did so in the barest whispers, leaning next to each other's ears. But mostly they communicated by signs, because Frau Jauch was supposed to be living alone, and a passerby might become suspicious if he heard voices. They would eat their meals together in silence in the kitchen. Afterward they would remain together either in the kitchen or the sitting-bedroom, because two lamps for one person in a frugal neighborhood would make the neighbors wonder.

Hans kept Frau Jauch's sales records for her, which she needed to obtain new merchandise. It was a small enough way to show his gratitude. Not only was she hiding him and emptying his chamber pot without complaint, she was also sharing her ration cards with him. Frau Jauch had two hens, which gave them a small supply of eggs, and she kept rabbits, which she insisted Hans learn to kill. "If you don't," she said in response to his initial squeamishness, "we won't have food to live on." She would bring a rabbit to his room, and Hans would kill it there, then cut it open and dress it.

Three antifascist families in the neighborhood knew about Hans and brought Frau Jauch extra supplies of food. His grandmother also came from time to time with provisions. He never asked her about the family. He did not want to know about anyone, lest he be captured and tortured into revealing their whereabouts. Similarly, he prayed that his grandmother wouldn't talk to the others about him.

Every morning Frau Jauch brought Hans a copy of the *Morgenpost,* and he would read every word—a four-hour task—even though he was certain that the paper was filled with propaganda. Frau Jauch had bought him a map; from the dispatches in the newspaper he could mark the location of the fronts. As good a face as the stories tried to put on the battles, it was obvious that the German armies in Russia had either been stalled or actually pushed back. Outright German victories were proclaimed with less and less frequency; when there was one, Hans took it as a personal defeat, an extension of his imprisonment. But German victories meant only that the war would be prolonged; Hans never doubted that the Allies would ultimately win the war, or that he himself would survive.

He prayed often for his brother, little Gert, who had had polio at the age of two, and whose blood serum, following his complete and rapid recovery, had thereafter been given to other polio victims in the hope that whatever had cured him so quickly might also cure them. (His blood ceased to be "acceptable" after the passage by the Nazis in 1935 of the Nuremberg Laws, which set forth the regulations by which the racial purity of "Aryans" was to be protected.) Gert had been ten when he was deported; Hans hadn't known then about the gas chambers. He prayed now that the rumors he had heard weren't true. Over and over again he chastised himself for not getting Gert out of that orphanage. Somehow he should have found a way. Again and again Hans prayed that after the war he would be reunited with his brother.

After the war he would do many things. First he would devote all of his time to finding and killing members of the S.S. The Nazis were murderers. They had started the war. They had killed the Jews. They did not deserve to live. Then he would go to the radio stations and broadcast to the German people, telling them that they must develop tolerance, that Jews were like other people. He would not leave Germany. He would stay and educate young Germans to democracy. He hated the Nazis. He could not hate the Germans. Right now a German woman was hiding him, feeding him, saving his life.

He could not understand the hatred of race. He spent hours wondering what was behind it, and other hours praying for the end of the war.

He slept lightly now. At the sound of footsteps he would awaken at once and grasp the knife he kept in his room. He quickly learned to distinguish between the footsteps of his neighbors and the jackboots of the Nazis.

13

SINCE THE MORNING after he had gone underground, early in
December 1942, Fritz Croner, the resilient jeweler, had scoured
the city for a sanctuary for himself, Marlitt and the baby, Lane,
to replace the one he would have to give up on January 1. When
the last days of December arrived and he had still found nothing, he felt that he had touched bottom. Perhaps, he told himself one morning, the time really had come for him and Marlitt
to place Lane with a friendly German woman and surrender to
the Gestapo.

And then that very morning the miracle happened.

Two hours later Fritz burst into their barren flat and took
Marlitt into his arms. "I found a place!" he said.

She sagged against him. "Thank God!"

Quickly he told her the details. The "place" was not a flat but
a store. He had rented it from a real estate agent, a non-Jew
married to a Jewish woman. The agent knew that he and Marlitt were Jewish, but it didn't matter, because he didn't have to
register them with the police. Only residents of apartments had
to be registered. There was no registration requirement for those
who rented stores, inasmuch as no one, presumably, lived in
them.

The store was in Halensee, just beyond the western terminus

of the Kurfürstendamm. The Croners moved in on January 1, 1943. There was only one bed, and a mattress for Lane, but its very improbability as a dwelling gave them added reassurance. Within a few days Fritz was able to secure a Telefunken radio, complete with short wave, and that brightened their lives even more.

Fritz told the caretaker of the building that he was an engineer stationed in Poland, and that his work brought him frequently back to Berlin. The caretaker accepted the story. But Fritz became restless. One hiding place didn't seem enough to him. He thought they needed two or three. They would be far safer if they could move around.

In late January he found a room in an apartment on the Mörchinger Strasse in Zehlendorf. He rented it under the name of Fritz Kramer. The woman from whom he sublet the room was paying 150 marks a month rent for the entire apartment; for his room—which he told her he planned to use only two or three days a week—she charged him 600 marks a month, even though she would rent the room to others when he wasn't there. Fritz didn't complain. When she asked him for his police registration, he told her that because he was in Berlin only a few days a week on business he wasn't required to have one. Had she believed his story, or had she reported him to the police? He couldn't know. He could only hope that she liked his rent enough to accept whatever risk was involved for herself in failing to report him.

Fritz and Marlitt agreed that it would be impossible to take Lane with them when they used the apartment in Zehlendorf. Someone would demand to know what a baby was doing with an itinerant merchant and his wife in a furnished room in Berlin. Why did not the mother and child remain at home? Where *was* home? And where were the papers to prove it? They still had no papers—and no convincing story for anyone more demanding than the landlady. And so they placed Lane with an old woman in Neukölln who had been recommended by others. Three times a week, Marlitt would go to Neukölln with food for the child. In addition they paid the woman 300 marks a month.

With Lane in safekeeping, and with two hiding places, Fritz was beginning to feel, if not secure, at least a little more comfortable.

And then, on February 4, 1943, Fritz Croner went to visit his parents at their apartment, only to learn that the event he had expected and dreaded since his own flight into illegality two months before had finally come to pass. That day the elder Croners had received an order to remain in their flat. They all knew what that meant: deportation. But no one had come. "Maybe tomorrow," Willy Croner said.

It was difficult for Fritz to look at his father. How proud a German he had once been. He had fought for his country and been crippled in its behalf; a wound suffered in the battle of Tannenberg in East Prussia, fighting against the Russians, had permanently disabled his right knee. He had received a medal for heroism. When the Nazis came to power, Jews from the nearby villages came to him and asked, "What are you going to do? Are you going to leave?"

"Leave Germany?" Willy Croner scoffed. "What for? I have my Iron Cross." Surely, Willy Croner believed, a man who had risked his life for the fatherland had nothing to fear.

Now, ten years later, the truth had worked like acid on Willy Croner's face, washing it of all illusion as well as the slightest sign of hope. It had been months since he had smiled. The pain that he wore so visibly worked doubly on Fritz. There was the empathy he felt for his father's suffering. There was also the devastating argument it raised against Fritz's own iron determination to survive.

The time came to say goodbye. Fritz embraced his mother. It registered on him that even in this moment she was being a predictable Jewish mother, making it easier for him by not crying. Then he turned to his father. They shook hands and then clasped each other. Fritz left the apartment sick with the knowledge that, in all probability, he would never see his parents again.

A week later he called the Jewish community headquarters. "What's with the Croners?" he asked.

"They were picked up February fifth," a voice on the other end said.

A few days later Fritz went to the apartment of his parents' neighbor, where Willy Croner had left a trunk with their papers, the papers that proved he had owned valuable property he had been forced to sell for a pittance. Fritz remembered the details of that humiliation all too clearly. One day in February 1938 Fritz was in Berlin on business when he received a frantic phone call from his father. "Come fast," he had said, "I'm in trouble with the Gestapo." When Fritz returned to Deutsch-Krone his father told him that he was being pressured by the Gestapo to sell his store and house and move to Berlin. The Gestapo said it had a buyer, but it wouldn't reveal the buyer's name or tell Willy Croner the price. Each day Willy was compelled to report to Gestapo headquarters, where he was made to stand for an hour and receive a barrage of insults, along with demands that he agree to sell out.

Several days passed, with the same routine. Then the Gestapo learned that Fritz was in Deutsch-Krone and ordered him to accompany his father. Finally Willy was excused because of his war injury, and Fritz was made to bear the Gestapo's hazing.

The Gestapo men in Deutsch-Krone were mostly peasants with little education. They delighted in making Fritz feel like a fool. They would stand him in front of one wall of their fifteen-by-eighteen-foot office, to which had been pinned the Nazi newspaper *Der Stürmer*. Then they would order him to do one hundred deep-knee bends.

"It will stop the moment your father says he will sell the shop and the house," one of them told him. "Be sure and tell your father."

Fritz was supposed to arrive for his daily ordeal at 7:00 A.M. One morning he overslept and arrived late without having shaved. Each morning thereafter he was compelled to announce his arrival. "I am the Jew, Croner," he would call out at the door. "I am clean-shaven."

The routine had continued every day for six months. Finally Fritz said to his father, "It's no use. We have to sell." Willy agreed. It wasn't just his son's ordeal; he knew that the same pressures were being exerted against Jews all over Germany. Inevitably they would be forced to succumb.

Willy Croner had calculated that if he ever had to sell the store he could get 500,000 Deutschmarks for it. He so informed the Gestapo. To his amazement the Gestapo agreed to the price—but then withheld all but 130,000 marks of the 500,000 paid by the buyer. Willy had been bitter about that to the last. He had worked hard for what he had earned, starting as a youth on a farm, then lugging a pack of textiles on his back through the countryside, selling to the farmers and their wives.

As he read through his father's papers Fritz made a vow. After the war he would be recompensed. The papers would help him get back what the Nazis had taken from his father. In his heart Fritz knew he would never be able to decorate his father's grave; the compensation would be his living memorial to Willy Croner.

14

NINE MONTHS had passed since his infant son had died, and in that period Hans Hirschel, the equable intellectual, had not once left the store in Wilmersdorf that Countess Maria von Maltzan, the baby's mother, had converted into an apartment. He spent the days alone with his memories, not simply of the child's death, or even of the deportation of his beloved mother to Theresienstadt the previous spring, but of how intoxicating life had been in Berlin before the Nazis came to power. That life was over now, and he was a prisoner, if not of the Nazis directly, at least of the hell they had made.

In order to maintain his sanity Hans followed a strict routine. Each morning at 6:15 exactly he would rise, draw Marushka's bath, then awaken her. While Marushka bathed and dressed—usually in pants, because she rode a bicycle to work—Hans would prepare her breakfast as well as a bag lunch of cut-up vegetables that she would take with her to the university, where she was finishing her studies in veterinary medicine. As soon as Marushka had departed Hans would wash the dishes, sweep the floors and tidy up the house. Then he would return to bed and read a book. Sometime after eight he would rise and begin his long ritual of preparing for the day. First he would bathe. Then he would ponder over his choice of clothing: he might wear the same suit and shirt two days in a row, but he always varied his bow ties. Finally he was ready to leave for the day—but of course he would go nowhere.

He had always been a fastidious man, and the best way to deal with his imprisonment, he had decided, was to retain as much as possible of the manner and appearance of the man he had known himself to be. The one great problem was the beard he had grown to alter his appearance. He loathed it. It did not become him, and it made him feel unkempt.

When he was dressed Hans would return to his self-appointed task of running the household. It was the least he could do, for Marushka was not only risking her life in his behalf, she was also virtually supporting him. Hans had brought a number of Indian bronzes with him from the apartment he had shared with his mother, which Marushka sold piecemeal from time to time as money was needed. However, the bronzes were not especially valuable and did not bring in enough money to cover expenses. It was Marushka who earned a steady income from her many odd jobs—she was now inspecting slaughterhouses and working for the German equivalent of the Society for the Prevention of Cruelty to Animals—and from black market trading. The fact was that Hans was now dependent on Marushka for everything—even his haircuts. Her hairdresser had told her of the many Jews who had been seized while visiting beauty and barber shops. Marushka told him she knew of a Jew in hiding, a man who desperately needed a haircut, and he had taught her how to cut hair.

Hans was not good at household tasks, nor did he enjoy them. It was not that he was unwilling or felt demeaned; it was just that he was inefficient, and nothing in his previous life had prepared him for such circumstances. All his life he had been attended to by either his mother or their housekeeper. Luzie Hirschel had encouraged her son's dependence as a means of keeping him for as long as she could. Ironically, certain women who were drawn to him initially because of his good looks became even more entranced when they discovered his dependency.

To a degree, Marushka was one of them. She enjoyed giving Hans his haircuts, or doing his wash—one household task Hans was never able to manage—but she was careful not to smother him. She esteemed what she called his "exquisite" brains, his philosophical bent, his cleverness, his wit. But she knew that Hans perceived himself in another light. Like many intellectuals, he wanted to be admired for his physical prowess almost more than his mind, and he would often boast about his accomplishments in such sports as tennis and boxing. The truth was that he was an all but hopeless athlete, and his boasts—considered in relation to his slim, almost frail physique—seemed like fantasies, which invariably sent Marushka into fits of laughter. One evening, recounting his experiences on the railroad gang before he went into hiding, he bragged of having lifted up a section of track that weighed 750 pounds. Marushka laughed so hard that she finally had to join her.

In the main, however, Hans was as well suited for a period of enforced seclusion as any man could be, and at the outset—before his mother's deportation and the baby's death—he had rather relished the privacy. Even now he admitted that the imprisonment had its uses. One of his greatest problems had always been to maintain his focus on the subject at hand. Coupled with the philosopher's love of abstractions, it had tended to make his writings diffuse and difficult to understand. Now, as his reality became more concrete and circumscribed, his work sharpened.

He had his one great intellectual passion to occupy him—his fascination with the dark side of even the most positive religious movement. But he also had a great deal of specific work—more, ironically, than he had ever had in normal times—articles, book reviews, radio plays, even short books. It was Marushka who would obtain the assignments, ostensibly for herself. She would then give them to Hans to do, along with the research materials he would need. When he finished a draft Marushka would re-write it, not out of vanity but from caution. Their styles were poles apart. It would not have done for anyone to question the authorship.

Hans did an article on Jan Hus, a radio play about a Finnish general, a play on Cromwell, one on the Boer War. The Cromwell play was intended to show how nasty the British had been to the Irish, the Boer War play how savagely they had treated the Boers, even putting them in concentration camps. Everything that Hans wrote, however, contained a guarded put-down of the Nazis, which only the Nazis failed to recognize.

In the evenings Hans and Marushka would listen to radio plays written by party hacks and laugh at the bad style and awful structure. Together they wrote a play about Louis Napoleon, trying, for once, to do it on a high level. The play was rejected.

"Let's write the worst possible play we can," Hans proposed. When they finished he said, "It's so vile, they'll never take it." The script was accepted without revision.

Hans's working day began after a lunch of oatmeal or other cereal, which he would dutifully prepare and then often forgo. When he had finished with the writing assignments he would either read or work on a poem. When a poem was finished he would place it on Marushka's pillow. It was in these poems that his true feelings came out—his gratitude to Marushka, his sense of lost potential, his feeling of alienation from the normal pulse of life.

"Our love fills the black void between us," he wrote in one of his poems. He was putting into as positive a context as he could the troubling knowledge that they had come from different worlds—Marushka from one dominated by an aristocratic mother who collected anti-Semitic literature, Hans from another, dominated by a worldly mother who moved in the highest literary circles. To an extent Hans's Jewishness—like his mother's and even his father's—had been largely replaced by his Germanness. He "felt" Jewish and was recognized as a Jew by others—the two fundamental criteria of whether one is or isn't a Jew—but he had no deep religious feeling. Because Marushka was such a free spirit, he had planned to defer to her in their child's religious training.

Since the 1870s, when Napoleonic concepts of equal rights gained acceptance in Germany, many Jews had shown their gratitude at being legitimized by becoming more German than the Germans. They supported the fatherland, both emotionally and practically. Yet even after Otto von Bismarck guaranteed civil rights to Jews in 1871, theory and reality were far apart. It took military service in World War I to make these rights, and full equality for Jews, an actuality. Almost 100,000 Jews had served in the army; 80,000 saw combat; 35,000 were decorated for bravery; 12,000 were killed. Hans himself had been decorated for his service in the final years of the great war, and he had supported Germany's aspirations wholeheartedly. He could not believe, let alone accept, what had happened since. In one poem, "The Song of a German Jew," he tried to express what it meant to feel so German and then suddenly not be permitted to *be* German.

The reality of Hans's confinement grew more vivid with each day. The longer it went on, the more troubled he became. Discourse had been his life, and now he was all but deprived of it. Occasionally Marushka would bring home some fellow students, and Hans, posing as "Professor Schoeler," would drill them in preparation for exams. The only friends Marushka could bring to him were those whose company tended to be unexciting; those friends engaged in touchy political work told Marushka it was better for everyone if they stayed away.

So, sadly, Hans's closest companions became the dogs—two Scotch terriers Marushka had bought to keep him company and also to breed for the income she could get from the puppies. Every morning Hans would groom the dogs and then play with them. When he did the household chores, he would talk to them. "Have you any idea where the towels might be?" he would ask. The dogs would stare at him and wag their tails. A little after ten Irmelin Patrick, the fiancée of one of Marushka's nephews, would come to take the dogs for their morning walk; Hans would peek through the curtain and watch them play. At eleven o'clock they would return for their meal. "I've got a lovely meal for you today," he would tell them. "You'll start off with a fine soup—bouillon with egg and cream. Then you're having venison with a cream sauce and red currant jelly. For dessert a splendid sorbet." Then he would serve them their dog food.

Despite his circumstances Hans rarely showed moodiness or despair. He refused to be destroyed, either by his own imprisonment or the threats of capture. His greatest problem was in coming to terms with the baby's death. He thought its moment of life had been senseless. "No!" Marushka argued one evening. "Every human being has some destiny to fulfill. This child, in one day, had a reason for his existence. If it wasn't for him you would have been killed in Poland." Hans looked away and closed his eyes. He was silent for several minutes. When he looked back at Marushka his eyes were shining. "I'll try to believe that," he said.

Only once did he raise his voice. "This damned war! This damned Hitler!" he shouted one day after his mother was deported. "You have to go out and do all this filthy work while I sit here helpless." But at all other times he remained amazingly equable, considering what he was going through. If he did feel himself slipping into despondency, he would play with the dogs or talk to the birds. Marushka had cages of them—finches, canaries, parrakeets. When Marushka arrived home in the evening his first order of business would be to tell her how the dogs had played that day and how the birds had sung.

With Marushka's return Hans would feel that he had been released from prison. If she looked particularly tired he would tell her to lie down and then bring her supper on a fastidiously arranged plate. He would try to convince her that his own day, spent in solitary confinement, had passed easily and happily. Only when he saw Marushka relaxing would he begin to bombard her with questions about her day. He had to know everything. He would open up her handbag, pull out its contents and demand to know where she had obtained each item. Usually there was a story attached to every object, because Marushka was such a proficient dealer on Berlin's black market. That market had commenced, as elsewhere in Germany, at the outset of the war. Within a few years it thrived to a degree the Nazis were reluctant to acknowledge. While food was the major trading item, false documents ran a close second, particularly as the war dragged on. Such documents—ration cards, priority cards, tickets, identifications—were Marushka's stock-in-trade. A false document could bring in hundreds of marks, which she would then exchange for food.

Marushka treasured her independence. She believed she could support herself and Hans by her black market transactions as well as her jobs. At the time Hans moved in with her, she estimated it would cost 1,000 marks a month to feed him, because all of his food came from the black market. Later the figure went much higher. But she always found a way—even performing an occasional abortion, for which she charged 3,000 marks.

One day a veterinarian Marushka knew was called upon to inspect a herd of cattle that had been shipped in from the Ukraine in an obviously unhealthy state. The veterinarian diagnosed a rare liver disease. Unfortunately for him that disease existed only in tropical climates. The man was fired, and Marushka got his job. Each Sunday when she went to the countryside to inspect the livestock, the peasants would load her up with fresh vegetables. What she didn't need she would trade for other foods.

To fill their stomachs she was not above a little mischief. One day she picked up her telephone and, because of crossed wires, overheard a conversation between a woman she knew, a Mrs. Zifkowitz, and a man who sold poultry on the black market. Mrs. Zifkowitz was in the process of ordering an extremely large goose. As soon as the conversation ended, Marushka telephoned

Mrs. Zifkowitz. Using a deep voice, she identified herself as a police officer and said that she had overheard the conversation and intended to report the episode. However, she said, she was the father of nine children; if Mrs. Zifkowitz agreed to leave the goose in a certain shed in a park near her home, she would not be reported. The next evening Marushka collected the goose.

Stories like these meant more to Hans than the food itself. He doted on Marushka. She was the most marvelous person he had ever known, a free and independent spirit, with an exotic background that he never tired of hearing about even when he had heard the same story dozens of times before.

She would tell him about her father, the count, the only member of her family she truly liked. He was descended from a line of Maltzans who had come into Germany from Sweden with Gustavus II, the "Lion of the North," during the first part of the seventeenth century—Protestant knights come to war upon the Catholics. They were granted estates in Silesia and East Prussia. Maltzan went one better; he married the only daughter of the ruler of Silesia—there were no sons—and thus succeeded to his title.

Marushka's father, Andreas von Maltzan, inherited a German estate of 18,000 acres. Although he lived in the twentieth century, he was as much a lord of the manor as his forebears. Any of the inhabitants of the estate who wished to marry were married by the count. Von Maltzan was respected—not liked, but he had a liberal conscience. He created hospitals, orphanages and old-age homes.

The Von Maltzan estate had passed rhythmically through the centuries between heirs with a head for business and those more interested in the arts. Marushka's father was in the latter category—his passions were paintings and antiques—but if he knew little about farming, he had the good sense to employ competent people.

When Andreas read to his daughter, he eschewed fairy tales in favor of more substantial works. By the time she enrolled in school she was reasonably well educated in history, and, not surprisingly, one of her first acts was to challenge her teacher's knowledge. In the ensuing uproar the count came to the school to investigate, and that evening he advised Maria: "Be kind to him. He doesn't know anything."

The count did his utmost to instill principles in Maria, but he was not a preacher. The lessons he taught her were usually given in a more practical form. One day Maria, then seven years old, rushed in to report that the cottage of her nursery maid had burned to the ground. "I know," her father said. "Don't worry, the insurance will pay for it."

"No, it won't," Maria said, and then repeated what she had heard her distraught guardian discussing with her husband. The family had been cutting hay the previous evening by the light of an open fire. Embers from the fire had started the blaze on the cottage roof. They knew that the fire had resulted from their own carelessness and that the insurance company wouldn't pay.

Count von Maltzan thought for a moment. "Maria," he said then, "how much money do you have in the bank?"

"Two hundred and seventeen marks."

"I suggest you go and get it. Berta has cleaned your shoes and taken care of you for a long time. Now you must take care of her."

That day Maria gave Berta two hundred marks.

Although Maria had three sisters and a brother, she led a fairly lonely life, which accounted considerably for the fierce love she developed for animals, including birds and even reptiles. The estate abounded in snakes; when Maria found one she would seize it, stroke it until it relaxed, examine it, and then let it go. One day she found a pile of dead snakes, and learned that the gardeners had killed them at the behest of her brother, who loathed reptiles. That day Maria invited her brother for a ride in her new boat, which she had bought with the proceeds from the sale of white mice and guinea pigs she had raised. When they were far enough out in the lake she pushed him overboard, grabbed his legs and held him so that his head remained under water. She would have drowned him if her father had not intervened.

To Maria, growing up was a war of survival. From her earliest years she believed that everyone ganged up on her, and with reason. When she was seven her sisters would contrive to send her to the stable on some pretext just before teatime. Their mother had an inviolable rule: anyone who did not have his or her feet under the table exactly at four o'clock got black bread at tea instead of buttered toast, jam and pastries. Each time Maria would be late, there would be more buttered toast and pastries for her sisters and brother to share. One day Maria finally figured it out. She went to the garden, grabbed a *Kreuzotter,* a poisonous three-foot snake, behind the head and marched with it into the dining room. "I want a good tea," she announced. "I want my buttered toast and jam and pastries. Either I get it or I let the snake go." She got her good tea.

She also ran her own little world. She made all her own decisions and took care of herself, partly because no one else would help her, partly because she surmised—correctly, in most cases—that she was more capable than the others involved, and only her combativeness would enable her to survive. Her mother had made it plain to her when she was very young that she didn't like her. "Every other child I delivered in less than three hours," she once said. "You took twenty-seven."

The countess made no effort to disguise her biases. She favored some of her children more than others. Her favorite of favorites was her son, the youngest child; her feeling for him was reinforced by the loss of an older boy. She cared for her husband, but was dismayed by their provincial life. Her most active biases were those against the Jews. Over the years a series of neighboring estates had been subdivided, and many of the smaller estates had been bought by Jews. Inevitably, intermarriages resulted, and when one countess converted to Judaism on her marriage to a Jew, Countess von Maltzan was beside herself. "I don't want *you* marrying a Jew," she warned Maria.

If Maria had any doubts about her mother's lack of affection, they were banished in her thirteenth year, at the bedside of her dying father. "Your mother doesn't like you," he told her. "But try to be polite and do what you should do."

To Hans the notion of an uncaring mother was all but incredible. His own grief at the departure and certain death of his cherished mother was minimized by Marushka's strength. He knew that in some respects he had traded one mother for another. He lived for Marushka's presence, and rejoiced at each return, as if it were a reunion following a prolonged separation.

Which made her abrupt, inexplicable departures in the night all the more painful.

They had begun almost at once after Hans moved in. There was no pattern to them. She might remain at home for weeks without going out in the evening. Then there would be weeks when she'd leave the house several evenings in a row. Often these sudden departures would be preceded by a phone call. It was obvious to Hans by the way she answered the phone that something was going on. Even if she was sitting right next to the phone, she wouldn't respond until it had rung three times. Sometimes the caller hung up after two rings. When that happened Marushka would look at her watch. About a minute later the phone would begin to ring again. Once more Marushka wouldn't answer—and once more the phone would ring twice and then stop. A minute later the phone would begin to ring again. Only then would Marushka answer.

Hans could never understand the conversation. It would be too fragmented, or oblique or guarded. Often she would leave at once after the call and be gone for several hours. On the few occasions when he had tried to find out what she was up to, she had brushed his queries aside.

One evening in the summer of 1942 Marushka came in especially late. Hans was waiting up for her. She went immediately to the bathroom and put some antiseptic on a neck wound.

"For God's sake, Marushka, that's a bullet wound!" he cried. "What the hell's going on?"

She looked at him coolly. "Hans . . . one thing. Never ask me about where I've been or what I've done. It's better that you don't know."

III

CAPTURE

15

SEVERAL WEEKS had passed since the seizure of Kurt Thomas and still there was no word from him. All of Ruth Thomas' anguished pleas for intervention by her husband's former wife, Lea, had been unavailing. He had simply vanished from her life. To Ruth it seemed that nothing the Nazis could do now would be worse than the seizure of her husband.

And then, one evening in March, Ruth learned how wrong she was. A doctor told her that she herself was being hunted— and that the hunter was a Jew working for the Gestapo.

Earlier that day, the doctor said, he had been visited by a young man who helped make up the transports. The young man had shown him a photograph of a woman whose maiden name had been Rosenthal and who had gone underground late in 1942. The picture had come with a letter from an anonymous informer who said that the Jewish woman was living with an S.S. officer's wife. "It was a picture of you," the doctor said softly.

Who could have denounced her? Ruth managed to ask herself in those first paralyzing moments of fright. Lisa Krauss! It had to be. Lisa, the young woman with whom Ruth had spent her first days of illegality and with whom she had remonstrated when she found that Lisa was using the possessions her Jewish employers—the pastry-shop owners named Dubrin—had left with her for safekeeping. One of the brothers had gone into exile in England. Two others had been sent to Theresienstadt but had bought their freedom. Here was Lisa wearing their wives' furs and displaying their works of art as though they belonged to her. Ruth had acted on impulse that day. She hadn't thought it through. What else was Lisa to do with the possessions? Why not use them? But none of these thoughts had occurred to her then. Instead she had lost her temper. "You don't really feel pity for the Jews," she had said, sobbing. "You just want to have our things."

A few days later a woman who knew them both said to Ruth, "Lisa is very annoyed with you."

"Why?" Ruth asked.

"Because you made those remarks to her."

And so Lisa had denounced her. It had to be.

Ruth rushed to a telephone to alert Hilde. "If the Gestapo comes, say you didn't know I was Jewish."

But Hilde had her own ideas about how to handle the Gestapo: no excuses, no apologies and, above all, no hints of the fear that was making her legs feel unsteady. When two men from the Gestapo arrived within the hour, she gave the performance of her life. "Oh!" she cried and stalked about the room, waving her arms in anger. "I don't know this woman—and I don't associate with Jews."

"But we have a report, Frau Doctor Hohn—"

"To hell with your report!" she shouted. "My husband's an officer in the S.S. I would have to be crazy to hide a Jew. Do you think I'm crazy? Do you?" She was screaming at them now, and while she was lying, her anger was no longer pretense. She could feel a surge of frenzy bordering on hysteria. "Here!" she ordered, stalking to a wardrobe. "Come here!" She threw open the doors. "Look at these dresses! They are all the same size." The Gestapo men hesitated. "Look!" she screamed. "I demand that you look!" She was crying now, all of her fear and anguish released into this confrontation.

Now the Gestapo men were nervous and obviously uncomfortable. "Frau Hohn, I assure you—"

"LOOK!" She was out of control now, and she knew it, but it didn't matter. She had them on the run.

Reluctantly one of the men moved forward and examined the dresses. He nodded to his partner. They were both eager to leave.

"Next time look for your Jews elsewhere, not in the house of an S.S. man!" she said as she opened the door. When they were outside she banged it shut and then leaned against the wall, afraid that her legs would give way if she tried to reach a chair.

In the next weeks Ruth moved ten times, carrying her belongings from place to place in a shopping bag as though she was returning from a trip to the store. Her first refuge was at the home of a "privileged" uncle. A few days later she joined her mother at the home of friends of her grandparents' housekeeper. Then she went to a house in Schöneberg maintained by a woman she scarcely knew, and then to the woman's sister, and then to several residences whose inhabitants were so anonymous that her existence there became a blur. Ruth refused to stay longer than a few days in any location, believing that it was safer for her to keep moving—and also safer for her benefactors, who were taking an enormous risk on her behalf.

During all this time Ruth went out of her way to avoid other Jews or to have any meetings with them, fearing they might fall into the hands of the Gestapo and reveal her whereabouts. But one day she chanced upon a Jewish girl friend, herself an illegal, and this friend recommended that Ruth hide with a woman named Louisa Knispel.

Tante Lisel—as Ruth immediately called Louisa Knispel because a niece of Frau Knispel's who lived with her called her that—looked like the typical German housewife. She was heavyset, with blue eyes and long blond braids wound around her head. As a young girl she had worked for a Jewish professor in Strasbourg and cared for his children. Before the war she had

been a Social Democrat and had despised the National Socialists. She was more than eager to help Ruth, and busied herself
with the task of making Ruth's stay enjoyable. She was a very
good cook, and she liked Ruth very much. But she was also difficult, principally because she was compulsively hygienic. If
Ruth would take a drink of water and forget to wash the glass,
Tante Lisel would run to the kitchen crying, "One can't live this
way. This is impossible." Ruth would want to explode in turn,
but her life depended on Tante Lisel and there was nothing she
could do.

For days the two women moved miserably about the house,
each one liking the other, each one knowing that it was the extraordinary time they were experiencing that was making them
act in such a high-strung manner, yet each one powerless to ease
the tension between them.

And then a friend of Tante Lisel's, a Frau Otto, a civil servant, was suddenly transferred to Posen. The first thing she did
was to call Tante Lisel to ask if she knew anyone reliable who
could sublet her apartment. It was imperative that she find
someone, Frau Otto explained, because if she left the apartment
vacant she might eventually lose it. Tante Lisel told Frau Otto
that her fears were over. She had the perfect tenants.

Ruth Thomas explained herself to Frau Otto by saying that
she was half Jewish. She introduced her mother as her aunt
from the non-Jewish side of the family. She said that they had
been bombed out of Schöneberg, where they had maintained a
home. She explained that Frau Otto could not register them
with the police, because if the police knew they were living
someplace else, they might lose title to their home.

As she listened to the story Frau Otto nodded sympatheti-
cally. She knew what it meant to be threatened with the loss of a
home, she told them. But Ruth surmised that Frau Otto probably suspected the truth and just as probably didn't want to
know. She asked no questions. When she departed it was with
the prayer that Ruth and her mother would preserve her home.

Tante Lisel had one word of advice for Ruth as she prepared

to move. "Forget that you're Jewish," she said. "Your mother too. You'll never make it if you keep going the way you are. Don't tell anyone your story."

Early in the fall Ruth and her mother moved into the apartment in Pankow, on the north side of Berlin. It was a small, three-room apartment on the top floor of a narrow building. It was not comfortable, but it did have a stove and hot water, and it was a hiding place.

And it also had a sewing machine.

To Ruth it seemed only natural that the sewing machine would be there. She was determined to survive, and she knew, beyond all doubt, that with a sewing machine she could—and pull Mother through, as well.

16

ON MARCH 20, 1943, Joseph Goebbels wrote in his diary: "The Fuehrer is happy over my report that the Jews for the most part have been evacuated from Berlin." But four weeks later, on April 18, he was not quite so sanguine: "The Jewish question in Berlin has not found its final solution yet. There still remain a considerable number of Jews by law, Jews in privileged mixed marriages and even Jews in simple mixed marriages, here in the city. This presents grave problems. At any rate I am issuing an order that all the Jews still living in Berlin be re-assessed. I do not want any more Jews wearing the Jewish star to be seen walking around in the capital of the Reich. They should either be allowed to go without the star and granted the rights of privileged ones, or be deported for good from the capital." Then Goebbels added a note of self-encouragement: "I am convinced," he wrote, "that purging Berlin of its Jews is the greatest of my political achievements. Whenever I remember the sight of Berlin on my arrival here in 1926 and compare it to its appearance in 1943, after the Jews have been evacuated, only then can I appreciate the greatness of our achievement in this field."

On May 19, 1943, the Nazis proclaimed Berlin *Judenfrei*. It was not true, as the Third Reich's Minister of Propaganda well knew. Official figures compiled by the Reichsvereinigung, the association of German Jews, at the behest of the Nazis, had listed 18,515 Jews still in Berlin as late as March 31. This figure, however, included all those Jews who were theoretically immune from deportation, the very Jews cited by Goebbels in his diary entry of March 20. ("Jews by law" were those Jews with one Jewish and one non-Jewish parent who themselves were practicing Jews as of September 15, 1935.)

The category of Jews to which the communique undoubtedly referred was the "nonprivileged" one, which was not protected in any way by the Third Reich's complex racial laws. It was this group Goebbels cited when he noted on March 11, "We . . . failed to lay our hands on 4,000." After the war the Jewish community of Berlin estimated on the basis of its own reconstruction that 5,000 Jews had gone underground. Other estimates ranged between 2,000 and 9,000.

Whatever the exact figure as of February 27, 1943, the date of Operation Factory, it is certain that by May 19 the number of illegal Jews remaining in Berlin had been drastically diminished. In that twelve-week period hundreds of underground Jews had been captured and deported or killed outright, or had committed suicide, or had died from malnutrition or fright or lack of medication.

On June 10 the Gestapo appeared at the main office of the Jewish community on the Oranienburger Strasse, announced that the community had ceased to exist and arrested all those employees with no "Aryan blood." At the same time, other Gestapo agents were arresting employees of the Reichsvereinigung, on the Kantstrasse. The Jews were taken to the Grosse Hamburger Strasse collection center. On June 16 a furniture van conveyed them to the Putlitzstrasse railway station, where they were put aboard a transport, along with five hundred Jews who had been taken from their sick-beds in the Jewish hospital on the Iranische Strasse early that morning.

But the hospital itself continued to function, manned by Jewish physicians, nurses and support personnel, and its administrative offices now became the headquarters of a new, curtailed

Reichsvereinigung set up to handle such Jewish affairs as remained, particularly the disposal of Jewish property. Many Jews who had escaped the deportations were pressed into administrative services by the Gestapo. In almost all cases these Jews were related by marriage to non-Jews. Few of them doubted, however, that as the number of Jews in Berlin continued to dwindle, they too would soon be on the transports.

With the help of the *Mundfunk,* Kurt and Hella Riede had kept abreast of developments. They knew that they were on the Reichsvereinigung lists, that they were unaccounted for, and that it was only a matter of time before they would be found and deported.

They had slipped back into their Kaiserstrasse apartment in Berlin without incident following their departure from Wittenau in mid-March. Kurt had even gone back to work at the leather-goods firm—yet another piece of luck.

In the firm was a Frau Hammerling who worked as a bookkeeper. On the floor of her apartment building in Reinickendorf, at the Scharfensee, lived a Gestapo civil servant with whom she had become friendly. He had confided to her one evening that he worked in the division responsible for making up the transports of Jews to the east. From the tone of his remarks Frau Hammerling got the idea that he didn't approve of the policy. She decided to take a chance. "Look," she said the next time they were together, "there's a man in our firm, a Jew, whom we all like very much. Do you suppose you could let me know when his name appears on the lists? I promise you complete silence."

The civil servant pursed his lips. Then he nodded. "I could do that," he said.

Only then did Frau Hammerling reveal Kurt's name—and even then she wondered if she had given his game away. It turned out that she hadn't.

One Monday morning Kurt walked into the office only to be summoned upstairs to see the baron. There, with the baron, was

Frau Hammerling. She explained what she had done. Then she said, "They're coming for you sometime Wednesday evening."

"Thank you," Kurt said. In the next moment he was gone.

That afternoon, six weeks after they had left, the Riedes appeared once more at the Wirkuses' house in Wittenau. Beppo was at work, but Kadi was there. Kurt was shaking, and even Hella, who was normally calm, seemed distraught. Kurt explained what had happened. He asked if they could stay.

Kadi bit her lip. "There's a complication," she told him. The look that crossed their faces made her ill. "There's a young woman living here. We had to take her in because we had so much space. Otherwise we would have lost the house." She squeezed Hella's arm. "I'm sure we can work something out," she said. "Beppo will think of something."

Beppo's decision, when he returned from work, was to tell the young woman that Kurt was his brother, that he had found work nearby and was therefore coming to live with them.

The new tenant, whose name was Ursula, believed the story. She was not a suspicious sort and cared nothing for politics. She was young and blond and pretty and very well pleased with her life. She worked as a secretary in a factory that produced aircraft motors; you could see the factory from the house. The room she rented from the Wirkuses was on the first floor, off a hallway, but it had its own private entrance. Aside from the times she was invited for an occasional glass of schnapps or wine, she did not enter the other parts of the house.

After the initial shock of the Riedes' reappearance had been absorbed, the original harmonies were reestablished. At first Kurt remained indoors, but as the weeks passed and his confidence increased, he ventured outside to water the garden and trim the shrubs. Hella journeyed to the central city and even strolled the Kurfürstendamm, almost as if to reassure herself that she was immune to the probing eyes of the catchers. One evening the two couples went to the Oranienburger Strasse in Wittenau to see a film. By then the Riedes were feeling so confident that they began making trips to Brandenburg to visit

Hella's parents. Kurt's heavy glasses were his pass in the neighborhood. All of the residents of Wittenau who saw him surmised that he had been exempted from military service because of poor eyesight and had a job in industry.

That was the story he told Ursula. Her own work began at seven, and she would not return home until after five. To explain why he was always at home when she left and returned, Kurt told her that his work started at eight and ended at four-thirty.

One evening Ursula left Kurt momentarily speechless when she announced she was taking the next day off. But he recovered quickly. "Great idea," he said. "We'll stay home together and spend a nice, lazy day."

Ursula never had a word to say about the war. Her one great interest was men. At home she flirted openly with both Beppo and Kurt whenever the chance presented itself, which delighted them and annoyed their wives. One evening the two couples were sitting in the kitchen when they heard a loud thump in the hallway, as though someone had dropped a sack of potatoes on the floor. The two men ran to see what had happened. There was Ursula, lying on the floor in a faint. They carried her to her room and put her on her bed. Hella came in a few moments later, pushed them from the room, and bathed Ursula's face with a wet towel. A few minutes later she emerged, disgusted. "This girl is faking," she announced. "She's whitened her face with powder and painted her lips blue."

One day in July, three months after the return of the Riedes, the Wirkuses had a visitor, an Augustine monk named Father Eusebius who lived in a nearby monastery. Father Eusebius had baptized their baby and had come to know the Wirkuses well because of their regular church attendance. He was surprised to see the Riedes, since the Wirkuses had never mentioned them. Now he asked who they were.

The Wirkuses told him the entire story. When they had finished he put his arms around both of them and said, "You mustn't be afraid. What you are doing is a good thing. I will include you in my prayers." A few weeks later, after Sunday Mass, he slipped them some extra ration cards.

The longer the Riedes remained, the more natural their presence seemed to the Wirkuses. When Kadi went off to her parents' farm, Hella would take charge of the house, cleaning, preparing the meals. No one was ever alone, and all of them worked together, not simply on household chores but to keep one another's spirits up.

They worked hard at laughing, but only at first. Soon there was no need to force it. They laughed about Ursula's fainting episode and joked about her flirtatiousness. Beppo would make fun of the daily stupidities at the office. They laughed over their lack of privacy and made fun of one another.

Often in the evenings they would share a bottle of wine. Through his office Beppo had access to liquor rations, which he could buy for very little money. Most of the liquor came from France. He would bring home a bottle of champagne to celebrate a birthday or some cognac to sip while they listened to the radio. It had been a medium-range radio until Beppo had had it modified to shortwave by some technicians at the factory who owed him a favor for expediting their orders. The two couples would sit and drink their brandies and listen to the BBC. It was in this manner that they learned the war had taken a frightening, if paradoxically hopeful, turn.

Berlin was to be leveled by bombs.

Bombs were not new to Berlin. The city had been bombed for the first time exactly three years earlier by the British, in retaliation for a Luftwaffe raid on London. Raids, some of them significant in size, had continued with increasing frequency since then. But the bombing that began in mid-August 1943 was of a scope and intensity such as the city had never experienced before.

Suddenly it was very hard to be gay, even though both young couples welcomed the attacks. The Riedes would now face a new danger. They could not go to the public bomb shelter, where patrols of the Wehrmacht might ask to see their papers.

They would have to sit out the raids in the basement of the Wirkuses' home, where a direct hit could either kill them outright or bury them alive.

17

To the non-Jewish residents of Berlin the bombs that began to fall upon them with such methodical rhythm and pulverizing force were more than portents of massive destruction and prospective injury or death. They were the explosion of the myth of German invincibility that had been so assiduously cultivated by the Nazis. Hermann Goering had boasted at the outset of the war that if enemy planes ever broke through the antiaircraft defenses around Berlin, his name would be "Meier." Now as the Germans sat in their air raid shelters listening to the roar of the approaching bombers, the screech of plummeting bombs, the booming concussions and the crash of falling buildings overhead, they whispered little jokes to one another about "Reichsmarschall Meier." They no longer believed the stories they were being told about the progress of the war in general, because the accounts in the newspapers and on the radio no longer accorded with their own perception of reality.

That reality, each day that they survived, was the certainty that there would be another raid the next day in which some bomber might be carrying a bomb destined for them. It was the possibility, after they had left the shelters in the wake of the all-clear signals, that they would find their homes destroyed and be forced to join the growing ranks of Berliners without a place to live or possessions of any kind. Each night they walked through streets clotted with fallen trees and masses of rubble. If there was a wind, the soot and ashes from hundreds of fires blew into their eyes. Fire engines, their sirens screaming, picked their way through the rubble, trying, often failing, to reach the worst conflagrations. Ambulances carrying the wounded careened through the passable streets, en route to hospitals. Each morning silence covered the city, as thick as the smoke still rising from the smoldering buildings.

For the few thousand Jews still hidden in Berlin, playing cat and mouse with the Gestapo, the air raids of the Allies meant all of this and more. For them the danger was greater, because they couldn't go to the shelters. A direct hit on their sanctuaries would be a calamity beyond the understanding of even the Berliners whose homes had been destroyed. But as great as the danger was, and as frightful as the raids were, the Jews rejoiced at the prospect of deliverance heralded by the bombs.

On an August night when the British bombers filled the sky in numbers such as Berlin had never before experienced, young Hans Rosenthal stepped cautiously and quietly from his hiding place for the first time in the six months since his grandmother had brought him to the house of Frau Jauch. Although he knew that the war was far from over, he could not help but believe that he had just been reprieved from a sentence of lifetime imprisonment.

Hans looked to his left and then to his right. There was not another human being in sight. Of course not; they had all taken shelter. He walked carefully out into the garden, his steps as tentative as those of a convalescent after a prolonged illness. His heart was beating so hard that he was afraid someone might hear it.

Only when he reached the little fruit trees twenty feet from the tool shed that had been his sanctuary since the previous March did Hans dare to look up. It was a clear night—the bombers seldom came in bad weather. If he looked away from the city he could see the stars. Turning, he could watch the searchlights crisscrossing the sky in their frantic search for the bombers.

He could hear the bombers' thunder and then see their flares. First came the lead plane, which set flares at four different points to mark the quadrangular target zone. And then came the squadrons. Their incendiary bombs lit up the city, sending the reflection skyward. Hans could see the bombs falling and, moments later, hear the dull thuds as they hit. Flak howled from the woods. Fighter planes covered the bombers, watching for Messerschmitts. Occasionally there would be a dogfight. Each time a Messerschmitt fell, Hans had to swallow a cheer.

He had no fear of the planes. They were his allies.

Every night that the bombers came Hans went outside to watch. Each raid was a turning point. It told him the Allies were still functioning.

He felt absolutely relaxed, because he knew the Gestapo wouldn't come. He stood next to the little fruit trees and prayed for each Allied pilot to stay in the sky.

For the Fritz Croners, as for Hans Rosenthal, the bombings had been a turning point—which had come none too soon. Since early February, seven months before, their lives had been haunted by the memory of Fritz's parents and their deportation to the camps. There had not been a word from them since then. God only knew what had happened to them; Fritz and Marlitt feared the worst and hoped for the best.

Their own lives had been filled with unremitting tension. The proceeds from Fritz's jewelry trade had been good enough to pay the exorbitant rents and black market food bills, all the higher now that Lane, who had rejoined them in March, following her two months with the woman who cared for her in Neukölln, was no longer an infant. But since then the strain on their resources had increased greatly because they had assumed responsibility for another underground Jewish family.

The family's name was Lissner. They had a tiny baby. Neither the father nor the mother dared go into the street because their features and coloring were so untypically German. Their plight had been brought to Fritz's attention by Joseph Drexel, a Catholic friend and business associate of Fritz's who for years had been president of the Berlin goldsmiths' association. Dr. Lissner had been his dentist. Drexel, a kind-looking man with a round face and soft eyes, told Fritz he had been caring for the Lissner family for some time but was unable to support them any longer. Could Fritz help?

Drexel had once said to Fritz, "If you need me, night or day, you come." His apartment was the Croners' last refuge if and when they needed it. Thus far they had managed without it, but Fritz felt a tremendous debt to Drexel for his offer. Now Fritz took Drexel's hand. "I'll do my best," he said.

Twice a week since then, every Tuesday and Friday, Marlitt had shopped for the Lissners and delivered food to the little flat where they were in hiding. She would knock on the door of a friendly neighbor, who would make certain all was clear. She always brought milk for the baby.

Each morning Marlitt would leave the Croners' hiding place to purchase food. They had no ration cards of course, so her shopping place was wherever the black market could be found. Fritz would be told by his jeweler associates where the dealers were. As she would leave she would say, "I'll be home about twelve." But twelve o'clock would come and she would not return; one o'clock, two o'clock, sometimes three o'clock would pass. Fritz would be so frightened he would be unable to work. His greatest fear was that Marlitt would be challenged by an S.S. patrol and be unable to produce a paper. But Marlitt always returned.

One summer day she came in badly shaken. She had gone to the Lissners and knocked on the neighbor's door. It had opened quickly. "The Gestapo is here," the neighbor whispered. Without a word Marlitt had turned and walked away, forcing herself not to run.

Both she and Fritz knew that they were using up their ration of luck. And how long could their nerves take the strain?

And then came the massive raid on the night of July 28–29, 1943, when 800 to 1,000 English bombers attacked Hamburg, Germany's second city. Although it was a hundred fifty miles away from Berlin, the raid would profoundly change the Croners' lives.

In his diary Joseph Goebbels wrote of "a catastrophe the extent of which simply staggers the imagination. A city of a million inhabitants has been destroyed in a manner unparalleled in history. We are faced with problems that are almost impossible of solution. Food must be found for this population of a million. They must be given clothing. In short, we are facing problems there of which we had no conception even a few weeks ago . . . 800,000 homeless people . . . are wandering up and down the streets not knowing what to do."

For the Croners, as for many other Jews, the key hit came during a raid a few weeks later when a bomb demolished the building that housed all of Hamburg's official records. A few days after the attack an old acquaintance of Fritz's, like himself an illegal Jew, approached him on the street. It flashed through Fritz's mind that the man might be a catcher, and for an instant he thought of fleeing. But the man, who was many years Fritz's senior, quickly reassured him. He was, he said, supporting himself by arranging black market papers. Would Fritz be interested in some? He could arrange it, he went on, for 5,000 marks. He had contact with someone in Hamburg who could obtain the official departure papers residents needed to move from the city. Since there were no longer any records for the officials to check, you could give a false name, place and date of birth, and tell the authorities that you had lived in a part of the city that had been destroyed and wished to visit elsewhere for several weeks. But the destination given would *not* be Berlin. That was the key. The Gestapo, knowing that records in Hamburg had been destroyed, was on the lookout for false papers from that city. What he would do, the old man said, was obtain departure papers for an intermediate city, one that had not been touched by the bombings. A few weeks later the papers from Hamburg to the intermediate city would be converted into departure papers from the intermediate city to Berlin. The police would be unlikely to suspect papers from a city that had not been hit by bombs.

For Fritz himself such papers were out of the question, because at his age he should have been in the army and civilian papers would do no good. But for Marlitt and Lane such papers would be a godsend.

Fritz agreed to the plan. Several weeks later the old man showed up with departure papers authorizing a move from Braunschweig to Berlin for a Vera Krauser, born in Lenz, and her daughter, Helena. The papers were exquisitely official.

To add to their good fortune, the Croners found a new sanctuary—two rooms in a seven-room apartment at Bayerische Strasse 5. It was an incongruously quiet residential street, with cobbled walks and stately trees and gaslights on slender poles, only a few hundred yards from the Olivaer Platz and the Kurfürstendamm. Fritz installed Marlitt and Lane there as the Krausers, mother and daughter. He continued to live in the store in Halensee, but the separation from Marlitt wasn't so painful, because the two dwellings were only a mile apart and he could make frequent visits.

For the first time since going underground nine months before, Fritz was beginning to believe they might survive.

18

For Hans Hirschel, confined since February 1942 to the Wilmersdorf store-turned-apartment of Countess Maria von Maltzan, the devastating new air raids were only the latest in a series of events that had radically altered his life.

He was still living with Marushka, but his long stretches of loneliness were now being broken up by a parade of Jewish illegals who had begun to pass through the flat on the Detmolder Strasse. How they had come to find Marushka, Hans didn't quite understand, and by now he knew better than to ask; but he also knew, to his immense delight, that his bouts of solitude were over. Every second or third evening there would be a knock on the door and it would be an illegal looking for a place to spend a few nights. The illegals always felt safer when they could move from place to place, so that their trail would never stay warm. "Can I stay with you Wednesday and Thursday?" one of them might say. "I've got someone lined up for Friday and Saturday."

One such itinerant was a carpet dealer in his fifties, with an appearance that Marushka sadly concluded resembled the anti-Semitic caricatures in *Der Stürmer*. He had a prominent nose and thick lips. Marushka considered it nothing less than a miracle that the man had not already been picked up, particularly since he was defensive about his appearance and wore the look of a hunted man. "Look here," she said to him one day, "you've simply got to take the offensive. What you should say to people is, 'Stop that staring! I know what you're thinking. Every three days somebody looks at me and says, "You're Jewish," and I'm just fed up with it.' " She also impressed on him that he must always do what others were doing. "The worst thing you can do is go into a *Stube,* where every German is ordering sausage and beer, and order cake and coffee."

But it was in a semipermanent resident named Hollander that Hans took the most delight. They had met in 1938, after Hans had lost his job and was being retrained as a metallurgist. Hollander was in the same class. They were approximately the same age, and while Hollander did not have Hans's intellectual gifts, he was nonetheless an intelligent and spirited man. Hans's one concern was that Hollander might be too spirited; he insisted on going out at some point each day to visit his mistress, a practice that Hans feared might jeopardize Marushka's safety, his own, and the safety of the other Jews sheltered in the flat.

But Hans said nothing for the moment, because he too had begun to leave the flat from time to time—an adventure made possible by yet another spectacular change in his life. With Marushka's help he had acquired an impressive piece of identity that could pass most normal checks.

Even though her sentiments were suspect, Marushka was still a countess and still immensely popular among Berlin's elite. Consequently she was often invited to dinner parties, and she almost always accepted—first, because it meant a good meal and, second, because she might pick up some valuable information. It was at one such party, given by the Ministry of Administration, that she had met Werner Keller, a tall, blond, good-looking man of thirty-two who had been a writer in civilian life and, after a brief career as a pilot, had gone to work for Albert Speer's Ministry of Armaments and War Production. Keller's look struck Marushka as both studious and thoughtful, which made his association with Speer seem incongruous.

Keller, as it turned out, was no Nazi. "I'd love to have a real conversation with you," he said after they had been introduced by a mutual friend. "We can't do that here." Marushka sensed that his interest wasn't romantic. She knew that Keller was married, and had sent his wife and children to their country home on the Elbe for their safety. Anti-Nazis, she believed, had a way of gravitating toward one another. When Keller telephoned her a few days after the dinner party, she remarked that she couldn't quite understand how he could be working where he was. It was an observation that could have meant a dozen things, but Keller knew what she was saying. "It's a very good place to be," he said. "You can help a lot of people." Another ambiguous statement—but now they both understood each other.

When she was certain she knew him well enough, Marushka invited Keller to the flat to meet Hans. It was at the end of Hans's longest period of isolation, and he was overjoyed to have a visitor. When he found out that Keller was a writer, Hans was beside himself. The two men talked for hours. Afterward Marushka said with great care, "Werner, what do you think the chances would be of getting some papers for Hans?"

"I think that could be arranged," Keller said after a silence that to Hans had seemed like an eternity.

The next time he appeared, Werner brought a paper that identified Hans as an official of the Ministry of Armaments and War Production. Marushka attached a photograph of Hans to the document, photograph and document were duly stamped, and Hans suddenly had a new identity. By way of celebration, Marushka took him out to Keller's country house late the following Saturday morning, and fetched him early Monday morning. She was willing to risk the trip with Hans's new document, but she did not quite trust him to brazen his way alone out of a tight spot if he should find himself in one.

A year had passed since Hans had moved into the flat. Marushka's thirty-fourth birthday, on March 25, 1943, was approaching. To Hans's astonishment she proposed that they have a party, and set about arranging it. Her guest list of twenty friends, most of whom knew about Hans, included an actor from Vienna, a girlhood friend, a writer and his wife, and two exquisite Jewish women, Maria Etlinger and Annchen Foss, who were also living illegally. But others would be coming who did not knows Hans—several young officers attached to the veterinary school where Marushka had been trained, and an army major named Von Borker, who had been flirting with Marushka for months now and pestering her to invite him to her house. Borker insisted that they had many mutual friends and that they might even be related by marriage. Marushka considered Borker such a fool that he wouldn't recognize a Jew when he saw one. She was sure that Hans could easily carry off a masquerade. He would pretend that he was "Professor Schoeler"—just as he had done when he had prepped her fellow students for their exams—with a chair in economics at the university. There was a certain risk involved, but there was a risk if she didn't dispose of Borker somehow; he might begin to disbelieve her story that she lived alone. Besides, he was on the verge of obtaining a Mauser pistol for her, because, she had told him, she felt unsafe living by herself. She very much wanted that pistol.

The party began at six o'clock. Marushka had collected a quantity of food from her black market sources as well as from peasants whose livestock she castrated. There was a greater variety of food, and in greater abundance, than the guests had seen in a long time—meats, sausages, cheese from France, dishes made with eggs. Marushka, carefully made up and wearing a brown dress, looked exceedingly feminine and beguiling. For her as well as for the others the party was a great release, and she proposed to make the most of it. There were many toasts, drunk with wine and schnapps. By the time Major von Borker arrived, the party was in high gear. He was astonished by the crowd—Marushka hadn't told him it was her birthday—and upset that he hadn't brought flowers.

There was no need to warn the others about Borker because

he was wearing his officer's uniform. Nonetheless there were some anxious looks when Marushka introduced him to "Professor Schoeler."

"How are your students these days?" Borker asked stiffly.

"Very poor," Hans replied. "All the good students are soldiers."

Before Hans could be tested any further Marushka led Borker over to Maria Etlinger and Annchen Foss. "This is the man I was telling you about, with such a wonderful feeling for race," she said with a smile.

From that moment on, Borker had eyes only for Annchen Foss, whose striking beauty blinded him to its Sephardic Jewish antecedents. "Have you children?" he asked after a bit.

"No," Annchen replied.

"What a pity," Borker sighed. "Children of yours would be such a credit to the German nation."

Behind Borker, Maria Etlinger leaned back against a wall, closed her eyes and put a hand across her mouth to stifle her helpless laughter.

An hour later, after voicing his approval of the recent mass deportation of Jews from Berlin, Borker departed. For a moment no one spoke. Then Marushka said, "Come on, everybody, let's dance." She put a fox trot on the phonograph and led Hans to the center of the room. All the guests applauded. It was after two when the last guest went home.

The next time he saw Marushka, Borker gave her the Mauser.

Six months had passed. The air raids had suddenly and dramatically intensified, a fact of life made all the more vivid for Hans and Marushka because their street, Detmolder Strasse, ran parallel to and fifty yards from an S-Bahn track along which flak trains—flat cars with antiaircraft guns mounted on them—ran during the raids. Their neighborhood got more than its share of bombs, but they welcomed the raids, and neither one of them was frightened, if only because it made no sense to fear something you welcomed. Hans even toyed with the idea of walking the deserted streets during the raids so that he might experience the feeling of absolute assurance that he wouldn't be detected. Everyone else would be in the air raid shelters.

He of course could not go to the shelters. His refuge was the cellar beneath their flat. The walls and ceilings of the cellar had been reinforced, and there were storage bins along each side. During the raids the shelter also served as a kennel for the dogs.

One evening in September, just as the diminishing sound of the planes indicated that a particularly heavy raid had ended, Marushka heard a bomb crash in the street. An instant later an explosion shattered the store window into thousands of pieces and scattered them throughout the flat. Later Hans discovered that tiny particles of glass had been driven through his wardrobe by the force of the explosion and had cut all of his shirts into tatters.

The explosion had also demolished the front entrance. Early the next morning Marushka foraged for some boards, then nailed them over the space where the window had been, and closed off the front entry as well. Now one could enter and leave the apartment only through the kitchen.

The pounding of the English bombs continued. Buildings at either side of theirs received direct hits. And then, one day, theirs did too.

In the cellar Hans thought the world had come to an end. He held the two Scotch terriers in his arms, trying to comfort them. At last the all clear sounded, and he and Marushka went upstairs to have a look at the damage. When they saw it they could only wonder how they were still alive. The explosion had destroyed all of their building, with the exception of their flat and the one above theirs. The ceiling of their living room sagged dangerously and looked as though it could give way at any moment. Marushka went out at once to scavenge for a beam with which to prop it up. By a great stroke of luck she found one, as well as a crew to help her carry it home and install it.

It was October now, and the weather had turned brisk. Each

day Marushka would eye the window frames stacked up outside the store of a glazier down the street. The frames had been brought to him to have the glass replaced. What a lovely supply of fuel, Marushka thought. The next chance she had, she approached the glazier, who she knew was an ardent Nazi, and gave him what he agreed was an inspired idea. He should segregate the frames—those of the good Nazis on the left side of the door, those of the nonparty members on the right. In that way he could attend to the good Nazis first. From that day on, that was how he did it, and from that evening on, Marushka helped herself to the window frames of the party members.

Marushka was often out in the evenings now, which would have bothered Hans even more than it did if he hadn't had one or more illegal Jews to keep him company. She never told him in advance that she would be going out, and she never said anything on her return. All he knew for certain was that her departures coincided with those mysterious phone calls: two rings, followed by a minute's interval, another two rings, another interval, and finally one more ring and a muffled conversation.

During the fall Marushka was also away from Berlin for several days, visiting one of her sisters in Munich. When she returned to Berlin she was aghast to see Hans waiting on the station platform to meet her. Even though he now had his false identification papers, each sortie was still a risk, and train stations were a special risk because they were so heavily patrolled.

"Please don't be angry," Hans pleaded. "I've missed you. I wanted to surprise you. And I just had to get out of the flat."

Marushka sighed. "Oh, God," she said. "Come on."

They boarded an S-Bahn train, but before they had gotten very far the bombing started, and passengers and crew abandoned the train for the nearest shelter. "Now we're in for it," Marushka muttered as she led a sheepish-looking Hans inside. She pulled Hans off to the darkest corner she could find, and they managed to find floor space in spite of the crowd. The raid went on and on, and as it did, Hans became increasingly fidgety. "Can't we go over there?" he whispered to Marushka, pointing to a space about thirty feet away that did not seem nearly so crowded.

"What's the matter with this space?" Marushka demanded.

"The crowd over there seems nicer," Hans said with a laugh, but Marushka figured he was only half kidding. In the center of that space sat a handsome, intelligent-looking man chatting with another man.

"We'd better stay where we are," Marushka said. "If we move we'll only draw attention to ourselves."

At last the all clear sounded. As Hans and Marushka rose to leave they happened to notice that as the handsome man across the way rose, the man he had been talking to rose with him. Then they saw why. The men were handcuffed together.

Hans and Marushka watched in silence as the two men walked away. All the way back to the apartment Hans did not make a comment.

19

THE AREA AROUND Wittenau, at the northern fringe of Berlin, was an inviting target for the Allied bombers because of its concentration of factories, supply yards and offices engaged in war production. No bomb had yet fallen near the house of Robert Jerneitzig occupied by the Wirkuses and the Riedes, but the noise of the explosion made the points of impact seem extremely close.

Night after night the bombers came, their arrival preceded by a period of grace when, warned of the imminent attack by German military broadcasts, residents of the presumed target areas could rush to the community shelters. Joseph Wirkus always took his wife, Kadi, and son, Wilfried, to their neighborhood shelter, five hundred yards away. It took them five minutes to get there, and then he would run back home to sit out the raid in his small basement shelter with Kurt and Hella Riede. He was less safe from the bombs in the basement than he would have been in the shelter, but there was a more important consideration. As illegal Jews the Riedes could not go to the community shelters without risking exposure; his own presence in the basement, Beppo reasoned, would reassure the Riedes—especially Kurt.

The bombs terrified Kurt. He readily admitted that he was

more afraid of them than he was of the Gestapo. It had nothing to do with cowardice; it was the vulnerability he felt because he was night-blind. Air raids meant dimness, even darkness, which meant, in turn, that he couldn't see. He felt trapped and helpless in the cellar, and often became so upset that he was forced to risk a trip upstairs, with Hella's assistance, to go to the bathroom.

Hella, on the other hand, was so calm that she would often read a novel by candlelight during the raids. Her courage amazed Beppo. "This house will not be hit by a bomb," she kept assuring them. "No house in which so much good has been done could be hit by a bomb." To Kurt she would say, softly but emphatically, "We are going to survive."

But as the attacks continued without letup, the strain became unbearable. Something had to be done. The more they talked about it, the more clear it became that Kurt would have to leave Berlin, if only for a while, in order to relieve the pressure. There was a perfect place for him to go—the farm in Pomerania owned by Kadi's parents. But how on earth would they get him there?

"I have said *A,* I must now say *B,*" Beppo told himself again and again, meaning that, having told Kurt he would help him initially, he must now meet his further needs. In his office one day Beppo executed an official leave-of-absence document, a pink piece of paper on which he listed his own name, his occupation, and the dates of his "leave." Then he gave the document to Kurt, to show to the authorities in case he was stopped on the train en route to the farm. Beppo could only pray that the leave paper, together with Kurt's fake postal identity, would be enough for the authorities. If the authorities became suspicious and checked back with Beppo's office, he knew that he was finished.

To minimize the risk of detection, the trip was scheduled for a time on the weekend when Beppo's office would be closed. Should the police request his military papers, Kurt could say that they were locked in his office for safekeeping. There would be no way the police could check that statement on the week-end, and so, rather than bother, they might let the matter slide.

But the trip passed without incident, and Kurt, Hella, Kadi and the baby arrived safely at Kadi's parents' farm in Pomerania. There was no question about the Riedes' welcome; there was the added practical advantage of having extra hands for the potato harvest at a time when farm labor was scarce. It was hard, monotonous work, done in an uncomfortable kneeling posture, but Kurt's joy was unbridled. At last he could do something that was tangible and physical and helpful to others as well as himself.

For four weeks they pushed their shovels into the rich soil and dug out potatoes, and lived with the assurance that the Allied planes passing overhead would not drop their bombs on them. If he could have, Kurt would have gladly spent the rest of the war working on the farm, but that, he knew, was impossible. He was being passed off to the neighbors as a soldier on convalescent leave; to stay longer than a month would be to invite suspicion and trouble, not only for himself but for Kadi's parents.

So at the end of the month Kadi's sister drove them in a horse-drawn cart to the farm of Beppo's parents, twenty kilometers away. Their reception here was very different. "Get these people away from me," Beppo's father muttered to Kadi when he learned who the Riedes were. Their presence endangered all of them, he argued. He was right, but no one else took his side, and eventually even he accepted their presence.

Four weeks later Kadi's sister came to collect them, and took them to the railway station, where they boarded a train for the return trip to Berlin, their satchels loaded with poultry, eggs, pork and produce. In his own suitcase Kurt proudly carried several geese back to the city.

Once again the journey was unquestioned.

Kurt felt reborn. Not only had he enjoyed a respite from the bombings for the better part of two months but he had met and passed a test of courage that had done wonders for his self-esteem. He had gone to the farms out of fear—but it had taken courage to go there. Twice he had run a gauntlet full of real and imagined dangers. The least display of anxiety on his part could have given him and the others away. As frightened as he had been, nothing outward had distinguished him from any other dispirited German traveler in the beginning of the fifth year of a war that all but the most fanatical of them now knew their country was going to lose.

Safely back in Wittenau, Kurt vowed not to let the bombings affect him, and he quietly went about arranging a way to express his gratitude to Kadi's parents. At their farm he had noticed that the drive belt on the flour grinder was so worn and frayed that it could scarcely power the mill. Now, from the baron's leather shop where he had once worked, he obtained a new belt to replace the old one—which, to Kadi's parents as well as all those the mill supplied with flour, was worth more at this moment than any sum of money.

There had been moments during his solitude when Willy Glaser would have traded a year of his life for an evening at the opera, but even he had to admit that life had improved. It had been six months since he had been forced to move from George Meier's summer home. A few days before he was supposed to vacate the house, and still with no place to go, he'd taken an enormous risk and told the truth to a neighbor. He'd just blurted it out on an impulse one day while he was working in the garden and the neighbor was leaning against the fence, exchanging pleasantries, all but inviting Willy to confide in him, hinting that he had already guessed Willy's story. Although the neighbor didn't look Jewish, and certainly hadn't said that he was, he made a point of using certain Yiddish expressions that had been adopted by many Germans. What was the man trying to convey? That he was friendly? That he had Jewish friends or business associates? That his wife was Jewish? Whatever the reason, Willy's surmise had been right. Once he had explained his predicament, the neighbor—who never told him his name—offered to let him use a small room on the second floor of his house. Conditions again. Willy was not to tell anyone where he was living. And he was never to be seen entering or leaving. Willy assured the man on both counts, and gratefully moved in.

Where his former house had been made of wood, and daylight was visible through the cracks, this one was built of stone and free of drafts. There were three rooms downstairs and a fourth on the second floor. That was where Willy lived.

In any other life this would have to be considered a wretched existence, but where the objective of life was survival alone, Willy could feel that he was doing well. Not only was he secure; for the first time since he had gone illegal he was warm. He could light a lamp at night. His benefactor extracted hard labor in exchange for the shelter—Willy chopped cords and cords of wood—but he was a kind man who had even lanced a dreadful boil on the back of Willy's neck.

Willy kept his word. He told no one where he lived. And on the days when he wanted to leave the house he would be gone by 5:00 A.M. and would not return until after dark. When the air raids began in the evenings he would run into the woods for shelter. From there he would watch the flares they called "Christmas trees" light up the ground, and the bombs burst near the antiaircraft emplacements a few miles away. But no bombs had even come close to his hiding place—still further evidence that divine Providence guarded him or that his life was somehow charmed.

And then one day in November 1943 Willy Glaser's luck ran out.

That morning he had chopped half a cord of wood for the owner, gotten tired and gone to his room to nap. He was awakened by voices in the garden. Instinctively he raised his head to peep out the window. It was at just that moment that one of the two men standing in the garden happened to look up.

"Who are you?" he called out.

Paralyzed with fear, Willy didn't answer.

"Come down here!" the man commanded.

In the garden, Willy could see a party insignia on the man's coat.

"What is your name?" the man said.

"Wilhelm Glaser."

"Are you a Jew?"

"No."

They handcuffed him and took him to the police station in Müggelheim. The police asked to see his papers. He had none. They asked where he had previously lived. He gave them his correct address. They called the police station in his old neighborhood and learned not only that he was Jewish but that he had escaped once before.

Several hours later Willy was in the basement of the heavy stone building on the Grosse Hamburger Strasse where Jews scheduled for deportation were gathered, the very building to which he had gone to say goodbye to his mother and to which he had been on his way ten months before. He was filled with bitterness. Ten months of cold, hunger, loneliness and danger endured, only to be captured.

20

FROM THE DAY that she and Mother had moved into Frau Otto's apartment in Pankow, Ruth Thomas had done her best to forget that she was a Jew, as Tante Lisel had admonished her to. It was an act of pretense that, given her upbringing and her memories, as well as the sheer joy she had experienced as a young Jewish woman, made all of her previous efforts at masking reality seem small by comparison. Not only could there be no religious observance of any kind, there could be no nostalgia for those culturally rich and festive times. Nor could she afford self-pity; whatever she felt about life in Berlin could be no more and no less than what any Berliner felt.

By way of commemorating her new identity, Ruth destroyed her Jewish star and her mother's as well. The only remnant of her past she kept was her identity card. She knew she would need the card when this nightmare ended, and so she sewed it into the hem of the gray flannel skirt she wore the most often.

In the first days on their own, both Ruth and her mother had been so frightened that they could not bring themselves to venture into the street. They would rise early and eat a meager breakfast. While Ruth sewed, Anna would clean the house and prepare food if they had it. Often they would go without lunch. Inevitably the day came when they had to risk a trip to the market, where they nervously bought a few turnips and potatoes with small bits of the money they had taken with them into exile. From then on, Mother went out only when she absolutely had to. Ruth's work, however, required that she leave the apartment more and more frequently—a fact of life that was as much a blessing as it was a danger. As she had known it would, the sewing machine had become their means of survival. Soon after she and Mother had moved into the Pankow apartment, word spread that there was a clever woman who could tailor very well. Before long she had all the customers she could handle, all of them happy to have someone fashioning the materials their husbands were bringing in from the conquered lands.

Whenever either Ruth or her mother went out, whether it was to pick up work or procure food, they carried all their money with them. It was a precaution against the possibility that they might be followed and therefore not be able to return to their sanctuary, or that the sanctuary itself might be discovered while they were away.

Every trip to the market was a gamble. Some of their food they bought on the black market, but Ruth hated to do it, certain that it had been the address book of a black marketeer that had brought them to the Gestapo's attention the previous November. Once a week a bakery woman in the Fasanenstrasse would give Ruth a loaf of bread. Another merchant would give her vegetables. Although the shopkeepers never spoke about it, Ruth knew that they were anti-Nazis. The people who didn't overcharge you were always those opposed to the regime.

As each day passed and nothing happened, Ruth's fantasy mechanism gradually became charged again and she could repress those awful memories that could destroy her will to resist. She had had one horrible relapse. A Belgian she knew had sold her a small radio. Each night Ruth would put the radio under her pillow and listen to the BBC and the Russian broadcasts. One night the Russians reported that the Nazis had been killing Jews in gas chambers and cremating their remains. Smoke was pouring from the crematoria chimneys, the Russians said. Ruth refused to believe it. She couldn't accept that Kurt Thomas would be killed in this way. She could not accept that Germans would be capable of such monstrosities.

But given her good fortune relative to other Jews, it was difficult for Ruth not to feel that she was living life in a protective bubble. Except for the fact that she was an illegal, being sought by the Gestapo, her existence was in truth no different from the average Berliner's. She walked the streets, took streetcars, shopped and from time to time even visited with friends. On streetcars men would stand and offer her their seats, even as they had before she had gone illegal.

Often Ruth would work in her customers' homes, and though she never told them that she was Jewish, she suspected that some of them knew. It was not insignificant that she never heard any discussions of the Jews, let alone an anti-Semitic remark, even though she was certain that some of her customers were Nazis. At that time only Nazis could afford the exquisite materials that Ruth worked on, and could pay for her work with food. They never asked her for her papers, because they were only too happy to have someone sewing for them, especially someone with Ruth's flair for design. If her customers offered her a choice of payment in either money or food and ration stamps, Ruth would choose the food and ration stamps. Between those payments and the food her friend Hilde Hohn was supplying, Ruth and her mother soon had enough to eat.

Hilde had an advantageous job. She was in charge of arranging documents and licenses for imports on behalf of a chain of small markets. So she had access to food. In addition, she traveled every weekend to the old manor house of her husband's parents and brought back supplies of food. Five persons, including Ruth and her mother, counted on her to supplement their diets. Ruth paid for what Hilde brought her, but there was always a little something extra from Hilde's in-laws, along with a message that they were praying for her to their patron saint, Saint Anthony.

Ruth and Hilde saw a great deal of each other. As they had

suspected from their first encounter, they were very much alike. Both were young and pretty and chic. Ruth made a dress for Hilde of dark blue and pink silk, with slightly puffed sleeves, a pink yoke, a dark blue bodice with a full skirt and three pink bands near the hem. Hilde was ecstatic. Twirling in front of the mirror, she announced, "I am the best-dressed woman in Berlin." A few days later Ruth accompanied Hilde on a drive to Gatow, a small community alongside the Havel River, on the southern outskirts of the city.

It was episodes such as this one that made Ruth believe she was secure. She became bolder and bolder. One day while she was in Berlin she decided on an impulse to go to a concert. Heart hammering, she bought a ticket and went inside. Memories flooded over her, carrying away the realization that she was the only Jew in the audience. The old concert crowd, the one she'd seen at concerts before the Nazis came to power, was gone. In its place were men in uniform and their women. I am as strange to them as they are to me, Ruth persuaded herself. I am secure.

But she could not quiet her heart. She was simply too excited. She couldn't remember the last time she had heard a live concert. The radio was a meager substitute, its sound small and scratchy. And the selections! Light operas and operettas, Johann Strauss at least once a day—a menu dictated partially by the exclusion of music composed by Jews, partially by the demand on the part of listeners weary of war work and air raid alarms for music to help them relax. Only on Sunday evening was there a good classical concert by either the Berlin or Vienna Philharmonic, but their programs were limited by the one-hour length of the program. Only rarely were long or challenging works performed.

This concert was a traditional one—Beethoven, Mozart, Bach, Haydn. Sadly Ruth noted the absence of music by such Jews as Mendelssohn and Meyerbeer. During the intermission Ruth remained in her seat. To stand or walk about would be to invite attention. She made it a point not to notice any interested males. Once when she looked to her left she saw a man staring at her. She had seen that stare a thousand times. It had nothing to do with suspicion; it was an announcement that said, "You attract me." She looked away.

After the concert Ruth departed quickly. But her success encouraged her to go again, and soon she was a frequent listener at concerts of the Berlin Philharmonic. Each time she went she would sit in a different place, in order to be certain that she was not seen more than once by season-ticket holders. Some tickets she would buy herself, but many she received as gifts from the desk clerks at the Central and Adlon hotels. They had known her for many years, from the time when the store was a place to send their guests. Ruth was certain that they knew she was Jewish. But they never discussed the matter. It was much easier to pretend ignorance.

Each time Ruth came to the center of the city she would look at the billboards to see if there was a good opera or concert being given. She went often to the opera until it was bombed, and to recitals, and most of all to films. She didn't think about the danger. She was very well dressed—better dressed, actually, than many of the people in the audiences—so she knew that she looked as if she belonged. Other than the interested looks from men, she never had any feeling that people were staring at her. She was never asked for papers—happily, because she had none to show. When she saw an S.S. patrol she would simply circle around it.

Ruth's sorties into the cultural world upset Anna terribly. She was afraid that Ruth would be caught; moreover, she felt much safer when Ruth was with her. On two occasions Ruth coaxed her mother into accompanying her, arguing that the safest place for them was the streets, that the safest course was to act normally. But Anna was too uncomfortable to enjoy herself, and besides, she didn't have the interest in music that her daughter did.

For Ruth, music was as much sustenance as food. For a few hours she could be like a child with forbidden sweets, daring to fill herself with the past she had trained herself to forget, to remember how life had been, to connect again with that time when fantasy and reality were synonymous. She could live for weeks on the memory of a concert. Those small moments gave her the equilibrium she needed when life did not go as she wished.

How *that* standard had changed! Once life, to be lived well, meant comforts, stimulation, lively company, a decent home—in Schöneberg, perhaps—frequent family reunions, success in business, personal growth, religious observance, leisure time, vacations in Baden-Baden and, of course, a marriage. Now all notions of the good life were compressed into a single word: survival. And not just her own—her mother's as well.

Six months had passed without incident since Ruth had learned that she was being sought by a catcher, but she was still always on her guard. Whenever she could she would avoid such streets as the Kurfürstendamm, where the Gestapo frequently checked papers. She had no plan for dealing with a sudden request to see her papers. She just watched out and tried not to think about it. On one occasion, however, she did have a close call—in, of all places, her own apartment building. The air raid warden for her block, a man named Knoll, lived on the floor below. He was a gaunt old man with white hair, and rather hard of hearing. Frequently Ruth would have to arouse him on her way to the bomb shelter, even though it was his duty to get the residents of the block into the shelter.

As block warden, Knoll had the right to inspect papers, and several times he asked Ruth for hers. Each time she told him the same story she had told Frau Otto when she rented the apartment: she had a house in Schöneberg and needed to retain her registration there in order to retain her rights to the home. But Knoll kept asking, and it was increasingly evident that the original story would not satisfy him much longer. So Ruth improvised ever wilder stories. First she told him that she was living with a man who was not her husband and that she was putting Knoll on his honor as a gentleman not to breathe a word of it, because she was certain that Frau Otto would not approve. Still the questions persisted. Finally Ruth spent a restless night thinking up a story, and the next day told it to Knoll.

She worked, she said, for the Gestapo. She was living here under an alias so that she might carry on her affair. Her real residence was in a pension in the Nymphenburger Strasse. The subterfuge was simply to protect her aunt—Frau Otto—who would never forgive her for having an affair. Again she called on Knoll to keep her secret. He assured her that he would. Just to be sure, Ruth called the pension she had referred to and alerted the woman who ran it, who was her friend, and who did have a boarder living there who worked for the Gestapo. If anyone came to check, she was to alert Ruth, who would then flee from the Pankow apartment. But no one came, and Knoll stopped asking questions.

And then, just as Ruth was beginning to believe that she had developed a feeling for danger and had learned to avoid it, she and danger came face to face.

She had set out one ominous afternoon to visit Hilde, whose office was a few hundred yards from the Bülowstrasse U-Bahn station—one of the U-Bahn's few elevated sections—near the center of the city. Black clouds moved over the city, heralded by thunder. By the time her train reached the station, it seemed that night had fallen. As Ruth walked toward Hilde's office she saw a familiar-looking man coming her way, a young, handsome man she remembered from the Jewish community. For a moment she thought, What a pleasant surprise! and was about to smile and say hello when she realized that she must be within ten feet of her catcher.

Ruth's expression froze and she looked away, but not before noticing that the man had noticed her. She began to move faster. Out of the corner of her eye she saw that the man had changed direction and was following her. She wanted to run, but knew that she shouldn't. Suddenly the clouds burst. Torrents of rain lashed the streets. It was a heaven-sent excuse for hurrying. Ruth raced to Hilde's office.

"My God, look at you," Hilde said.

Ruth blurted out her story and asked if she could remain overnight in the office.

"Don't be afraid," Hilde said. "We'll leave together. As long as you're with me, nothing will happen."

Ruth didn't believe her, but she had no alternative. Together they walked to the U-Bahn station. Ruth did not see the catcher, but she was positive he was following them.

They took the train to the Bahnhof Zoo, where Ruth was to transfer to a train for Pankow. Hilde walked her up the stairs, crowded with commuters going home. At the top of the steps Ruth bolted to the other side of the stairway and, head down, followed the crowd going down. Hilde kept on walking—luring away anyone who was still following Ruth.

A minute later Ruth boarded another train. She didn't know where it was going. She didn't care. She had lost her pursuer.

21

THERE WERE TWO ironic compensations for his capture and incarceration in the deportation center on the Grosse Hamburger Strasse for Willy Glaser. The first was that he had been permitted to take a bath, the first he had had since going into hiding ten months before. He had been so dirty that a crust had formed on his skin. The second compensation was warm food. The food, prepared by a Jewish woman, Frau Harpruder, wasn't good by normal standards, but Willy savored every bite.

The compensations, however, were of little comfort. Willy knew why he was there. It would be only a matter of time before he was on his way to Auschwitz.

Several days passed without incident. Willy spent hours looking out the barred window of his room, watching the guards play soccer. The building backed onto the oldest Jewish cemetery in Berlin. It was overgrown now, with many of the gravestones lying on their sides, but it had once been the burial place of the most important Jews in Berlin. It was said that Moses Mendelssohn, the great scholar and philosopher who lived in the time of Frederick the Great, was buried in the cemetery. Mendelssohn had translated the Pentateuch, the first five books of the Old Testament, into German. He had also been—yet another irony—a leading proponent of German-Jewish assimilation.

The guards were playing in a clearing and laughing very loudly. It wasn't the kind of laughter you normally associated with soccer. Then the play moved Willy's way, and suddenly he understood why they were laughing, and he had to bite hard on his lip to keep from crying out. It was not a ball the guards were kicking; it was a human skull.

Six days after his capture Willy got his transportation number to Auschwitz. "I'm not giving up yet," he told one of the other prisoners. "If I get a chance I'll try something. I'd rather have a bullet in me than be shipped to Auschwitz."

The other prisoner, a reed of a man, also in his forties, eyed Willy critically. "I'd like to come along," he said at last. "I have money outside. If we make it we can live well."

"That's great," Willy said. "I have no money at all."

The day before the transport was scheduled to depart, the guards took the prisoners outside to exercise in the cemetery.

"Now's our chance," Willy whispered to the reedy man.

But the man shook his head. "I can't," he whispered back.

Willy nodded. "I've got a coat and a briefcase back in the basement. Take them with you," he said.

The guards made them line up and count off and then sent them marching around the cemetery. Once, twice, three times they went around. By now the guards were off in a small group, talking, laughing, kicking the skulls, not watching the prisoners any longer. As they passed some shrubs Willy darted through them and toward the cemetery wall. He saw a headstone next to the wall. His senses were so clear he even noted that the inscription was in memory of a couple. He put his foot on the headstone and vaulted to the top of the wall. He heard no shouts and he did not look back. Seeing a garbage can on the other side of the wall, he accepted it as yet another sign that his life was charmed. He jumped onto the can, and then to the ground, and ran to the first door he saw. Then he raced through a corridor and out into the street. He knew exactly where he was—on the

Oranienburger Strasse, not far from an S-Bahn station. He walked as rapidly as he could without running to the station. The minutes that he waited for the train were the longest in his life. He could feel his throbbing temples and his banging heart.

Finally the train came and Willy got in. He rode over viaducts, arches and bridges, through tunnels and forests and along canals and rivers—stunning views, all of them, of what had once been a magnificent city. Now it was being ground to pieces by the Allied bombs. As frightened and self-absorbed as he was, Willy could not help but be shocked by the devastation he saw from his vantage point on the elevated S-Bahn. How right he had been: it would take a bloody war to finish Hitler. Well, they had it now, their "total war," these crazy Nazis. When would they learn they had lost?

When the S-Bahn reached the Tempelhof station, Willy Glaser got off.

On November 17, 1943, a Wednesday, Fritz Croner set out from his store residence in Halensee to deliver some gems to a jeweler friend. It was a warm day for November in Berlin. He walked slowly, limping, swinging his right leg ahead with the help of his cane. As he moved along the crowded Kurfürstendamm in the direction of the Olivaer Platz, he felt completely at ease. For months now his limp and his cane had been his unstated answer to any questions in the minds of passersby. The trick, he had learned, was to walk the streets as though you had every right to be on them. At first it had required a monumental effort of will to do that, but now he felt so absorbed by the city and its multitudes that he was certain his inner confidence expressed itself in his face. His sense of security was such that in recent months he and Marlitt had even gone to restaurants and movies.

And why shouldn't he be confident? The war was going his way. A permanent reddish haze hung over the city from the smoke of the incessant fires set by the incendiary bombs—proof, if such were still needed, of the ability of the English to bomb

Berlin at will. It was only a matter of time, he thought. The war
would end and he would be free. In the interim he was sure he
could survive. His black market contacts were the strongest they
had ever been. His jewelry business was thriving. Most important, the Croners' two hiding places had met the test of time. He
was secure in Halensee, and Marlitt and Lane, with their official identification papers, had been accepted without question
by their new neighbors at Bayerische Strasse 5. The papers
themselves had held up under scrutiny when Lane, her eyes injured by flying fragments during a raid, had to be taken to a
hospital for treatment. Given the realities of Nazi Germany for
a Jew, Fritz could, and did, thank God for his good fortune.

As he waited at a corner of the Olivaer Platz a young man
came up to him and held out a Gestapo card. "Mr. Croner," he
said, "you're under arrest."

Fritz's heart exploded. Slowly he turned to look at the man.
He knew he had never seen him before. It took every bit of effort
he had, but he managed to force a frown. "You're mistaken," he
said. "My name is Kramer."

"Turn around," the young man said.

Fritz turned around. Standing against a building on the other
side of the Olivaer Platz was Fedor Friedlander, the man who
had stolen his jewels and been forced to give them back.

Caught! Fritz turned back to the young man, the only
thought in his mind to shove him and run. But the young man
showed him a gun. "If you're thinking of doing anything, I
wouldn't advise it," he said.

The young man took Fritz with him to a beauty shop on the
Kurfürstendamm a few blocks from the Olivaer Platz. There he
spoke to a young and beautiful blond woman who was having
her hair done. "I've got one," he said. "I'll take him to Grolmanstrasse."

The woman nodded. She would not look at Fritz.

The young man went to make a phone call. "I've got someone
to be picked up," Fritz heard him say. "I'm taking him to the
police station. You can collect him there."

Half an hour later the young man dropped Fritz off at the Grolmanstrasse police station. Then he left. Fritz spent the afternoon waiting. There was an elderly police officer at the station who passed by him several times. Perhaps it was his imagination, but Fritz thought the officer seemed upset for some reason. Finally Fritz took a chance. "Who was the man who brought me? Do you know?" he asked.

The policeman looked to his left and right. No one was within hearing distance. "That's the tragedy of the situation," he said then. "One Jew brings another Jew to the knife."

22

FOR WEEKS NOW those mysterious evening telephone calls to Marushka had been coming with increasing frequency, until she was averaging almost one a night. And always it was the same. Two rings, then silence. A minute later another two rings, and then another minute's silence. Then the telephone would ring a third time, and finally Marushka would answer, only to speak so softly and in such an elliptical manner that Hans had no idea what she was discussing.

One morning as she was leaving for work Marushka said to Hans, "I'll be home quite late this evening. I've got something to do."

Hans's question died on his lips. He knew that asking would yield nothing. In vain he searched her face for clues.

Late that afternoon Marushka took the train from Berlin. Two young men went with her. They were in their twenties. She knew nothing about them, only that they had been assigned to accompany her. All the way out no one spoke a word. At Frohnau they got off the train and walked north, through the square, its lush lawns faded now and covered with dead leaves. The air was crisp but not cold. Good, Marushka thought. There was almost no movement on the streets. She had been worried about encountering patrols, but had been assured there would be none, and there were none this night. They walked a mile from the town, to the beginning of a forest. Then they turned off and walked into the woods. A hundred yards in, they found the people.

It was dark now, but not so dark that she couldn't see them. There were twenty of them. She motioned them to come close. As they approached she noted that they were of all ages. Some appeared to be Jews; others didn't. All of them looked haggard and badly frightened. They pressed tightly together, as though taking comfort from their proximity. "Will you try to walk very carefully," she began, "taking care not to stumble or to step on anything that will break. Don't walk on the road. Stay in the woods. Don't crowd. Just follow the person in front of you." She hesitated, wondering if it was even necessary to emphasize the seriousness of the moment, wondering whether anything she could say to these people would add to what they already felt. "This is the last short step to freedom," she said at last. "Be very careful." All of them nodded in unison.

They walked for a mile in the woods. Then Marushka halted the column. She motioned for the young men to approach. "Look, I can't explain it, but I've got a bad feeling," she told them. "I want you to get home. If anything happens, it will happen on your way back." One of the young men began to argue, but Marushka held up her hand. "I know you were told that I was in charge. Please do as I say." Without another word the two young men left. The column moved on. The group was being very good, but to Marushka their footfalls sounded like the pounding of timpanists.

At last they came to a clearing. Marushka held up her hand and they stopped. Then she beckoned and they came and huddled next to her again. She pointed to the clearing. "Look," she whispered. In the broken light they could see a tiny shack next to some railroad tracks at a point where a dirt road crossed the tracks.

"You're to hide in the woods on the other side, fifty meters

from that shack. When the train comes, stay hidden until someone fetches you. You'll be told what to do. Now move out, one
at a time, and God be with you."

One by one they crossed the clearing and disappeared into
the woods on the other side. At last all was still.

Marushka would have liked to stay, to watch the operation.
But her assignment was only halfway to completion. She'd been
instructed to retrace her path now, in order to be certain no one
had followed them. If she encountered a patrol she was to side-
track it somehow, so that she would avert the danger from the
people in the woods.

That bad feeling was still with her. Even though they had
planned carefully, it did not seem logical that they should get
away with the operation so easily. There were forced-labor
camps in the area. The laborers were forever breaking out and
the Germans forever tracking them with dogs. If it happened tonight the dogs could pick up the group's scent.

The group. Marushka wondered who they were. Most of
them Jews probably, but a few of them political dissidents. How
wildly terror and hope must be warring in their minds now.
They knew nothing about what would happen—only that they
were being smuggled out of Germany.

It would happen any time now. A freight train bound for the
north of Germany would make an unscheduled stop on the des-
olate stretch of track that cut through the woods. Suddenly a
group of men the illegals hadn't seen would rush from the
woods and open one of the boxcars. Then they would break the
seals on a number of large crates and carefully pry them open.
There would be furniture in the crates, which they would remove and throw from the boxcar. At a signal the illegals would
run from the woods, be lifted into the boxcar and placed inside
the crates. The crates would be nailed up once more. Counterfeit seals would replace those that had been broken. The men
would jump from the boxcar and close the door. The train
would move down the track once more, bound for the port city
of Lübeck. In the morning the crates would be loaded aboard a

freighter. The next day they would be unloaded in Sweden. The furniture—property of Swedish diplomats and their families— would have long since been hauled into the woods and destroyed.

An exquisite operation. The best yet—if it worked. If it didn't—well, she didn't want to think about that. It would be very messy for all of them—for the Swede Erik Wesslen most of all. The operation had been his idea. He was the one who had smuggled a Jew out of Berlin to Sweden in a crate that was supposed to contain a piano. But she was the one who had said to him, after he'd told her the plan in an unguarded moment, "Well, get a pot under his behind or the piano will be leaking."

Wesslen had said nothing more. He never said more than he had to. That was his operating principle. Except that he was under such strain, and he liked her so much, and she had proved to him many times over that she could keep a secret, and so she had become something of a safety valve for him. One day he'd told her that they were going to smuggle a big group out, and because he needed her help, he had to tell her the circumstances. The operation had suddenly become possible because the Germans had unexpectedly given the Swedish diplomats, whose families were being evacuated, permission to ship their furniture back to Sweden.

To make the plan work they would need the cooperation of the crew of the train on which the furniture was to be shipped. The crew would be told nothing of the plan of course; they would simply be asked to stop the train in the woods outside Berlin for the amount of time it would take to make the switch. Usually the men crewing trains were elderly, not such strong, pig-headed Nazis as the young trainmen who had gone off to war. Wesslen could offer something to the engineer and conductor for their cooperation—food, coffee, cigarettes, money. These days that was a lot.

Then there was the matter of the seals that would need to be broken. How could they be replaced? That was solved simply enough: a counterfeit stamp was copied from a used seal.

Then there was the matter of providing for the stowaways while they were crated in the lift vans. They would need food. They would need pots for their wastes. They would need codeine to suppress coughs.

And then Marushka brought up a point that had been overlooked. "Don't forget that humans weigh far less than furniture. You'll have to add some weights."

"Good idea," Wesslen said. "I hadn't thought of that."

Marushka had been brought into the operation only toward the end. The counterfeit seal had been obtained, the railwaymen had been bribed, all was in readiness. It was then that Wesslen had asked her if she would lead the illegals through the woods.

"How will you get them to the woods?" she had asked.

"Never mind how," he replied. "We'll get them there. All you do is lead them."

Now that part, at least, was over. She walked back through the woods in a stillness so deep that she could hear her own breathing. Just as she reached the edge of the woods she heard the sound of barking dogs. And then—or was it her imagination?—the thud of marching boots on pavement. Suddenly the darkness was pierced by a curtain of light thrown across the clearing a hundred yards ahead of her. She knew then that it wasn't her imagination. Seconds later another curtain of light appeared behind her. She knew, without seeing the two other light curtains, that she was caught in a quadrangle—and, by the sound of their baying, that the dogs had picked up her scent.

In front of Marushka was a brook, and beyond it, if her nostrils told the truth, a pile of manure. Quickly she ran to the brook, leaped across it and raced to the manure pile. Then she buried her feet in the pile. When she was sure that her feet and legs were covered with manure, she ran back to the brook—effectively having stopped her scent at the pile. As rapidly as she could she waded with the current until she reached a pond that was overhung with trees. She swam to the far side and then waited under the trees until the sounds of the frustrated dogs receded. Only then did she lift herself onto the shore.

She no longer knew where she was. Even if she did, in her condition she would have to wait out at least the night, and then figure out a miracle that would get her back to Berlin. In the meanwhile she prayed that the illegals had fared better than she had. And she worried about Hans, who might almost die of worry when she didn't come home. Her wet clothes clung to her skin and she was shaking uncontrollably from the cold, but she thought, Poor Hans—at least *I* know I'm alive.

It hadn't been easy to keep the other half of her life hidden from the man she loved. But she had felt she had no alternative. She wasn't at all sure that Hans would be able to withstand torture if the Gestapo ever caught him. More than her own life was at stake in the event that Hans broke and identified his benefactress, because Marushka was heavily involved with the resistance movement, and had been even before her relationship with Hans. "I love this country so much, and I'm just beside myself with what's happening," she confided miserably to a friend after the Nazis took power.

She was studying in Munich at the time, nearing a doctoral degree in natural history but wracking her brain at the same time for ways to combat this new political scourge. She played a small part in helping two outspoken opponents of the Nazis, one a priest, the other a genetics professor, to leave Germany just as they were about to be arrested. She worked briefly on a newspaper, whose editor taught her how to pass confidential information secretly to like-minded journalists throughout the country by writing between the lines of printing mats. And she broke with her brother, who had inherited the family estate and become a fervent Nazi. But publicly she maintained quite another profile—that of a charming, well-bred young countess who was splendid company at dinner parties and completely naïve about politics. Her seemingly innocent questions, asked of the high

Nazi officials who were invariably present at embassy functions and high society dinners, produced harvests of useful information, which she passed along to other anti-Nazis.

She had made contact with these people almost immediately after arriving in Berlin from Munich in 1936, following a brief marriage to an architect. She had one narrow escape when she decided at the last minute not to attend an organizing meeting of opponents of the regime that was masked as a social tea. The next day she learned that everyone at the tea had been arrested. Later, because of her command of languages—she spoke English, French, Spanish and Greek—she was pressed into censorship work by the military. All of the correspondence of certain suspect persons came to her for review. After censoring the letters she would contact the writers privately and chastise them for being stupid and indiscreet. Then someone—she never learned who—reported her to the Gestapo for warning anti-Nazis. She was held several days but finally dismissed without charge, due in part to the fact that her superior was a family friend but also because she had raged so vociferously at being suspected as an enemy of the state that the Gestapo was glad to get rid of her. But in the meanwhile she had learned what the censors knew about finding hidden messages, and was able to relay that information to the resistance.

"Resistance" was the word they used, but it did not adequately convey the activity that went on. There was almost no resistance in the accepted sense of the term—saboteurs, assassins, provocateurs. Rather, almost all of the work was defensive, attempts to save the lives of endangered persons—Jews for the most part, but also political dissidents as well as those who were trying to help the oppressed. Much of this help came from individuals, who might offer nothing more than money or a hiding place for a fugitive to stay overnight. But most of the help came from several church groups, one German, the others Scandinavian. It was with one of the latter, the Church of Sweden, that Marushka became involved.

It had begun innocuously enough in a chance meeting with a Protestant priest named Sivkowicz at a 1939 birthday party for a mutual friend. In the course of their conversation Marushka suggested that the most valuable service persons like themselves could perform was to help people get away. Sivkowicz made no comment. A few moments later he drifted away. In the next half hour he did a lot of checking up on Marushka. As they parted he said, "About that thought you had. You might want to get in touch with the pastor at the Swedish church."

A few days later Marushka called on the pastor, Birger Forell. He acted as though he didn't quite understand what she was talking about. He said simply, "We'll be in touch."

Whatever it was that these Swedes were attempting, they couldn't succeed without the help of Germans. An offer from a well placed countess with impeccable references was not to be taken lightly. Several weeks after her first contact with the church Marushka received a call from Forell. "There's a man we know who needs a place to stay for a few days," he said. "Do you suppose you could find him something?"

She passed that test, and several like it in the next few years, until finally, in 1942, she met Eric Wesslen. He was a young, almost cherubic-looking Swede, with atypically dark straight hair, who had originally come to Berlin earlier that year ostensibly to study landscape architecture. He had an informal relationship with the church as a sort of parish worker. Wesslen's real work was to free certain people from the S.S.—to "buy them back," as he would say—then hide them and eventually export them. Many were Jews, but some were political people. He never explained his priorities. His contact was supposedly a high official of the S.S. He never told Marushka the man's name, and she never asked him for it. He would simply say, "Tonight I'm getting some people back. Can you get them under a roof and find them some food?" She never asked who the people were. She had her one segment of the operation to perform, and that was it.

But gradually, as his respect for Marushka deepened, Wesslen came to rely on her more and more. Often it was Marushka who would propose whom to buy back. She would hear from her neighborhood sources—apartment managers, housewives, merchants, sometimes even the police—when a special person had been taken, and she would then tell Wesslen.

It was a dangerous game he was playing. He knew that if he was caught he could expect no help from the Swedish legation. He did not even like to contemplate the consequences. He simply kept to his task in as straightforward a manner as he could. "You have so-and-so," he would say. "How much?"

"A kilo of coffee, a kilo of sugar, two cartons of cigarettes, and he's yours," would come the typical reply. Once the payment was made, the captive would be released.

Inevitably the work got to him. Marushka could see it in the set line of his mouth or the strain in his face when he dropped into her flat. "I had a rough day today," he told her once. "I bought back several people. The S.S. was really tough. They want more and more. They saw we really wanted those people. They drove a hard bargain." He sagged against his chair and rubbed his face and let out a long sigh. "Isn't it disgusting to barter a pack of cigarettes or a jar of marmalade or a kilo of coffee for a human life?"

Once they had the people back they had to provide them with lodging, food and papers showing that they were authorized to live or work in Berlin. Often that was where Marushka came in. She had a network of safe houses in which the fugitives could stay for a night or two at a time, as well as an excellent source for counterfeit ration cards, a Chinese printer who worked out of a cellar on the north side of Berlin. Counterfeit identity papers required valid blank forms, but those could be obtained with the help of friendly policemen—sometimes for a bribe, often for nothing. After a document had been forged, there remained the problem of an official stamp. It had to be lifted from some old document and placed on the new one. Marushka accomplished that with an old trick borrowed from her school days, rolling a shelled hard-boiled egg over the old stamp, then transferring the ink onto the new document.

Most of the old documents came from black market sources. Some of the documents were collected from fugitives being smuggled from the country who no longer had need of them. On at least one occasion a document came from an outright theft. Marushka was in line at the grocery one day behind a woman whose pocketbook, hanging from her arm, was gaping open. Inside was the woman's passport. While the woman intently watched the clerk totting up her bill, Marushka gently relieved her of the passport.

The longer the war against the Jews ground on, the more difficult it became to buy them back. Not only did the prices continue to rise, the sellers became more devious. One day Wesslen grimly reported a new tactic by the sellers: to chase after the people they'd just released, take them back into custody and ransom them once more.

Over the weeks Wesslen developed a series of escape routes designed to prevent recapture. He enlisted Marushka's help. One evening he picked up a group of six elderly Jews from the Gestapo and drove them to a rendezvous point, where he turned them over to Marushka. As she led them through a culvert she realized she was being followed. She hid at a bend in the culvert until her pursuer overtook her and then shot him in the leg. The sound of the shot reverberated as though a dozen cannons had gone off. Marushka and the Jews rushed away.

The next day Marushka reported the incident to Wesslen. He was enraged. "That was the stupidest thing you ever did," he shouted. "You should have killed him."

Marushka held out her hands imploringly. "I can't kill a man who hasn't got a gun," she said.

"Of course he had a gun."

"But he didn't have it out."

"You're useless," Wesslen said. "Now we can never use that route again." He refused to talk to Marushka for several days.

But eventually he forgave her—first, because she was the

most valuable ally he had and, second, because he needed her for a vital role in the best plan ever hatched to smuggle Jews out of Berlin.

And now, six weeks later, having played her role, she was trapped in a forest without the slightest clue as to how to get out alive.

Dawn came. Marushka was frozen and hungry, but she was still afraid to move. Whoever had tracked her through the night would be waiting for her to leave the woods. With her wet and filthy clothes she would give herself away.

She waited through the day, praying for an air raid, the only diversion she could imagine that would enable her to escape. As darkness fell, the four curtains of lights came on again. She was still trapped, still hunted.

And then she heard the sirens. Sweet, sweet sound!

Moments later the curtains of lights went out. She heard the bombers droning in and then the thudding explosions. Now or never, she thought. Crouching, weaving, she made her way through the trees until she reached the edge of the forest. Just then there was a tremendous explosion as a bomb hit a factory. Soon the factory was blazing, turning night to dawn. Marushka could see that the road was empty. The moment the all clear sounded she made a dash for the factory. As she had hoped, everyone was suddenly too busy with the fire to pay attention to a lone figure running down the road.

For an hour she helped fight the fire. Soon her clothes were no more wet and soiled than those of the others around her. As soon as the fire was under control she approached an official. "I'm not from this area," she said. "I was here visiting friends and got caught by the raid, and then I helped put out your fire. Now can you give me some kind of paper saying that's what I've done?" She got the paper without question.

By the next afternoon Marushka had made her way back to Wilmersdorf. When no one was looking she scaled the wall of the churchyard on the Kaiserallee. Wesslen opened to her

knock. With him was Erik Perwe, the minister who had succeeded Birger Forell the year before. "Are you going to faint?"
he asked.

"I don't think so," she said.

Perwe grabbed her and led her to a couch.

"How about the people?" she asked.

"They made it," Wesslen said. "They should be on their way
to Sweden."

Perwe handed her a glass of champagne. She took a sip and
fainted.

Involved as she was and great as were the risks she took,
Marushka never would learn the depth of the involvement of
the Church of Sweden in efforts to assist Jews. Even those persons who worked for the church, either formally or, like Wesslen, informally, did not know everything that was going on.
There was only one person who did.

23

HE WOULD SIT for hours in the churchyard, working on his ancient charcoal-powered automobile. His staff never understood what he accomplished by his endless tinkering, so they invented an expression to describe it. He was, they said, "polishing his screws." Wearing a smock and beret, he looked like a French mechanic. Strangers to the church would invariably approach him to ask where they might find the minister. "Well, sit down," Erik Perwe would say. It would take the strangers several moments to realize that they stood before the brains and guts of the most organized effort in all Berlin to save its remaining Jews.

He was a small but sturdily built man in his late thirties, with burrowing brown eyes that peered out from under protruding brows. Most of the time he walked about with an intense, preoccupied look, as though to warn others away from the secret knowledge he kept. But his smile, when he flashed it, was as hearty as a clown's, and he had the polished diplomat's gift for saying and doing all the right things at the right times. He never said more than a situation demanded, but if the situation demanded a story that would cheer up his listeners, he'd tell that story. While he was concerned with the plight of all oppressed persons, he spent most of his spiritual and psychological resources on the Jews who came to him for help.

One day in September 1942, two weeks after he and his family had settled into the large city villa that served as church, community house and home, Martha Perwe, a striking woman whose beauty was not disguised by the prim garb of a preacher's wife, went down to her husband's basement office to fetch him for lunch. To her astonishment she found a crowd of Jews waiting outside his door, their heads bowed, the Star of David on their coats.

Perwe did not take lunch that day. Instead he sat through the afternoon in his oak chair at his oak desk, listening to his visitors' stories. When he finally came upstairs that evening he removed his horn-rimmed spectacles, rubbed his bloodshot eyes, and said to Martha, "I feel like a lemon squeezed dry."

"What can you do for them?" she asked.

"I can get them food. I can arrange housing. I can send letters for them."

"Does that satisfy them?"

"Seldom."

"What do you do then?"

"I take them in my arms. I cry with them."

Perwe's dedication to his work was rooted in his belief that God had called him to it. His Church's dedication, no less intense, was both mystical and historical. Its fascination with the Jews went back a hundred years to the time when Jews first began migrating to Sweden. The Church's reaction then had been twofold. First, it attacked the Jews as Christ killers, the classic but superficial response. Second, it sought to convert them.

But the fascination that the Jews held for the Church of Sweden in modern times was only partially explained by its desire for conversions. What lay behind the Church's concern was a sense of guilt for the suspicion in which it had initially held the Jews. The Church's efforts during the Hitler era sprang from a strong desire to atone for its initial attitude.

Coincidentally there existed a practical mechanism for atonement. In 1903 the Church of Sweden had begun to establish missions in those foreign cities in which many of its members had foundered after emigrating from Sweden in the hope of reaching America. Once the plight of the Jews became evident, it was only natural that the Church's Swedish-Israel Mission, founded in the 1870s to assist Jews socially and spiritually—and to convert them—would work through these outlets.

The first major rescue operation began in Vienna in the 1930s, after Austrian priests had been frustrated by the Nazis in their own efforts to help baptized Jews escape the persecutions. Göte Hedenqvist, a minister of the Church of Sweden, was asked by the headquarters of the Austrian Evangelical Church to come to Vienna to assist the converts. But once on the scene, Hedenqvist began to give help to nonbaptized Jews as well. "If they come to me for help, I can't ask them if they are Christians or not," he told his superiors.

One thousand children and two thousand adult Jews were rescued from Austria before the war made further efforts there impossible. Hedenqvist returned to Sweden and took over the Swedish Mission to the Jews—another name for the Swedish-Israel Mission—as well as the task of resettling Jews then coming to Sweden from Germany with the help of the Church.

The pastor of the Swedish church in Berlin at that time was Birger Forell, a man "as single-minded," one of his parishioners once observed, "as a dog who's got hold of your pants." Forell had been in Berlin since 1929; from the moment of the Nazi takeover in 1933 he had been helping Jews and other oppressed persons with a tenacity that often overpowered local authorities. But by 1941 Forell had received so many warnings from powerful Nazis to stop his rescue efforts that he knew his usefulness had ended. In a letter to Perwe, he said, "You should prepare yourself to take over."

Perwe's first involvement with the beleaguered Jews had occurred in 1935 when he went to Vienna to observe the rescue efforts of Hedenqvist, an old friend and colleague. On his return to Sweden, Perwe lectured extensively on the plight of the Jews in Austria; one by one, he stated, they were disappearing. At each of his lectures Swedish Nazis would march noisily into the meeting place and heckle him. But Perwe kept talking, and his speeches came to the attention of Archbishop Earling Eidem, who decided that Perwe, whom he had known since his student days, belonged in Berlin. In 1939 the archbishop sent him there. His specific mission: to get Jews out of Germany.

What Perwe found dismayed him. It was not simply that by then the Jews were being persecuted in a manner and on a scale that had been unimaginable to him, it was that his German brothers in God were, for the most part, doing nothing about it. Individual ministers and their congregants were trying to save baptized Jews, but, with a few courageous exceptions, almost nothing was being done to help the overwhelming majority of nonbaptized Jews, and—worst of all—the churches were officially silent. A few scattered sermons here and there, but otherwise no protests of any kind.

Why? Perwe asked himself. Was it because the churches feared for their own survival in the Third Reich, resounding with pagan overtones and the deification of Hitler? Or was it because they were so frightened of socialism and so nationalistic that they considered it necessary to support the Reich uncritically as it brought Germany back to life? Was it because they too, like most other Germans, had felt it would be good for the country to reduce the Jewish presence in business, the professions and the arts? Was it, finally, because the German churches, deep down, were uncomfortable about the Jews, saw them as aliens whose participation in the society somehow diluted the Germanic essence—because, in short, the churches, their clergy and parishioners, in the overwhelming majority of cases, simply didn't like Jews?

Whatever the reasons, whatever the answers, Perwe was appalled. He returned to Sweden in 1941 badly shaken by his experience. Forell's letter, which he received soon after his return, threw him into a quandary. He was not at all keen about taking his wife and three daughters—the eldest was only seven—into a war zone. And yet how could he refuse to go if his presence in

Berlin might save the lives of even a few persecuted Jews? "Is this the answer to the question of the future?" he asked himself on one of the lined pages of the black soft-cover diary he filled regularly with brief yet tantalizing notes.

In the spring of 1942 the Nazis told Forell that he was no longer welcome in Germany. Forell informed Perwe. "God calls. I must obey," Perwe wrote in his diary. On June 21 he received a telegram from Berlin confirming his election to the parish priesthood there. "God help me and us all," he noted. The Perwe family left Sweden for Germany on the last day of August, an emotionally taxing transition he covered with two cryptic entries in his diary: *"August 31, 1942:* Departure from Norrköping to Berlin. Many people at the train to see me off. Touching, painful, encouraging. *September 1, 1942:* Train to Berlin. Many people. Very warm. Met by legation's car. At residence met Sister Vide. God bless our arrival."

The Swedish church was in the reception hall of a large and gracious villa on the Landhausstrasse, in Wilmersdorf, an attractive residential neighborhood. The street was lined with linden trees. In the back of the villa was an enormous informal garden that ran the length of the block to the Kaiserallee, one of the major thoroughfares leading to the center of the city two miles to the north. To those who worked in the church or came to it for help the villa and garden, which was like a private park, seemed a world apart in wartime Berlin. The bombings would soon make it that almost literally. So many houses and apartment buildings at both sides of the villa were flattened that the church stood virtually alone.

But it was the emotional ambience even more than its physical isolation that set the church apart. Whereas before the war the atmosphere had been moral, pious, even narrow, now it was expansive and often explosive—merry, easygoing, elastic, tolerant. Visitors to the church might be offered brandy and cigars—something seldom if ever observed there prior to the war. There was always a pot of soup and another of coffee on the stove; anyone who needed a meal got one, whatever the hour. Sides of pork hung from the pegs on which women parishioners had once placed their fur coats. There were so many unexpected visitors that the staff's sleeping quarters were often preempted, forcing them to double up. They didn't mind that or the eighteen hours of work they often put in each day. They knew that they were experiencing the kind of community they had always hoped to find in service to the Church but had never previously encountered. The people they helped helped them in turn, looking upon them as saviors, operators of a way station on the road to salvation. They knew they weren't superfluous, and no matter how difficult their work became, that knowledge made life easy—at least for the kind of people they were.

The most exuberant among them was Sister Vide Ohmann, a trained nurse functioning additionally as a social worker in these emergency times. Sister Vide was a vivacious young woman whose lovely face, as fresh as a milkmaid's, broadcast her turbulent emotions. A lifelong resident of Berlin, she had translated all the anguish and anger and confusion she felt over the changes produced by the Nazis into a single, powerful desire to help the victims of its policies. She walked about the church and residence with a look that said, "If you want my hands, here they are." There was little that she and her colleagues were not prepared to do to make life easier for the Jews.

The major job of the women in the church was to care for the Jewish itinerants who regularly inhabited the building. There might be twenty at a time—bent, thin, seemingly without hope. Perwe would see them all. One day he said to Vide, "I'm not living one life. I'm living twenty every day." Precisely how the minister helped the Jews the women never knew. They put it out of their minds. "Please never ask when you see anything here," Perwe had told them. "It's better that you don't know."

Part of what the minister was doing was creating false identities. The best possible paper was the *Kennkarte,* the obligatory national identity card. To obtain it one had to show a certificate of baptism. Such certificates could be readily counterfeited, but they had to be backed by the church's records. Accordingly,

Jews who were given false baptismal certificates were also "inscribed" in the church's baptismal records, which went back to 1905.

And then, of course, there was the clandestine purchase of Jews from contacts in the Gestapo. Perwe was in charge of that operation as well, but he left it mostly in Wesslen's hands. He could not get over Wesslen. The man seemed drawn to danger. Why else would a man choose Berlin in the early 1940s, when the bombings had already begun, for his studies in landscape architecture? Wesslen was thirty years old, but he seemed at times to have the outlook of an adventure-loving schoolboy. The greater the risk, the more he liked it. He still looked somewhat like a schoolboy too, innocent and good-natured. His manner was so open that no one would ever have suspected him of wrongdoing. In fact, he had a flair for anything and everything crooked. He was a master at getting along with and using the Gestapo. His underground contacts were seemingly inexhaustible. A feverishly active man, he knew where to trade a bottle of brandy for a set of tires, a pound of butter for a tank of gas. His bartering supplies—food, wine and cigarettes obtained from Sweden—were as plentiful as his contacts and his energy.

The most valuable thing the church could give the Jews was, ultimately, a safe place to stay. It was Perwe who would give out these addresses, most of which he obtained from a man named Reuter, the maintenance chief of the church. Reuter was an elderly German of medium stature, with white hair, a sad, bleak face and a big nose on which was precariously perched an ancient pair of glasses. His clothes were old and baggy. He gave every appearance of being a poor, insignificant man, and he frightened the women in the church because he was often so disagreeable. He would appear fairly regularly to have a meal, with a pack of papers or a bag stuffed under his arm, but he rarely ate with the staff, and he almost never spoke to them. Once in a great while he would smile, and then he seemed like another person. Where Reuter got his list of safe houses not even

Perwe knew. All he knew was that if Reuter offered them, they were safe.

But within two or three weeks after the Jews had gone to the safe houses they would be back at the church, saying that the Gestapo was on their trail. Perwe never knew if this was true. It might be the Jews' imagination; it might be that the Germans sheltering them were also getting nervous. In any case, he would have to find them new places to stay. Sometimes there would be no places, and when that happened Perwe would let the Jews remain in the basement of the church for several days, even weeks. Inevitably there came the day when, of necessity, a Jew became a quasi-permanent resident of the church.

His name was Erich Müller. He was a violinist from Leipzig, in his forties, a seemingly inconsequential man who did not attract attention both because his manner and appearance were so unprepossessing and because he did not have Semitic features. Until this moment the combination had helped him survive. But when the Perwes met him during their first weeks in Berlin he had all but lost control. Several years before, Perwe's predecessor, Birger Forell, had slipped Müller's son into Sweden; now Müller desperately needed another favor. He'd been living with his fiancée, who was also Jewish, and her mother, he explained. His fiancée was pregnant, and he had to arrange an abortion. Would the minister help him?

Before Perwe's conscience could be tested, Müller's fiancée miscarried. When she recovered she determined to leave Berlin for Fribourg, Switzerland, where she planned to live with relatives. Müller did his best to dissuade her, but she was adamant. Perwe supplied her with a backpack, clothes and food, and she set out. Weeks passed without word from her. Müller became so depressed that he threatened to take his life. His fiancée's mother ordered him from her home. On December 1, 1942, Müller moved into the church. He was quartered in a room in the attic, a tiny space that Forell had used as a study. The terms of his agreement with Perwe were that he confine himself to his room until ten o'clock each evening. Then he was permitted to walk outside on the terrace facing the garden.

Müller more than kept his part of the bargain. He would not even open the door when Martha Perwe brought him his tray of food. When she returned an hour later the tray would be where she had left it and the food would be untouched. In vain she implored him through the door to take some nourishment, but often he did not even respond. For days they neither saw nor heard him, and his fast went on. They feared that his confinement and his fiancée's disappearance were slowly driving him mad. In desperation one day, Martha laced some tea with amphetamines and took it to his door. That evening Müller appeared at last and said that he felt better. On Christmas Eve he came down again and played to them on his violin.

In March of 1943 two more Jews moved into the church on a semipermanent basis. Until that time Martin Weissenberg, a man in his early sixties, and his wife Margot, a woman twenty years younger, had managed to elude the Nazis, principally through the help of the sister of Horst Wessel, whose composition had become the party's official song and the secondary anthem of the Third Reich. Horst Wessel had been a childhood friend of Margot's. When the Nazis took power it was his sister who prevailed upon the Weissenbergs to send their children to England, provided them with food, clothing and medicine from her own scarce reserves, warned them when actions against the Jews were imminent, and once got them away from a hiding place minutes before the arrival of the Gestapo. Their resources exhausted, the Weissenbergs had walked the streets at night, hiding in abandoned buildings or in doorways or parks, until Perwe began to help them.

A friend, an active Social Democrat until Hitler took power and banned all parties but his own, had suggested they contact Perwe, who had already found refuges for several other Jewish friends. Three days after they saw him Perwe sent word that he had arranged quarters for them in a retirement home near the southern outskirts of Berlin. The home was run by an elderly German woman who not only took them in but did her best to stiffen their spirits. Other Jews had lived there before moving on to even safer lives, she confided, and not once had the Gestapo bothered them.

A few weeks later, however, the Gestapo did make a surprise visit, following a report by one of the elderly residents that Jews were living in the home. Luckily the Weissenbergs were away at the time shopping for food with ration cards just supplied them by Perwe, an adventure made somewhat safer by two postal identification cards Weissenberg had arranged through their former postman in exchange for ten cigars. After finding no Jews on the premises and hearing the administrator's fervent denials, the Gestapo dismissed the report as the product of a senile mind, and did not return.

The Weissenbergs lived in the retirement home without further incident through January and February of 1943. Mrs. Perwe brought them food to supplement their rations, and Perwe himself came to visit from time to time. To Martin Weissenberg, who in 1940 alone had lost twenty of his closest relatives, among them six brothers and sisters, whose own health had been undermined by forced labor, shoveling coal, his present life might have seemed, by comparison, a form of deliverance, except for one daily reminder: a song sung early each morning by S.S. troops quartered in a nearby barracks about how Jewish blood would spurt around their knives.

And then in March the retirement home was destroyed by a bomb. There were no casualties, because all the residents had been in bomb shelters, but the Weissenbergs were so distraught at the loss of their sanctuary that there were moments when they wondered if death was not preferable to the uncertainty that once again was their lot.

It was then that Perwe moved them into the church.

The staff had never liked the violinist Müller—he was testy, complained a great deal and kept insisting that Perwe arrange his escape to Sweden—but they responded powerfully to the

Weissenbergs, who were so obviously grateful for the assistance they had been proferred, so cheerful and so eager to help in any way they could. Margot Weissenberg busied herself with household work, and Martin Weissenberg became the house expert on air raids. He had a large map of Berlin that looked something like a game board. Letters ran along the top and numbers along the side. As Allied planes approached, the flak center near the zoo would track their flight and broadcast the patterns on the radio. "Bomber squadron entering A2. Heading direction G5." By plotting the information on his map Weissenberg could tell the others whether there was a chance that their building might be hit.

The staff had access to the bomb shelter at the Swedish legation in the Tiergarten, and, while the legation was several miles away, there was always sufficient warning of a raid for them to get there if they wished. But they vastly preferred to remain at the church during the raids, because they knew from experience that this was when many Jews and other hunted persons—using the cover of the raids—would come to them for assistance. So most of the time the staff used a homemade shelter they had rigged up in a potato bin in the garden. If the bombs came very close, the illegals joined them.

Martin Weissenberg was listening to a radio broadcast one day when two uniformed policemen walked unannounced into his sanctuary. His heart turned over. They immediately made it clear, however, that they were there not to pick him up but to monitor the broadcast with him. It was Weissenberg's first encounter with Erik Perwe's two greatest allies—the constable and chief of the police station across the street. The constable's name was Hoffman. He was a stocky, middle-aged German, with a bushy mustache, who managed to look well fed in a period when no one got very much to eat. The chief's name was Mattek. He was a small and sturdy man, also middle-aged, with a dapper mustache, a dimpled chin, and a perpetual grin that could turn into a magnificent smile that wrinkled his face. Both men had been old-guard Social Democrats, but they were Prussian to the core. Like many policemen, they resented the crude, unprofessional and illegal methods of the Nazis; policemen, in their book, did not seize people late at night and without proper papers.

Hoffman was in charge of all outside investigations for the station; he was anti-Nazi and didn't try to hide it. But it was Mattek, the chief, who was the more outspoken of the two. He hated Joseph Goebbels. "The little clumpfoot's telling fairy tales again," he would announce after each pronouncement by the propaganda minister.

Both Hoffman and Mattek were regulars at the church. They would come to listen to the BBC or to have an occasional game of chess with the pastor. Both of them not only knew that Jews were being hidden in the church but went out of their way to converse with them. Perwe made certain that both men received coffee, butter, liquor, cigars and whatever staples they might need to feed their families—which, in Mattek's case, eventually included a deserter he kept hidden in the cellar of the police station. The policemen, in turn, made certain that no unsympathetic-looking visitors lurked about the church. On one occasion Hoffman arrested two men who had been prowling in the vicinity of the church, and pretended to be very surprised when he found out that they were from the Gestapo. On another occasion a man from the Gestapo came to the police station and seated himself at a window that looked out onto the street, from where he could observe anyone who entered or left the church. Moments later Mattek slipped out the back door of the station, walked down the block, cut across the street and made his way through a series of connecting basement passages to the church, where he told Perwe about the Gestapo observer. The minister posted sentries at either end of the block to warn illegals away.

Perwe of course was his own best sentry, given his innate capacity for caution and his guarded, watchful manner. Part of his defense was to maintain the appearance of the person he was supposed to be—the minister of the church of a neutral country—and he worked hard at doing that. He was a frequent guest at diplomatic receptions, where he mixed amiably—or so he made it seem—with Nazi party officials. Martha always went with him, an incongruous presence in her drab dress of a preacher's wife, dark stockings and Salvation Army-type shoes, and chaste hairdo. But the hair, pulled back into a bun, only served to heighten the lines of her chiseled face, and the guests were invariably fascinated with this woman, who held a wine glass from which she never drank and chatted with diplomats as though she had done it all her life. If anything, it was her husband who was occasionally lacking in tact. At one reception he watched a brother of Heinrich Himmler smoking a cigarette whose ash grew longer and longer. "Ah," Perwe said at last, "the final solution." Himmler's brother quickly flicked off the ash.

Perwe knew that he was suspect, if only because of his predecessor's reputation, so he was constantly on the alert. One day a woman appeared at the church and told Perwe a classic tale of deprivation. She had been separated from her family, she was without papers and food, she had no place to stay, and had been walking the streets for weeks. Could he help her? she asked. Perwe eyed her coldly. "Anyone who is as well combed, well dressed and well fed as you hasn't been walking the streets for weeks." He stood and gestured toward the door. "If you please," he said.

Incredibly, another woman tried the same inept routine a few weeks later. Perwe was sure they were from the Gestapo. He could only wonder how much the Gestapo knew.

Throughout, Perwe continued to keep his diary. His commentary was invariably terse, but it aptly summarized the troubles with which he was engaged, the uncertainties he suffered and the rewards he experienced as he helped someone to freedom.

September 7, 1942: Visit from Miss Elias, "non-Aryan," from the refugee staff in town.

September 11, 1942: The Jew Müller concerning his son Rolf living in Sweden.

September 16, 1942: Müller with fiancée—in deep distress and great danger.

September 30, 1942: Reception. Several inquiries regarding relatives in Theresienstadt.

October 16, 1942: At the legation, concerning permission to communicate to Eidem information on certain significant circumstances for Christianity ... Permission denied.

October 17, 1942: Burial of a young man, Nyberg, who had been mentally ill and "as usual" put to death at the hospital.

October 21, 1942: Mrs. Ida Kuransky, concerning her child whom she wishes to send to Sweden.

October 23, 1942: A number of German authorities in the area of education, among them a government secretary and a brother of Himmler's. A great deal of Heiling and such.

October 31, 1942: A woman, Jewish, with two small, star-marked girls. Wanted to have the children adopted in Sweden.

November 17, 1942: Reception. A woman concerning the Swedish Red Cross's relationship to Theresienstadt, to which her mother had been deported.

November 18, 1942: Received as a guest for a few days Miss Rubin, Jewish, who is bound for Sweden.

December 11, 1942: Received word that the German author, Klepper, took his, his wife's and daughter's life last night. His wife and daughter had been threatened with deportation. They were *Mischlinge!* [*Mischlinge,* progeny of mixed marriages, were of special concern to Perwe, but the case of Jochen Klepper was not quite what the minister thought it was. Klepper, a devout German author and hymn writer, was a pure Gentile who had married a Jewish widow and then adopted her two daughters. The elder daughter had emigrated to England in the mid-1930s, but the younger elected to remain with her mother. Klepper was despondent at the failure of his own Evangelical Church to make more than a few feeble protests against the treatment of the Jews.]

December 12, 1942: Car to Tempelhof with Miss Jenny Rubin, who happily moves to Sweden.

December 14, 1942: Reception. Among others Miss Tali Paul, who criticized the party yesterday, defended Jewish politics and revealed a distorted view of Christianity: God bears responsibility—guilt—for everything. Mrs. Wehmeir, who also criticized the party, discussed politics and persecution of the Jews among others.

December 16, 1942: Supper with Bishop Meiser. Interesting man but exceptionally careful. [Bishop Meiser, a German, told Perwe he had three pieces of advice for him: "One: Be careful. Two: Be careful. Three: Be careful." "Then I might just as well pack my bags and return to Sweden," Perwe replied.]

December 29, 1942: Many "non-Aryans" because of the aggravated situation.

January 1, 1943: Visit from a Jewish couple who needed housing. Berg-Weissenberg.

January 4, 1943: Many homeless Jews.

January 13, 1943: Many unhappy non-Aryans.

March 1, 1943: Air raid of worst kind. Three fire bombs in the house, one of which in my room in the apartment. The blue hundred-year-old sofa and a black table destroyed. We succeeded in the nick of time in dousing the flames. Berlin is a sea of fire.

March 2, 1943: Worked at home preparing for air raids to come. God be with us!

March 5, 1943: Martha and the children to Sweden. Sad but necessary. God keep them all!

March 7, 1943: Worked late with Dr. Lehfeld on a report to the Swedish government re persecution of Jews.

August 17, 1943: Air raid. A terrible attack by 900 planes with five thousand men. Seventeen hundred tons of bombs.

Two bombs at a distance of 300 meters, phosphorous bombs in the park, twenty meters from the house . . . two burning houses next to ours, many broken windows . . . Church and house all undamaged. Helped at the house next door. To bed at 6:30 A.M.

August 24, 1943: Worked with our broken windows. The city looks horrible.

November 22, 1943: Air raid, the worst of them all. The home, legation's house in ruins, city in turmoil. Helped evacuate legation. Then by car to the church. Three hours struggle against fire and smoke.

November 26, 1943: Air raid, two hours. Horrible. New and terrible damage. Thirty percent of Berlin gone. The church stands. Praise God.

December 31, 1943: So ends this year, a terrible year. May God have mercy on the deeds of this year, their perpetrators and their victims.

24

So HE'D BEEN CAUGHT by a Jew! Fritz Croner could hardly believe it. He'd been warned about the catchers months before. "These people are working for the Gestapo," another underground Jew had told him. At first he'd all but dismissed the notion, because the idea was so repellent. Nonetheless, he'd taken no chances. A few weeks after the warning he'd seen another Jew approaching him on the street and ducked inside a building before the man could spot him. But he had slipped up this time, and so now, thanks to Fedor Friedlander, he was a prisoner, awaiting shipment to Auschwitz.

Although Fritz had no way of knowing it that day, he had been arrested by one of the two most notorious catchers who roamed the streets of Berlin and other major cities between 1942 and 1944, under instructions from the Gestapo to look for "black hair and big noses." His name was Rolf Isaaksohn, he was young and short and pretentious, and for a long time before he himself was captured by the Gestapo he had traded in false identification papers for illegal Jews.

On the day of his arrest Isaaksohn had been arranging to sell identification papers to a woman tailor who was working for a non-Jewish friend and living in the friend's home. Isaaksohn

collected the payment—money and a suit—and said he would
return with papers. He never did. The tailor, a Mrs. Mecklen-
burg, became frightened and fled from her friend's apartment.
The next day the Gestapo arrived to inquire of her whereabouts.
Mrs. Mecklenburg was probably the first Jewish "U-boat"
Isaaksohn denounced.

The only catcher whose reputation exceeded Isaaksohn's was
the woman he had spoken to in the beauty parlor just after cap-
turing Fritz. Her name was Stella Kübler; at the height of her
activity she was just twenty years old, an extravagantly pretty
woman who came to be called the "blond ghost." Kübler and
Isaaksohn often worked as a team; between them they were said
to have accounted for the arrest of 2,300 Jews but that figure
has never been corroborated.

Kübler was born Stella Goldflack in 1923. Her father was a
well known composer, her mother a cabaret entertainer. During
her schooldays she was always prominent and popular because
of her good looks. She was particularly popular with a boy
named Manfred Kübler. Stella and Manfred were married in
1941, but she was only eighteen at the time, and the marriage
didn't last. By 1943 Stella and her mother were working together in a large factory; they were at their jobs on February 27,
but managed to avoid being taken in the roundup by hiding in
a crate filled with sand. By morning they were near suffocation;
the sound of their gasping attracted two foremen who were
having breakfast on the crate.

There are contradictory accounts as to when Kübler began to
work for the Gestapo and under what circumstances. One story
is that she volunteered for the work after factory employees
turned her and her mother in. Another story is that she was arrested with Isaaksohn in a cafe in March 1943 as he was in the
process of selling her false identity papers for herself and her father. As proof of her willingness to cooperate with the Gestapo,
she was asked by her interrogator, one S.S. Hauptscharführer
Doberke, to denounce her husband. She did. Kübler agreed to

work with Isaaksohn, and other catchers, one of them Fedor Friedlander, Fritz Croner's tormentor.

Kübler's greatest asset in her work was her attractive appearance. One day she stopped a man walking down the street and asked him to invite her to lunch because she hadn't eaten anything for some time and didn't have any money. As they sat in the restaurant she confided to him that she was an illegal Jew. He told her that he was too. A few minutes later Kübler excused herself to go to the powder room. Not long after that the Gestapo arrived.

That Kübler was troubled about her activities is indicated by the help she gave the Jews awaiting the transports, smuggling food and carrying mail in and out of the building.

By comparing notes with other Jews who had been caught, Fritz eventually surmised who it was who had caught him, and who the woman was who had been sitting under the hair dryer. Now that he understood what was happening, he had no doubt that the two men who had come to collect him at the police station that first evening of his capture were also Jews. Both had been young and dark and very tall. When they took him to the street, the light was so faint because of the dimout that again he thought about making a run for it. But once more a captor showed him a gun and said, "If you try to get away, I'll shoot you on the spot."

They took him to the Grosse Hamburger Strasse detention center. Inside, his interrogators told him to empty his briefcase and pockets. When he did, they gaped and then looked at him in astonishment. On the table before them was a small fortune in money and jewelry.

Fritz swallowed and looked away, fighting to maintain his composure. It was not money and jewelry he was giving up, it was life. He had always carried his valuables on his person in case the Gestapo raided one of his hiding places in his absence. Thank God, he thought, Marlitt has her half. That was how they had done it—sharing the custody of the valuables so that even if one was taken the other could still survive.

They returned his empty briefcase. Then they took him to the cellar of the building and put him in a small and crowded room and locked him up for the night.

For several days after his capture Fritz Croner was questioned by Jews. They were to him literally beneath contempt. *Dreck,* shit. The Gestapo were Germans, under orders to bring the Jews to Auschwitz. But the Jews who worked for the Gestapo were worse than the Gestapo. He mocked their efforts to obtain information from him.

His interrogators had obtained his record from the files of the Jewish community organization and knew therefore that he was married and had a child. It was obvious that all of their questions were directed toward learning the location of two more Jews.

"Where are your wife and child?" one of them asked him.

"I don't know," he answered. "My wife has been living with a German for some time now, and has kept the child away from me. It's been months since I've seen them."

"Where have you been living?"

"With whores on the Augsburger Strasse."

"Where are your clothes?"

"In the luggage checkroom at the Bahnhof Zoo."

"Then where is your claim check?"

"In my wallet."

They looked in his wallet. There was no ticket.

"I'm sorry," Fritz said, "but it was there when you took my wallet."

"What does your luggage look like?"

Fritz described his suitcase for them—an invention, of course. Then they let him go.

Two days later the questioning resumed.

"There was no such suitcase in the checkroom," one of his interrogators told him.

Fritz held out his hands. "I'm sure there wasn't," he said. "Whoever stole the ticket from my wallet has also stolen the suitcase."

The interrogator glared at him angrily. Then he demanded to know where Fritz had obtained the ration cards he'd been carrying when he was arrested.

"I don't know his name," Fritz said, "but on the first day of every month I meet a man at the Bahnhof Zoo and pay him a thousand marks for the cards." A thousand marks was, in fact, the going price for ration cards at the time.

"Describe the man."

Fritz described an imaginary man. Then the interrogator dismissed him.

A few days later Fritz was summoned once more for questioning.

"No such man was there," the interrogator said.

Once again Fritz shrugged. "All I can tell you is that for the last four months he has been there on the first of the month. I'm sure he took precautions. Undoubtedly, when he didn't see me, he looked around and saw someone waiting and figured out what had happened."

For hours on end it went like this, Fritz playing with his captors, inventing stories, telling them what they wanted to hear. The more he toyed with them, the smaller they became to him.

At last they made him an offer. "Name ten Jews who are living illegally, and tell us how to find them, and you can stay here until the end of the war."

Fritz held out his hands, palms up. "I don't *know* any illegal Jews," he pleaded. "How many times must I tell you?"

Another day passed. Then, two weeks after he had arrived at the Grosse Hamburger Strasse building, Fritz received a visitor, a short, thin, coarse-looking man in his middle fifties.

"My name is Koplowitz," he said. "May I sit down?"

Fritz indicated the cot. Koplowitz sat beside him, and gave him a look of commiseration that has passed between Jews for centuries, identifying himself as a fellow sufferer who understood the misery that Fritz was going through. He told Fritz that he was living in a privileged marriage—his wife was Gentile—and therefore not yet subject to deportation. He indicated that he did not expect this immunity to last forever. In the meanwhile he had been pressed into service by the Gestapo. It was not volunteer work, he stressed. It ate his insides out. His one consolation was that, in his hands, the work went more gently and with more consideration for those Jews he dealt with than if they were handled by the Gestapo.

Fritz listened in silence. He had a thought he would have liked to express. "And if you did not cooperate, whatever the consequences to yourself, all the Jews you've sent to the camps would still be free," he would say. But he said nothing, only waiting to find out what it was Koplowitz would offer. He did not have long to wait.

Koplowitz spoke about how terrible the war was. He spoke about how terrible it was to be a Jew in Germany at this time. He spoke about how terrible it must be to go alone to Auschwitz and how much better it would be to be resettled as a family. Then he asked about Fritz's family.

"I don't know anything about my family," Fritz said.

"But you must know."

Fritz repeated the story he had told the others.

"Look," Koplowitz said, putting a hand on Fritz's knee, "I'm a Jew. You're going to Auschwitz in the next few days. What can your wife and child do here alone without you? Either they'll starve or they'll be found. And then they'll have to face their ordeal alone. Better you tell me where they are, and then they can go with you."

Fritz held out his hands. "I tell you, I don't know where they are. And if I did know, I wouldn't want my wife to go with me. She's a terrible woman. She deserted me. Imagine, a Jewish woman in this time taking up with a non-Jew."

Koplowitz sagged visibly. "Maybe it's true what you're saying. But if it's not true, let me make you an offer. If you will give me the names of two illegal Jews and their whereabouts, you can go visit your wife and child. How about it?"

"It's impossible," Fritz said. He almost felt sorry for the man—so coarse, so crude, so stupid, so willing to do anything to save his own precious skin.

Without another word Koplowitz walked from the room.

25

THERE WAS a famous Hungarian fortune teller in Berlin whom even certain Nazis would consult, although such a practice was illegal. Her name was Ursula Kardosch. She was a vivacious woman in her early forties, whom Marushka had met during her student days a decade before when she had accompanied a friend to an appointment at the fortune teller's home. When they had finished, Frau Kardosch emerged, looked at Marushka and said, "You'll have a place with lots of animals." Over the years Marushka and Frau Kardosch became friends. One day Frau Kardosch told Marushka to check her bank account for two months, because she had been cheated. Marushka found the errors. Now, as 1943 was ending, the fortune teller sent her maid around to Marushka's flat with a note. "Something around three o'clock," it said. "I can't see whether it will be day or night."

Marushka was scarcely a superstitious woman, but she was bothered nonetheless. In the last few months, she knew, she had flirted with disaster. Getting those people onto the train for Sweden had nearly cost her life. Since then she'd become even more heavily involved in underground work. The number of illegal Jews living in the flat on any one night had risen dangerously. One night she counted twenty. They were there only briefly for the most part, until papers could be arranged. Traffic in counterfeit papers had become much more brisk as a consequence of the bombings. Out of fear that the city's data bank on its residents would be destroyed, Berlin authorities had removed the central card file to a bunker outside the city, where it was effectively unusable. There was a second set of cards for residents, in the various police precinct stations around the city. It was their registration at these stations that entitled residents to live where they did and to obtain ration cards. But a number of these stations had been hit and their records destroyed. With the central data bank stored in the country, there was no way to verify identities in cases where the second set of cards had been destroyed. It was a heaven-sent opportunity to create new identities for Jews who had no papers at all.

Accompanied by someone who, for fifty marks or half a pound of butter, would attest to their identity, Jews would tell the authorities that they had lived in a building that had been destroyed, and that all personal papers had been destroyed as well. The address would have been chosen with care—a building that had been flattened or gutted by the bombs, its residents killed in the process. The Jews would explain that they had been in another part of the city when their buildings were hit. Some Jews would maintain that they had been bombed out in Hamburg, in the devastating August raid when 800,000 persons had been made homeless, and had moved to Berlin from there. Four months earlier that story might have been brought to the attention of the Gestapo, but so many persons had been made homeless by the bombings since then that it no longer aroused suspicion. To the contrary, a person who had been twice bombed out was a focus of great pity, and so the police would issue the new papers without much ado.

Although most policemen cooperated with the Gestapo, there were numerous police officers such as Mattek and Hoffman who disliked the Nazis for the same reason those two friends of the Swedish church did: the Nazis' methods were not correct—certainly not for Prussians. By now Marushka and others working for the church knew who these sympathetic policemen were, knew which might even be willing, for a little bribe or sometimes even for nothing, to obtain blank documents with which the church could forge false identities. They had all become adept at transferring stamps from old documents to new ones, using hard-boiled eggs. But even that crude technique had become unnecessary for the most part, because a counterfeit rubber stamp had been fabricated in Sweden and smuggled back to Berlin.

So, all in all, as the daily pounding of the bombers kept the authorities focused on the increasing problems of a troubled citizenry, as the growing destruction and disorganization worked in their favor, many illegal Jews—far too many, in Marushka's opinion—had not only begun to believe that they would survive the war, they had actually become bold and careless, endangering not only themselves but those who were helping them. You could scarcely blame the Jews; they had been cooped up for so long in their attics and basements and offices. But the *Mundfunk* told stories of Jews who had gone for their first walk outdoors in years only to be spotted by the catchers.

It was for many of these reasons that Marushka had finally evicted Hollander, Hans's friend and former colleague, who had been living in the flat for almost a year. The man had insisted on leaving the flat during the day because this was the only time he could visit the woman with whom he was having an affair. Marushka had proposed to his lover that she keep Hollander during the week, and Marushka would personally escort him back to her flat for the weekend. But the woman was unwilling to take the chance, and Hollander was unwilling to discontinue his daytime visits, and so Marushka had had no other alternative but to send him packing. As badly as Hans felt, he not only supported the action but recommended it.

And now this note from the Hungarian fortune teller: "Something at three o'clock." What? And when? In the afternoon? In the middle of the night? Today? Next week? Next month? Marushka could not let her life pivot on such an uncertainty, let alone one based on a vision. So she went about her life, a little more carefully, perhaps, but with the increasing conviction, as the days passed and nothing happened, that the vision had been just that.

And then one day it happened, at three in the afternoon.

It had been a good day for Marushka. She was always looking for ways to supplement the money she needed to feed Hans and the other illegals who occasionally congregated in her flat. This day she had found a treasure—a collection of leatherbound English books left by a Jewish woman who had emigrated before the war. A doctor had lent her his car to fetch the books, and now, at three in the afternoon, she was bringing them home. As she was carrying the first batch of books into her flat, a neighbor, the wife of a tailor, stopped her.

"I found this card with your name on it," she said. "Is it of any use?" The woman handed Marushka a yellow card. On it, handwritten, were the words "Bei Maltzan wohnen J."

Marushka could not believe what she saw. She knew the *J* stood for "Jews." "Jews are living with Maltzan" was what that card said. She darted a look at the tailor's wife. Was there the slightest sign of suspicion in her eyes? If there was, Marushka couldn't see it. "Where did you find this?" she asked.

"On the floor. Two gentlemen came and asked for you early this afternoon. One of them must have dropped it."

"What did you tell them?"

"I said you were at work."

Marushka mumbled her thanks, turned and ran into the flat. She dumped the books on the kitchen counter and rushed into the sitting room. "For God's sake, Hans, it's the Gestapo," she whispered. "Get into the couch." The greeting he had been about to give her died on his lips. Without a word he rushed for the couch.

Marushka took several deep breaths to calm herself. In vain she tried to will her thundering heart into silence. At last she swallowed, and walked to the street to get another load of books.

It was then that she saw them—a woman and two men. The

woman was young, blond, attractive, and fashionably dressed.

Out of the corner of her eye Marushka saw the two men move toward her as she picked up a fresh load of books. She carried the books into her flat. By the time she had dumped them on the kitchen table the men were at her back door. One was a small man, overdressed, wearing a gold bracelet and diamond ring. He was about thirty, and when he looked at her he scowled. The second man was about forty, blond, with an open, friendly look.

"We're Gestapo," the small man said.

"What do you want from me?"

"We understand that you have Jews living here."

"What? That's ridiculous."

"We know that a Jewish girl used your place for two weeks."

Marushka gaped at them. "That's simply not true."

"Do you deny that a girl lived here?" the small man asked.

"No. A girl did live here. But she wasn't Jewish. She had perfectly good papers."

"Those papers were forgeries."

Marushka threw up her hands. "How should I have known that?"

The little man looked at her contemptuously. "The girl was not the only one. We know you've been hiding Jews."

Marushka pulled herself erect. She advanced on the little man, all but backing him up with her breasts. "Look *here*, whoever you are. I'm not going to stand such insults." Without taking her eyes from the man she stretched out her arm and pointed at the picture of her father hanging on the wall. "My father was the Count von Maltzan and an officer under the Kaiser. My mother was a well known anti-Semite. I am a good German. What makes you think I would have anything to do with Jews?"

The smile the smaller man gave her now was more like a smirk. "Then I'm sure you won't mind if we search your flat?"

"Whatever you like," Marushka said, dismissing him with a wave.

The older man came up to her now. "I hope you understand," he said apologetically. "It's just a formality."

The old game, Marushka thought. One's the villain, the
other's friendly.

The small man searched everywhere, even in cupboards. Finally he came to the wardrobe where Hans kept his clothes. "To
whom do these belong?" he asked triumphantly.

"If you know so much about me, you must surely know that I
gave birth to a child not so long ago," Marushka said icily. "I
can assure you that the child wasn't made by the Holy Ghost."

"Then may we know who the father was?"

"Of course. His name is Eric Svensson. He is a Swede."

While the men poked about the house Marushka tried to affect nonchalance while at the same time observing whether they
looked with any suspicion at the couch. Twice the small man
looked at it, then looked away.

In the kitchen the two men found a cache of coffee in Swedish
bags, which Marushka had obtained from the church. The
small man called to her. She came into the kitchen. "Where did
you get this?" he demanded.

"I just told you that my boyfriend is a Swede." Marushka
looked at them mischievously. "I'd offer you a cup of coffee—
but then you'd accuse me of bribery."

The small man's face clouded. "Look here, Countess, don't be
so smart. I can have you put into a concentration camp."

"On what grounds?" Marushka demanded.

The older man stepped in now. "Please!" he said. "There's no
point in arguments. We're just doing our job." He smiled at her
as though he was a priest and she was a penitent. "If you've
done anything you shouldn't have, won't you relieve your conscience?"

This time Marushka could not suppress her laugh.

For more than an hour the two men went over and over every
item in the small flat. The small man kept returning to the
middle room to look at the couch. At last he went over and sat
on it, and said, "How do I know someone isn't in there?"

Marushka held up her palms once more. "You're welcome to look."

The small man pulled aside the cushions and tried to pry open the top. When he couldn't budge it he said, "Please open it up."

"I don't believe it opens," Marushka said. "I've only had the piece three weeks. I bought it when my other furniture was destroyed. I tried to open it, and I can't."

"I don't believe you. Someone could easily be hiding in there."

"*Oh!*" Marushka shouted. "Enough! I'm tired of this. I have work to do. You think there's someone in the couch, there's one way you can find out. I'm sure you have a gun. Take your gun and shoot through the couch. But you had better understand one thing: *You* pay for the fabric and repairs to put it back in shape."

The small man hesitated, obviously flustered.

"Go on! Shoot! And then get out! I haven't got all day!"

They glared at each other. Marushka stared him down. He turned away. "Ah!" he said. "I still don't believe you." Then he stalked from the flat. The older man followed.

For the next ten minutes Marushka sat, trying to calm herself. She did not try to speak to Hans, nor he to her. When she heard a knock on the back door she almost jumped from the seat. It was a Jewish girl wanting a counterfeit residence permit. "Go away," Marushka whispered. "The Gestapo's just been here." The girl's eyes opened to twice their normal size. In a second she was gone.

Half an hour later Marushka heard Hans unlatch the lid. She had to help him from the couch.

26

WILLY GLASER had gone to Tempelhof after his escape from the Grosse Hamburger Strasse detention center in the hope of finding a Gentile boyhood friend. He had met Gilbert Mach when he was seventeen and they had served as extras at the opera. Neither had money, but both loved music, so being extras had solved their problem. When they were not performing they would attend the opera together, sitting in the highest, cheapest seats. They had one other passion in common: both had been fervent Social Democrats in the time before Hitler. On his birthday in 1924 Willy had received a biography of Beethoven from Mach. In the flyleaf Mach had written: "All men shall become brothers. This be our highest goal." Surely now Mach would redeem that pledge, Willy thought as he rode the S-Bahn to Tempelhof.

But Mach, a producer of fruit juices, was away on a business trip. Willy had so counted on his presence that he was momentarily paralyzed by the news. When he recovered he went to the store of a grocer he knew and slipped in the back. The grocer told him that a man from the Gestapo had been in to inquire about him and was this very moment standing across the street. Apparently someone eager to get in favor with the Gestapo had supplied the police with a list of all Willy's non-Jewish friends. The grocer begged Willy to leave, and he did.

That night he slept in the woods. The next morning he walked the streets. He was without money and had not eaten since the previous morning. He stood in front of a bakery and inhaled the aroma of baking bread. When he was certain that no one was looking he picked cigarette butts off the sidewalks and smoked them until they burned his fingers. That night he slept again in the woods.

The next day Gilbert Mach returned to Tempelhof and took charge of Willy's life. He could not take Willy in because there was no way to hide his presence from the neighbors, but he managed to find Willy a place to stay. He also, miraculously, found Willy a job as a glazier, mending some of the thousands of windows that were being broken daily in the bombings.

Mach seemed to be without fear. Willy was not the only Jew he was helping. Nor was his help confined to Jews. For a while he had sheltered a woman whose husband had been executed by the Nazis for Communist activities. Mach did not even try to disguise his contempt for the Nazis. "Heil Hitler," the mailman would say to him each morning. "Good morning," Mach would reply.

Mach instructed Willy to maintain his appearance as well as he could in order to avoid attracting attention. That was not an easy job. The suit Willy wore was his only one; the material was shiny and thin. Because he had lost so much weight he was hard pressed to keep his pants up. His shoes were scuffed, the soles worn through. Nonetheless he tried. Wherever he went he carried a small briefcase with shaving equipment. On the days when he did not have a lodging he would shave in train stations. The risk of walking about unshaven was greater than the risk of using the restrooms. Most nights Willy did have a place to stay, but occasionally he would have to sleep in the woods, and so he also carried a small blanket in his briefcase.

On his first day off Willy took a train to the center of Berlin and went to the Philharmonic. He stood in the front hall, near the ticket windows, and scanned the seating charts as though he was choosing a place, all the while listening to the orchestra rehearse as he kept an eye out for guards. The music thrilled him.

The next morning Willy walked to work. Half a block from his destination he stopped in dismay. Where the glazier's shop had been there now lay a pile of rubble.

Only a handful of Jews had been in the Grosse Hamburger Strasse building on November 17, 1943, when Fritz Croner was picked up and brought there. The story was that a transport had left with fifty Jews just a few days earlier. Each day thereafter one or two more Jews arrived. As soon as another fifty were collected, they too would be put on a transport and shipped to the east. The word was that they would travel in a boxcar with straw on the floor; they would eat and sleep and dispose of their wastes in this boxcar, not leaving it until they arrived in Auschwitz. What happened after that was a source of endless debate. Many of the prisoners insisted that they would be put to some kind of forced labor, but others passed along the rumors that the Jews were being gassed.

In the first days of Fritz's confinement all of the prisoners were locked up throughout the day. This precaution had been taken, it was said, because a Jew had escaped the day before the last shipment was to leave, creating consternation among the guards. Exercise periods in the cemetery behind the building had been banned. After a week, however, the prisoners were permitted to mingle with one another in the corridors.

It struck Fritz that he was meeting the kind of Jews with whom he had never had dealings before. Except for his time on the railroad, his own life had been spent with middle- and upper-class Jews—professionals, merchants. His companions now were almost all working-class Jews. Conversation was not a problem, though; they had their common plight to discuss.

Each of them had a story, which he desperately wanted to share. There was the shoemaker of approximately thirty-five years, a diminutive man with red hair and a self-consciousness about his lack of education. His parents, who were Polish, had lived in Berlin since before World War I. They had had a difficult time. Germans disliked Poles to begin with; to be Polish *and* Jewish was to invite multiples of contempt. The thought of Auschwitz terrified the shoemaker. Each day he sought out Fritz, not to talk—because he had nothing more to say—but simply to be near him, which he found comforting. One day, as they sat alone in the hallway, the shoemaker leaned close to Fritz and whispered, "I have ten one-hundred-dollar bills in my left shoe and two diamonds in my right shoe. They are sewn into the soles. I put them there because I was sure they wouldn't take our shoes." He hesitated. "If something happens to me, I want you to take my shoes." Where the shoemaker had obtained the dollars Fritz never learned, but he was deeply touched by the offer.

In the hall one day Fritz noticed a woman of forty whom he hadn't seen before. He surmised that she had been captured the previous day. She was crying. He didn't approach her. When he returned, she hadn't moved, and she was still crying. He walked up to her and tried to console her, but what she told him then threw his own feelings into a turmoil. She had been living in the underground with her niece. Her niece had been picked up; the Gestapo had told her that she could go free if she would turn in two other Jews. She had turned in her aunt and another woman, a family friend. "My own niece," the aunt sobbed.

Oh, God, Fritz thought, what has become of our people?

And then came a man who had escaped from Auschwitz. His arrival electrified the prisoners. Fritz judged him to be forty, but he was only twenty-five. He was six feet tall, with dark hair and a face that remained handsome in spite of his almost skeletal appearance. From his features Fritz would never have guessed that he was Jewish. He told Fritz that he had escaped while on a work detail outside the camp. A Polish farmer had given him some clothes and burned his prison garb. Traveling only at night, he had made it back to Berlin in three weeks. Berlin had been his city, and he had thought that he could hide there. But all of his family was gone now, and he had been unable to find any of his friends. Without money, without a place to stay, he had had no alternative but to wander the streets. Inevitably he had been challenged by soldiers who patrolled the streets looking for deserters. And now here he was, on his way back to Auschwitz.

"Is it true that they're killing Jews?" Fritz asked.

"It's true," he said. The weak and the strong were segregated on their arrival. The weak disappeared at once, never to be seen again. The strong ones worked until they became weak, and then they too disappeared.

They were sitting on the floor in the hallway. The young man leaned his head against the wall and closed his eyes and began to breathe deeply through his nostrils. "I saw a child separated from his mother," he said at last. "The mother went off with the strong, and the child was kept with the weak. He became hysterical. His screams annoyed the guards. They picked him up by the legs and swung him against a wall until his head was smashed."

Fritz covered his eyes with his hands and, moaning softly, began to rock back and forth. Almighty God, he prayed, please never let them get Lane.

From the moment of his capture Fritz had been looking for ways to escape. It seemed hopeless. There were bars on all the windows. The doors were locked. They were never let outside. At night the prison was bathed in light and patrolled by guards with rifles and dogs.

Fritz, however, had managed to communicate with Marlitt. There was a barber, a Jew, who came every day to shave the prisoners because they were not permitted to have razors. He was a privileged Jew because his wife was non-Jewish and his children were being raised as Christians. He still lived at home. One day as Fritz was being shaved he said to the barber, "I would like to ask a favor. I have a girl friend. I would like you to contact her and tell her that I'm being held." Fritz offered the barber his briefcase, which had been returned to him after it had been emptied of money and jewels. "It's yours," he said.

"I'll give it to my son for Christmas," the barber said.

Had he heard the line in a play Fritz would have laughed aloud. Now he simply stared at the barber and turned silently away.

Fritz had given the barber the telephone number of his Russian friend Makarow, knowing that Makarow would contact Marlitt. The next day the barber told Fritz that his girl friend had been to see him. He had told her that Fritz had "gone out of this life" and was on his way to Auschwitz. She had brought along several pair of wool socks and some underwear, which the barber now slipped to him. With the clothes was a note. It said that they were well and he was not to worry. It said nothing of her anguish.

Each day the barber returned with little bits of clothing and another note. Each night he left the building with a note from Fritz to Marlitt. Most of the notes contained nothing but small talk. But on December 5 Fritz wrote, "Leave Berlin. Berlin will be destroyed."

He did not tell Marlitt that the Jewish prisoners now numbered fifty.

It was time for his last desperate try. For days he had been conspiring with a man named Metz, who seemed to exist in some kind of twilight zone. Perhaps he was half Jewish; whatever the reason, he had a privileged status, something like that of a prison trusty. But Metz had one important privilege that trusties seldom have: he was allowed to leave the prison. Some of Fritz's fellow prisoners thought Metz worked as a catcher when he was away from the Grosse Hamburger Strasse building. He was scarcely a reliable ally, but he was the only chance Fritz had.

It was Metz who had made the approach. He had seen thousands of Jews come and go, he said. He knew that the number of deportable Jews in Berlin had dwindled to almost nothing, because whereas each of the first transports had consisted of a thousand Jews, now they were leaving with fifty. When the last Jews had gone off to Auschwitz and he was no longer needed, what would happen to him, he had asked himself. The answer was not comforting. It was time for him to walk from the prison and disappear into the underground. But he also knew how much money it would take to survive as a "U-boat," and he didn't have a pfennig.

That was where Fritz came in.

He knew all about the jewels Fritz had been carrying when he was arrested, Metz said. He assumed that Fritz had good contacts in the city. Metz had access to the keys to all the locks; he was sure their escape would go smoothly. He wanted 5,000 marks at the outset, and another 5,000 marks as soon as they were free. Could Fritz arrange for that kind of money?

He could, Fritz said.

Fritz gave Metz a note to the Russian Makarow instructing him to pay Metz 5,000 marks. The note was signed with a number: 5.39. That was the weight in carats of a stone Fritz and Makarow had recently bought together.

Later, as Fritz was being shaved by the barber for what they both supposed would be the last time, Fritz asked, "Do you have ten pfennigs?"

"What do you need ten pfennigs for in Auschwitz?"

"Just a souvenir," Fritz said idly.

The barber shrugged and gave him a ten-pfennig coin. Then he turned away. As he did, Fritz grabbed a pair of the barber's scissors and put them in his pocket. He had never stolen anything before. He did not even know what use he would make of the scissors, only that they were a weapon of sorts.

Through the day and evening Fritz prayed. The next morning he looked at Metz's face to see if his prayers had been answered. But Metz refused to look at him. Finally Fritz walked up to him. "Did you get the money?" he asked.

When Metz looked at him, Fritz could not read what was in his eyes. "Yes, I got the money," Metz said. "But I was searched when I returned."

Without a word Fritz turned away. He did not believe Metz. He did not think he had been searched. He believed that the man had lost his nerve and turned the money over to the Gestapo, sucking up, trying to make an impression, believing the money would somehow buy him his life. Whether he was right or wrong, Fritz knew that his last hope was gone, that he was on his way to Auschwitz—and that his last, bungled attempt to save himself could have compromised Makarow.

That night the Jews were lined up in the corridor and informed that the next morning they would be taken to the freight yards in Charlottenburg to be placed on a train. It was a man from the Gestapo who made the announcement, a rough-looking, middle-aged man. When he finished he walked down the line and stood in front of Fritz and, his head not a foot away, glared into his eyes. "Are you Croner?" he demanded in a loud voice.

Suddenly the figure in front of Fritz did not seem to be standing still any more. This is the moment, he thought. He crumpled to the floor.

"A doctor! A.doctor!" the Gestapo officer called.

One of the prisoners stepped from the line, bent over Fritz and listened to his chest. "It's his heart," he told the officer.

"Get him into my office!" the officer demanded.

Several prisoners carried Fritz into the office of the commandant. He waited until Fritz opened his eyes and then he said, "Croner, I've got your money."

"What money?" Fritz said. "I gave you all my money when I came here."

The commandant smiled. "Here," he said, opening his desk drawer. "I've got your five thousand marks." He took out the money. "You were going to escape with this money, weren't you? How? Whom were you going to bribe?"

"I don't know what you're talking about."

But the Gestapo officer obviously thought that he was onto something big. If there was corruption in his administration, he would find out where it was. For this inquiry he needed a healthy witness. "Take him up to the sick bay," he told the guards.

As the guards led him away Fritz could not help thinking how ludicrous it was. He was too sick to go to Auschwitz! In a few days he would be murdered, but he was too sick to keep the appointment.

The sick bay was on the third floor. It was a small room with two beds. A man of thirty and a little boy were lying on one of the beds. Between the beds was a window. Fritz walked to it. He could not believe his eyes. The window had no bars. He turned to the man, an obvious question on his face. The man nodded his understanding. "I couldn't try it because of the boy," he said. He reached under the mattress and began to pull out a homemade rope.

"Wait!" Fritz whispered. He took a broom handle and inserted it through a handle on the door, so that anyone pulling on the door from the outside could not open it.

The rope had been fashioned from strips of blanket. The moment he tugged at it, Fritz knew it would never hold. But there was more material. Fritz made another rope. Then he braided the two ropes together. As he worked he told the man about the transport that was scheduled to leave for Auschwitz in the morning. They agreed that they would try to escape that night.

That evening the lights outside the building went out, and a few moments later Fritz could hear the drone of the approaching bombers. Soon the bombs were whistling down on the city. The first explosions sounded like the beat of muffled drums. The fires from the incendiary bombs slowly spread along the horizon, and the darkness of the night lifted like a curtain rising on hell. At ten o'clock Fritz opened the window very slowly and eased his head outside. The guards were gone—in their shelters, no doubt.

There were several raids that evening. Each time a new wave of bombers came over, the explosions moved closer. Now all of the sky was red, and there were fires only a few blocks away.

Several times during the raids Fritz peered out the window. There were no guards, and the street was empty.

"We'll go at two," Fritz whispered. The man nodded. "I'll go one way, you go the other," Fritz said. They played a game from childhood to determine who would choose. The game was rock / scissors / paper. Fritz showed scissors. The man showed rock; rock dulls scissors, so he had won. He elected to go to the left.

Fritz undid his belt and extracted two hundred marks from a secret pouch and gave it to the man. Then he gave him a fresh pair of socks from the supply that Marlitt had sent and told him to pull the socks over his shoes so that they would cut the scent.

At a few minutes before two Fritz lashed the little boy to his father's back. Then he eased the window open and nodded to the man. The man stepped over the sill. Even in the darkness Fritz could see the whites of his eyes. The little boy was also frightened, but he didn't make a sound.

As soon as the man reached the ground Fritz went over the side. They waited together on the ground for an instant. "Go," Fritz whispered. The man disappeared to the left, the boy still on his back.

Then Fritz began to run. It was as though all of his life he had been tied to the earth with ropes and they had suddenly been cut from his feet. The socks on his shoes muted his footfalls, but they echoed through the darkness nonetheless. He heard shouting behind him then, and knew the man and boy had been caught. The sounds drove him even faster. Five hundred yards from the building he ducked into a bombed-out house, found the cellar, and leaned against a wall, trying to still his breath. He could hear the dogs. Their barking grew stronger and stronger. They were no more than a hundred yards away now. He could no longer make a break for it—the dogs would run him down.

Then, miraculously, the barking sounds receded.

Fritz remained in the cellar for an hour. While he waited he used the scissors he had stolen from the barber to clip off his mustache. At last he went up to the street. The streetlights were out and there was no moon. He walked so close to the buildings that he brushed the walls with his shoulder. He walked for half an hour, moving south, until he was well out of the neighborhood. Only then did he go into a phone booth.

He reached into his pocket for the ten-pfennig "souvenir" he had been given by the barber, placed it in the telephone and raised his finger to dial Makarow's number.

He could not remember the number. He had dialed it hundreds of times, but as much as his life depended on it, he could not remember it now.

Only Makarow could get word to Marlitt; he, Fritz, would not dare jeopardize her and Lane by going directly to them. He would have to go to Makarow's, he decided now. He would still be taking a risk, because Metz might have given the Gestapo Makarow's name. But he had no other choice.

He walked through the empty streets until he reached Makarow's block. Fifty yards from his building he stopped. Were his eyes playing tricks or was that the glow of a cigarette in the dark? Fritz edged backward until he reached the corner. Then he walked around the block and approached the building from the other side. Once more he could see the tip of a cigarette, and now he saw a man. He turned quickly and walked away. Were those footsteps behind him? He walked faster. The footsteps sounded closer. He looked around. Two men were following him. He ran then, and they ran after him, but he had that feeling again that he had been cut loose from the earth, and he was sure they wouldn't catch him unless they used a gun. He ran to the Hauptstrasse. A tram was coming down the tracks. It was not yet in service, on its way from the barn to where it would begin its run. Only a motorman was aboard; there was no conductor. Fritz ran into the street and jumped onto the open platform. Only then did he look back. His two pursuers had stopped running. He wasn't sure, but he thought he recognized them. They were from the Grosse Hamburger Strasse building, privileged Jews, *Mischlinge,* perhaps, or Jews married to Gentile women. If so, they hadn't been that interested in catching him. Had they been catchers, he would have been a dead man.

Just then Makarow's phone number flashed into his head. A few blocks farther on, Fritz dropped from the tram and telephoned. "It's Fritz," he said. "I escaped."

"Thank God."

"The Gestapo may be watching your house. Go see if anyone's outside."

A moment later Makarow returned and told him no one was there.

"Get in touch with Marlitt. Tell her I'm in Halensee. She'll understand." Even Makarow hadn't known that Fritz had a hiding place there.

The streets were filling now as the working day began. Fritz lost himself in the crowd and walked to Halensee. There he found the caretaker, who let him into the store after he explained that he had just returned from his engineering job in Poland and had forgotten his key. He drank several glasses of water. Then he undressed, put on his pajamas and lay down on the bed. An hour later a knock on the door awakened him. It was Marlitt. She fell into his arms.

27

THE GAME WAS ON in earnest now. No more loud singing of Hebrew prayers at night. No more capricious walks in the streets.
No more restlessness translated into spontaneous trips to the
railway station to meet Marushka. At last Hans was willing to
take his enemy seriously, to see him for what he was. He knew
that his lair had been marked. Officially he no longer existed,
but it would take only one insistent catcher or a Gestapo agent
to remedy that.

The first order of business after the catcher's visit was to stop
all traffic to the flat. At least ten illegals might show up the next
day to get their ration cards. Marushka telephoned a friend, a
Fraulein von During, and arranged a meeting. At the rendezvous she gave her a list of names and addresses. Each person she
found was to receive the same message: "Stay away from the
flat."

The next order of business was to get Hans away for a while,
because Marushka was sure that the Gestapo would be back.
She called friends who owned a home on the Lake of Ferch,
near Potsdam. They agreed to shelter him. Now the problem
was how to get him out of the house without being observed.
They knew they were under surveillance. The morning after the
catchers' visit a man with a newspaper was standing under the

streetlight across from the flat when Marushka left for the university in the morning. He was there again the next morning.

On the third morning Marushka crossed the street and went up to him. "Look," she said, "I'm quite late for an appointment. Your taxis are paid for by the Gestapo. Could you give me a lift?"

For a moment the man looked at her incredulously. Then suddenly he grinned. "By all means," he said.

The next day he was back, but a day later he was gone. Were there others, in other places? They couldn't take a chance. That weekend Hans slipped out the back and went through a passageway of a neighboring building that led to the cross street. For good measure, he took the dogs with him. Who would suspect a man who was walking his dogs?

As it turned out, Hans had left just in time. That evening one of the cats tensed as she sat next to the kitchen window. Marushka looked out the window but saw nothing. She was fairly sure, however, that she heard what the cat had heard—the movement of people.

Each evening for the next week the cat noticed something, and then Marushka would hear the noises. Finally she determined to put an end to whatever was going on. Early the next evening she went into the garden and rigged several trip wires. Then she poured hot water—which freezes very quickly—over the stone path. An hour later there was a tremendous thud and a lot of swearing. Marushka immediately called the police. They were there within minutes, confronting—along with a dozen neighbors—two agents of the Gestapo.

A few days later the Gestapo dropped its surveillance. After a fortnight Marushka brought Hans home.

Wilhelm Glaser had been raised in a religious home. He had been bar-mitzvahed in the Lindenstrasse synagogue. By 1920, however, his religious enthusiasm had lapsed considerably under the influence of scientific explanations of the creation of the universe and the arguments of his Marxist friends. But in the time since his life had come apart he had begun to pray once again, and he had prayed in recent months more than he ever had before. When misery is the greatest, God is the closest, he would tell himself.

He was homeless once again. He had run through all of the safe houses Gilbert Mach could find him; friends of Mach's had been willing to hide him for a night or two but not longer. And although Mach had found him a series of part-time jobs, he was currently unemployed and almost out of money. And yet, in the bitter cold of the winter of 1944, Willy was beginning to believe once more that he was being watched over by God. One could say that he had been lucky—but, then, the luck had to have come from somewhere. God must have apportioned him an extra share.

There had been the day a few weeks after the destruction of the glazier's shop when, achingly cold from a night of sleeping in the park, he had gone to a popular coffeehouse on the Moritzplatz. Drinking his coffee, and hungry for news of any kind, he had just gotten his turn at the *Völkische Beobachter* when he heard a voice say, "Let me see your papers." He looked up slowly from the newspaper. A man from the Gestapo stood before a customer at the table next to his. Willy reached for his hat and briefcase, rose and, nodding to the Gestapo man, returned the newspaper to its rack. Then he walked from the coffeehouse and sauntered away, his body tensed for the command to halt that would hit him like a bullet in the back.

Much later, when he had stopped shaking, Willy would conclude that it had been his choice of newspaper that had saved him. Since the advent of the Nazis the *Völkische Beobachter* had been Germany's leading newspaper—which was not saying much. It had achieved some degree of sobriety since its pre-power days as a cheap and lusty tabloid, and it did manage to contain some bits and pieces of real news—the reason that Willy had chosen it—but it was still a party-line newspaper. If you were a member of the Nazi party, or even a nonparty member who wished to demonstrate your devotion to the state, you read the *Völkische Beobachter.* Seeing Willy with the newspaper, the Gestapo man must have assumed that he was loyal to the cause.

Another day, waiting for a train at an S-Bahn platform, Willy was aghast to see two soldiers with dogs appear on the platform. It was part of the dreaded *Kettenhunde* patrol, which combed the streets for deserters. One of the soldiers looked Willy's way, then turned and spoke to his companion. The two of them started down the platform with the dogs. Just then the train rolled in. Willy got on board, waited until he saw the soldiers board another car, and stepped out of his car as the doors were closing.

But Willy's best break by far was his chance encounter with a woman at the workshop of a tailor named Lowental. He went to Lowental's shop every so often to deliver some textiles he had managed to acquire on the black market. From time to time Lowental let him spend the night on his cutting table. One day, just as Willy was leaving, the woman came in to Lowental's shop. "Who is that man?" she asked the tailor. He replied that Willy was in essential war work. Hearing this, the woman turned at once to Willy. "Sir," she said, "my husband is in the army, I live alone with my daughter, and I'm deathly afraid of the air raids. I assume you live in a furnished room. Perhaps you would like to move in with us."

Willy could scarcely believe his luck, but in his wildest dreams he couldn't imagine the reception that awaited him when he arrived at five o'clock that evening. There on the table was the best dinner he had seen in years.

That night he slept in the woman's bed, with her daughter between them. If it was a precaution on the woman's part, it was needless, because she was so unattractive he did not even consider sex. In the morning she gave him coffee and rolls, and then made him some sandwiches on the assumption that he was going to work. Dutifully Willy left, spent the day walking around, and returned that night.

It went on like that for several weeks. Each night they would undress in the kitchen and go to sleep to the sound of music on the radio. When the air raid alarm sounded, Willy led them to the shelter. The woman marveled at his courage and was more than content with their bargain.

Then one day her husband returned. He was not the least bit bothered that a man had been sleeping in his bed. In fact, he expressed his gratitude to Willy for taking care of his family.

But then, once more, Willy Glaser was homeless.

28

SINCE AUGUST 1943 young Hans Rosenthal had been a conscientious spectator of the Allied bombers' massive nightly attacks on Berlin. The attacks were the highlight of his existence, not because he wished ill-fortune for the mass of Berliners whose city was being destroyed, but because he knew that each attack brought the end of the war closer, and also because each night he could stand outside, under the fruit trees twenty feet from Frau Jauch's house, and feel that he was free. He was absolutely certain that his presence would be unobserved. Not only did prudence dictate to the Germans that they remain in their shelters during air raids but the law forbade them to be on the streets. Of one thing he could be certain, Hans knew: Germans obeyed the law.

In the last months, however, Hans too had been driven indoors, partially by the onset of winter, with its wet and penetrating cold, and also because the bombs were coming closer with every attack. Hans knew that a direct hit would kill him whether he stood in the garden or remained in the tool shack, and he was resigned to that, but he saw no point in shortening his odds by making himself a target for shrapnel.

And then one night, as he huddled in his shack, a bomb came whistling down as though it were aimed at his head. It exploded no more than twenty yards from Frau Jauch's house, in a corner of the garden. The explosion collapsed three houses around hers, but her own house remained standing. Only its windows were shattered. Hans was shaken but unhurt.

To Frau Jauch it was clear that God had spared her house in order to save her Jew. Hans knew better: the explosion had created a vacuum that sheltered objects nearest it. But he said nothing.

The next morning danger appeared, in a form far more threatening to Hans than the bombs. Two S.S. officials arrived to inspect the damage. As they walked from garden to garden Hans could hear their voices. Frantically he hid all objects in the room that might give away his presence, and then he crawled behind the couch and lay against the wall, an open knife in his hand.

He had been there only a minute when the S.S. officers arrived at Frau Jauch's house. They explained to her that if she wished to replace the windows they must first make out a request. "Please," she said.

The S.S. officers began to inventory the broken windows. "What about that one over there?" one of them said, pointing to the tool shed.

"Yes, that one too," Frau Jauch said.

"Perhaps we should look inside," the other S.S. man said then.

"By all means," Frau Jauch said as loudly as she dared.

Hans's grip tightened on the knife. If they find me, I'll take at least one of them, he vowed.

He heard their steps in the kitchen, and then he heard Frau Jauch pull aside the curtain and open the tool shed door. They were within five feet of him now.

And then he felt the couch pressing hard against him. The S.S. men had sat down. He could hear papers rustling. One of the men must be making out a report, he concluded.

"Would you like some tea?" he heard Frau Jauch say. Her voice sounded calm. She seemed completely composed. The S.S.

officers accepted with thanks. Frau Jauch left the room. Neither of the men spoke. Hans could hear their breathing. He was certain his own was audible; only because they suspected no other presence was it going undetected. But if he coughed . . .

He felt a tickle in his throat. He shut his eyes and willed his mind against it, constricting his throat, swallowing, praying. But the tickle persisted, and became more intense. Slowly, carefully, he took an enormous breath through his mouth and held it in his lungs, and at last he felt the tickle subside, just as Frau Jauch came in with the tea.

The pressure against him eased as the S.S. men leaned forward. Hans knew they must be picking up their tea. A moment later the couch pressed against him again as the visitors settled back. Hans could hear their slurping, and then one of them was telling Frau Jauch not to be excited or upset by the bombing. "We'll win the war," he assured her. "Everything will be over soon."

Suddenly the tickle returned, so surprisingly and forcefully that Hans was sure he would cough. Again he opened his mouth and swallowed air, but this time it did no good. And then he heard Frau Jauch's voice, and he thought, If I cough, it's all over for her too.

He was gripping the knife so firmly now that his right hand shook from the effort and his nails dug into his palm. With the utmost care he moved his left hand to his throat and scratched the skin in the little hollow between the collarbones. Somehow that sensation seemed to draw his mind from the tickling in his throat.

Leave! he prayed. Leave!

Five minutes later they did. As soon as he heard the door close Hans began to cough. For a long while he couldn't stop coughing or shaking.

At last the long winter ended. The frozen ground began to soften. The fruit trees flowered. Their fragrance filled the air—a scent as incongruous as perfume on a corpse. Anyone with the least amount of objective vision could see that Berlin was doomed, its life inexorably destroyed a little more each day by the fusillade of bombs.

One night a fire bomb landed thirty yards from Frau Jauch's house and set a neighboring cottage on fire. A strong wind showered sparks directly onto her house, as well as many others. Hans could hear the neighbors outside agreeing that the only way to save the other cottages was to push down the one on fire. He knew that if he ran outside to help them they would wonder who he was. But if he didn't go and the fire spread, he could burn to death. There was really no choice. He eased himself outside.

A few of the neighbors were fighting the fire with picks and shovels, but most of them worked with their bare hands, trying to drag away the parts of the house that hadn't yet caught fire. The roof was the greatest problem; like those of the other cottages around it, it was covered with tar paper, and now the heat was melting the tar and turning it to liquid. As Hans grabbed a portion of the roof he could feel the tar burning the skin on his left hand.

As soon as he saw that the fire was under control Hans drew slowly back from the crowd, then turned and retreated to Frau Jauch's house, making certain that no one was watching as he stepped through the door. Inside, he looked at his hand. The molten tar had burned away the skin on his palm and little finger. The pain was so intense and the burn so ugly that Hans knew he would have to see a doctor.

For the first time in more than a year he left the vicinity of Frau Jauch's cottage and ran through the street, past the burning cottages and buildings, toward the S.S. hospital in Herzberge, two miles away. Leaving his sanctuary after all this time should have terrified him, but the pain drove everything else from his mind.

At the hospital he ran up to the admitting desk, cracked his arm into a salute and shouted, "Heil Hitler!" as he had seen the Nazis do so often.

"What is your name?" the receptionist said.

"Hans Busch," Hans answered, giving the name of a Christian school friend he knew to be a soldier.

"Your papers?"

"I got burned while putting out a fire. I came straight here. My papers are at home."

An S.S. doctor treated Hans's hand. He instructed Hans to come back the next morning to have the bandage changed, and reminded him to bring his papers. Hans said he would.

"Heil Hitler," the doctor said.

"Heil Hitler," Hans said.

He did not return the next day.

29

Hans Hirschel was once again experiencing life within the small space of Marushka's three-room ground-floor flat on the Detmolder Strasse in Wilmersdorf. He did not dare to go outside lest he be spotted by a catcher. The only exception was a nightly visit to the yard, but it might as well have been a prison yard for all the sense of freedom it gave him. The small plot of ground was surrounded by apartment buildings; he could not look out, only up, into the black, unpromising sky.

Marushka was not much help either. She spent long hours at the animal protection society, where she had become the chief veterinarian. She would arrive home usually between seven and eight, have dinner, chat with Hans for a bit, and then go out again. She was still working, mostly with the Swedish church but sometimes on her own or with other groups, trying to find shelter for Jews and other illegals, getting them ration cards and phony identities. As a precaution she had arranged for her own false identity, a student card made out in the name of Maria Mueller. Other than her place of birth, all of the facts were the same as those on her legitimate papers, so that if she were questioned she would have no trouble remembering. During the day she carried her legal papers; in the evening she would change them for the false one. As Maria von Maltzan she would be a giveaway lead to the Gestapo if captured; as Maria Mueller she would not lead them back to Hans.

She was desperately tired, not simply from the long hours but from the incessant tension. The little triumphs kept her going. One day Hoffman, the police constable, came to the flat, ostensibly to investigate two complaints: first, that the dogs were making a racket, second, that Marushka had failed to display the Nazi flag on April 20, Hitler's birthday. Regarding the first complaint, Marushka assured him that she was in the process of selling several of the dogs; regarding the second, she said, "I don't have a flag. I have no money for flags."

"I didn't think you would have," Hoffman said. They laughed together. He was the same constable who was so helpful to the Swedish church and Erik Perwe, and his views were well known to Marushka. He could have sent someone else around to investigate the complaint, but, in addition to protecting her, he had wanted to unburden himself. "I hate it," he said now, sighing. "What they ask of us has nothing to do with human decency. Taking people from their flats whom I know to be decent people—what has this to do with order and justice?"

Marushka thought for a moment. "You know, it would be quite nice if you could manage to obtain a list of the people to be arrested, and give me some of the names in advance."

Hoffman nodded. "That *would* be quite nice," he said.

She got several people away that time, and the triumph fueled her spirit for days. But there were other, bitter, occasions, and these threw her into despair. A nurse at the Jewish Hospital in Berlin had come to the flat. Marushka had helped her to obtain papers from the German Red Cross authorizing her transfer, under an assumed name, from Berlin to a post near the Swiss frontier. From there she was to cross the frontier on foot with the help of underground allies. A fortnight after Marushka had put the nurse on the train she got word that she had gotten to the border undetected, but then, thinking she was across, had sat on a rock to eat her lunch and had been captured by a German border patrol. The news all but demolished Marushka. It was not simply a case of a life needlessly lost; it was an escape route permanently closed.

There was yet another cause of tension in the flat: money. Saving lives had become an unbelievably expensive proposition. Marushka's salary, her black market activities and her annuity from the estate were not nearly enough any longer to maintain herself, Hans and the steady stream of illegals who came to her door for help. More and more Marushka became fixated on the idea that the solution to her financial predicament was to be found in the family estate. The castle was packed with valuables, many of which might be sold for cash provided Marushka could persuade her brother's wife to do so. Her brother, the rabid Nazi, had been killed in the French campaign in 1940. Years before, he had inherited the bulk of the estate on the death of their mother and had paid an ample sum to each of his three elder sisters, but nothing to Marushka, the youngest, who as a child had once almost drowned him for ordering the gardeners to kill the snakes. All that was in the past now; what mattered was to convert the estate and its valuables into cash and safe assets before everything was lost. One day late in the spring, after leaving the dogs with a friend and arranging for another friend to bring food to Hans each day, Marushka went off to Silesia for a week to try to talk some sense into her sister-in-law, who now effectively controlled the estate.

She returned and mournfully recounted the details of her trip to Hans. She had suggested to her sister-in-law that she sell all of the valuables, as well as the estate itself, if she could, distribute a certain amount of cash to the family, keep a reserve and use the very substantial remainder to buy land in Austria, where it could be gotten cheap. "You see, we're losing the war," she had argued, "and we will lose the estate as well as every other bloody thing we have unless we do something now." Unfortunately her sister-in-law now had a boyfriend, an army man who had convinced her that Germany was winning the war.

Hans had never seen Marushka so defeated as she was after her return from Silesia. He did everything he could to cheer her up. When she finally did begin to come around, he credited his efforts somewhat, but he was sure that much of the boost had come from two other sources. The first of these was the litter of four Scotch terrier puppies, which, six weeks after their birth, had become the object of his adoration as well as Marushka's. They named them Archibald, Anne, Amy and Andy. As the weeks passed and the puppies grew big enough to play, Hans and Marushka could forget the bombs and pressures and intrigues for a few moments a day. Neither mentioned what was on both their minds, that the puppies must soon be sold, for this was why they had been bred.

The second source of replenishment for Marushka's spirit was the frequent appearances of her favorite nephew, Brumm— Friedrich Karl von Reichenau—son of her second sister, Alix, and Field Marshal Walter von Reichenau, her baffling brother-in-law, one of the first, if not the first, important army officers to embrace the Nazis, who nonetheless knew of and liked Hans; who always came to Marushka's flat when he was in Berlin to have several glasses of his favorite drink, Turk's Blood, a half-and-half mixture of Burgundy and champagne; who once offered to give Marushka anything she wanted as a present and, when she told him she wanted a red cardinal, found one; who one day, just before his death of a stroke in January 1942, warned Marushka that even he would be unable to help her if she ran afoul of the Gestapo for associating with a Jew.

Walter von Reichenau's son Brumm was no Nazi, and scarcely a soldier. He had forsaken a commission for duty as an enlisted man. He was in a combat unit, but he drove a motorbike, which had enabled him to avoid shooting at people he had no desire to kill. Until Russia. There, one day, he had driven into a small woods just retaken from the Russians by the Germans, and there he found many of his comrades smashed against trees by Russian tanks. The next morning Brumm's unit captured some Russian troops and massacred them. Brumm killed his share. Later, back in Berlin on leave, he recounted the story to Marushka and confessed that he was thinking of suicide. She took Brumm into her arms and let him cry and assured him that war makes people go out of their minds. As sick as she was about what he had done, she was privately elated with this proof that there *were* decent young Germans.

Not that Marushka had ever really had doubts about her nephew. An exquisite skier, he had once, with the help of friends on the Austrian-Swiss border, arranged to have Jews escape to Switzerland on skis. Brought to trial on another occasion on a charge of conspiring with an anti-Nazi group—which, in fact, he had done—he had been spared only because the judge, awed by the knowledge of whose son Brumm was, had virtually put words into his mouth when he testified. "Surely you didn't know with whom you had been," the judge had said. "No, your honor," Brumm had replied.

Now Brumm had come to Berlin on leave and had put up at Marushka's apartment, which pleased her enormously because it gave her a chance to mother him, although he was only twelve years her junior. Brumm, a fantastically good-looking young man, was an inveterate womanizer; how or why Irmelin, his equally good-looking fiancée, put up with his escapades Marushka never understood. Yet, seeing them together, so young and beautiful, so obviously in love, Marushka stirred with hope that there was some future beyond all the pain.

30

FIVE MONTHS had passed since Fritz Croner's escape from the Gestapo prison on the Grosse Hamburger Strasse. When he walked the streets now he did so with the knowledge that his face was known. After his escape he had vowed that the catchers would never arrest him again. His eyes methodically scanned the faces of the pedestrians coming his way, and his right hand remained in his coat pocket, loosely curled around the butt of a small pistol.

But rather than appear furtive, he had elected to be obvious. He had abandoned his cane at the Grosse Hamburger Strasse, and with it the limp he had affected. His disguise now was a style of dress that suggested a special importance. He wore his leather coat and trousers and boots in combination with a wide-brimmed gray felt hat encircled by a narrow band. It was a common enough hat, but it happened to be the kind that Gestapo agents wore, and they wore it differently from other people, the brim lower in front than in back. That was how Fritz wore his hat. If others surmised that he was from the Gestapo, so much the better.

Fritz continued to live in the store in Halensee. He came to Bayerische Strasse only late at night, in the twenty-minute interval between the radio announcement that Allied bombers were over Hannover and Braunschweig and the time they would arrive over Berlin. The warning almost always came at 12:30 or 1:00 in the morning. It was a distance of well over a mile, but by walking fast he could make it. In the shelter of the sturdy stone apartment building Marlitt would introduce Fritz as Wilhelm Kramer, a cousin of her husband, which explained, they hoped, the resemblance between him and Lane. Lane called him "Uncle Fritz," as she had been taught to do from the time that she was two.

The cellar was dark and dank, and when a bomb exploded nearby, it was almost instantly filled with plaster dust, which set all of the inhabitants to coughing. The coughing, together with their fright, made them breathe even harder, which only compounded their problems. When the whistling of the bombs became very loud they would all cringe, waiting for the impact. After an hour one of the women might begin to cry, at which point those nearest her would try to reassure her. There was a feeling, unusual among a people not noted for their friendliness, that they were all in this together.

Each time Fritz entered the cellar he gave the Nazi salute. During the raids he often sat next to one of the tenants, Standartenführer Adam, a calm middle-aged man with a military bearing, who was stationed outside Berlin but frequently arrived with his driver to spend the night in his flat on the first floor of the building.

"Why aren't you in uniform?" Adam asked him one evening.

"It's secret," Fritz said sternly, which seemed to satisfy Adam, because he pursed his lips and nodded his understanding. As soon as he could, Fritz got hold of some technical drawings, mastered the terminology and, the next time he and Adam met in the cellar, confided that he worked in an aircraft factory just outside the city. At that point, in any case, he didn't think Adam would press him; from what the man said and didn't say, Fritz judged him to be a rational man with no love for the Nazis.

And then, early one morning, after the all clear had sounded, Fritz left Marlitt and Lane and returned to Halensee, only to discover that the store had been demolished and with it everything he owned except what he was wearing and carrying— which, he thanked God, included the jewels. He had no alternative now except to move in with Marlitt and Lane, a mixed blessing that created grave new problems and risks.

All of the problems and risks of course stemmed from the fact that Fritz was not supposed to be in the building during the daytime, when he presumably worked at his secret job in the aircraft factory. This meant not only that he could not leave the building to conduct his business but that he could not go into the cellar shelter during the daytime air raids. Of the two, he did not really know which was worse. A bomb hit could kill him, but without money to live on the black market he might just as well be dead.

It did not take long to solve his business problem. Within a few weeks jewelers, most of them in uniform, were coming to the Bayerische Strasse apartment at the rate of one and two a day. They came ostensibly to see "Frau Krauser." Fritz trusted them implicitly; he had known and dealt with all of them for years. In the jewelry trade the amounts of money involved were such that trust had to be either 100 percent or nothing. The jewelers came because, week after week, Fritz managed to have the best supply of jewels in Berlin. His source, unknown to anyone but Marlitt, was a courier for the Minister of Trade who, for a large commission, went back and forth each week between Amsterdam and Berlin. Fritz gave him 50,000 to 100,000 marks; he brought back English, Dutch and French gold coins, as well as gems.

The problem of shelter during the raids was something else again. Fritz would have to wait until all of the building's residents had gone to the main shelter in the cellar. Then he would sneak down the stairs and into that part of the cellar in which the individual storage bins for each apartment were located. There he would sit and listen to the bombs and wonder what would happen if the building were hit. As buildings near theirs were demolished one by one, it became increasingly evident that he was pushing his luck.

And then, one night several weeks later, the building was finally hit. They could feel the impact in the cellar. As soon as the all clear sounded they rushed upstairs. A fire raged on the roof. All of the tenants pumped and carried water until the fire was out. Exhausted, they left the roof, only to discover that the floor of the flat just below the roof was still burning. There were only two men present, Fritz and a sixty-five-year-old man named Koch, whose left side was paralyzed. Fritz took an axe and ripped out the floor and threw the burning planks from the window until the fire was out.

His efforts made him the unofficial hero of Bayerische Strasse 5. From that day on, the tenants all smiled whenever they saw him, as if to say, "It's okay. Herr Kramer is here."

31

BY THE END of spring 1944, almost a year and a half after he had gone underground, the most that Willy Glaser could say for his existence was that he was still alive. For months now, ever since her husband's return had forced him from the home of his homely angel, Willy had been sleeping in the woods, wondering if he would ever again sleep in a bed. His clothing was all but in tatters. He had lost fifty pounds and was now so thin that he had to hold his pants up with a piece of rope. The soles of his shoes were so worn and his socks so full of holes that when he walked his bare feet scaped the pavement. He was constantly wet and cold, and developing chronic bronchitis. The days when he didn't eat outnumbered the days when he did. There were times when he could go to the back door of the grocery owned by his friend and get a small supply of provisions. Once the grocer gave him some butter, which he sold to other friends; that money kept him in food for several days. On another occasion a friend gave him ration tickets for bread. From time to time he was able to make himself useful to black marketeers, which earned him carrots and lettuce. But his hunger was never appeased. The most mournful fact of all, however, was not Willy's constant hunger; it was the realization that he was now a beggar. He would have joyfully worked if he could, but there was no way that he could. So he spent his days asking for food and searching for cigarette butts. These he would either smoke as they were or hoard for his pipe until he had enough tobacco for a bowlful.

Each day Willy wandered the streets, his thoughts his only companions. As hungry as he was, there was a greater problem than food. It was shoes. The grocer and other friends found new shoes for him from time to time, but each pair wore out quickly because of the miles and miles of walking.

He kept moving, knowing that if he loitered he would attract attention. In the morning he watched the Berliners on their way to work, and in the evening he stood at the Friedrichstrasse railway station feeling a heaviness in his throat as he watched them go home. He watched the audiences filing into the opera. On two occasions he risked going to the Metropol Theater—sympathetic ushers let him in—but attending the opera was out of the question because of his clothes. It was astounding if you reflected on it—as Willy, given all his idle time, often did: Here was the city being ground down further and further each day to rubble and ash and pretzel-shaped girders, and yet each day the Berliners formed long lines at the cinemas and supported more than one hundred plays.

Germans have a word to describe that devious response by which humans sometimes rejoice over others' misfortunes. They call it *Schadenfreude*. But Willy's emotions as he viewed the ever greater destruction of the city on his daily walks were a good deal more complex than that. He wanted the destruction, to be sure—more ruinous and punishing and faster than it was being meted out. But the Berliners rushing to their concerts and operas and plays and films reminded him of what the city had once been and what it had meant to him.

If Willy had a home it was a bench in a little corner of a park in Pankow known as the Kissing Place. He thought of it as his corner. Jews were not permitted to sit on park benches, but he did it anyway, just as he continued to wash and shave in public restrooms, where Jews weren't permitted either. Inasmuch as

Berlin had been officially *Judenfrei* since May 19, 1943, it was
important to act like the increasing numbers of Germans whose
lives had been disrupted, even devastated, by the bombings.
Willy knew that the official pronouncement had been a lie, that
even now, more than a year later, Jewish "U-boats" still sur-
faced to prowl the streets, just as he did, in search of food and
objects for barter. But he was as alert for other Jews as he was
for the police patrols; who knew which Jew he met might not see
in him an object to be traded for his own salvation?

So Willy thought of his park bench as a sanctuary where,
alone for a few hours, he could relax a little. There he would sit
and study the trees and watch the birds and sometimes inadvertently fall asleep even though it was dangerous to do that.

As Willy approached his bench one day he saw, to his dismay,
that it was occupied. A young woman was sitting there sewing
uniforms. He judged that she was in forced labor. He wondered
if she was Jewish, a privileged Jew of some kind. Her features
were little help. She was certainly not a prototypical blond and
blue-eyed "Aryan"; yet many Germans had such dark hair and
chiseled features. Maybe yes, maybe no; he couldn't take the
chance. He walked on without stopping or speaking.

But when Willy returned to the Kissing Place the next day
the woman was there again. She looked up and smiled at him.
This time he sat down.

"Good day," she said.

Willy muttered a greeting that was deliberately unintelligi-
ble.

"How is it that you're not at work?"

"I work the night shift," Willy lied.

The following day the woman, whom Willy judged to be in
her early thirties, ten years younger than himself, told him that
her name was Ruth Gomma. Willy nodded but did not tell her
his name.

Each day that he came to the bench from then on, Ruth
Gomma was there. Each day she did such talking as passed between them. One day Willy fell asleep, and Ruth Gomma

opened the briefcase that he always carried with him, both as a status symbol and a repository for his toilet articles. Inside, in addition to his toilet kit and blanket, she found a copy of *Crime and Punishment*. She knew then that Willy had no job, because a real worker would be carrying a meal with him to his shift.

Willy was not reading *Crime and Punishment*—he had read it years before and hadn't liked it—but was carrying it around to give his briefcase a weight identical to what it would have if, in fact, he was carrying a meal.

When Willy awakened he found that Ruth's questions had taken another tack. It seemed to him that she was testing him now to determine how well he had been educated. Again he hedged his answers, giving nothing away, not even the background that might identify him in the smallest degree. He did not want this woman to have a single clue in the event that she was questioned about him.

But then Ruth asked Willy if he was interested in the theater, and for the first time in years a tiny crack appeared in the wall of misery that had encircled this passionate lover of the arts. They talked for an hour about favorite plays and playwrights. By the time they had finished they were smiling at each other, if not as old and cherished friends, then as two people who had discovered the possibility of friendship. Ruth confirmed then what Willy had suspected; she was a privileged Jew. Her father, now dead, had been Jewish, but her mother was a Christian. She lived with her mother in an apartment nearby, she told him. And then, in an offhand manner, she asked if he would like to come to her house for a bite to eat. Willy wanted that bite to eat, and those few hours of shelter, more than anything he had ever wanted in his life. But he refused the invitation because he had no proof that Ruth Gomma was who she said she was, and he couldn't take the chance that accompanying her might somehow lead to his discovery.

The next day Ruth invited him again. And the next, and each day thereafter, until Willy finally succumbed. She gave him supper; it was a simple meal, but it nearly made him weep.

Then she asked him his name. He refused to tell her. "It's better that you don't know," Willy said.

Willy became a regular visitor to Ruth Gomma's house. Time and time again she tried to tease him into revealing his name. Time and again he refused. One day he quoted Lohengrin: "Never you ask me whence I came, nor what my name."

"I have it!" Ruth said with a laugh. "I'll call you 'Lo.' "

There was really no doubt in Ruth's mind at this point about the basic identity of "Lo." When she had seen him for the first time in the park she noted his black hair and long sideburns and mustache and thought perhaps that he was a foreign worker. But such remarks as he had made to her at first had been in faultless high German, which few foreign workers would speak, and so she had concluded that this man must be an illegal Jew. She had not particularly liked him at first, but he had intrigued her, and his knowledge of the performing arts had impressed her. For Ruth as well their conversations had opened a crack in the misery that had enveloped her since 1940, when she had begun to work at forced labor.

Four months had passed since those initial conversations. During that time the crack had widened considerably. As improbable and crazy as it was, Ruth had to admit that she had fallen in love—and she was as sure as a woman can be that her Lo had too.

32

THE BOMBS continued to rain on the industrial works in Wittenau, as well as on the gas works and Tegel airfield nearby. Considering the destruction that daily increased around them, Joseph and Kadi Wirkus had to consider themselves extremely fortunate. Their house had not been hit in the eight months since the massive Allied bombings of Berlin had begun. And considering the risk they were taking, their blessings were more numerous still. Kurt and Hella Riede had been with them for a year now, but not once in that time had there been so much as a hint that the Gestapo was on their trail. More than that, the bonds between the two couples had continued to strengthen, to the point that they thought of themselves as one family. Thanks to the food the elder Wirkuses sent from the farm, there was always plenty to eat. And Wilfried, the baby, was now a lusty one and a half years old. Given such evidence, Beppo and Kadi could be excused for wondering if God wasn't rewarding them, after all, for saving Kurt and Hella.

In May, Beppo received a bonanza, a four-week trip to Marienbad, Czechoslovakia, courtesy of the federal insurance agency, for himself, Kadi and the baby. Ostensibly the trip was for therapy. His elbow, the one he'd injured permanently as a child—which had kept him out of the service—had been giving him trouble, and it was thought that the baths might help him. But it was also a glorious chance for a respite from the bombings and, even more, for the first real vacation they had had since the beginning of the war.

But the trip finally made real a question both couples had often pondered in theory: What to do if and when the Wirkuses left Wittenau for any length of time and the Riedes remained? All of their discussions had led to only one plan. In the event that they were challenged, Kurt was to pose as Beppo, and Hella as Kadi, using their false identity cards as proof. If anyone asked about another couple that was said to be living in the house, they were to say that a man and a woman whose house had been bombed out had lived with them for a while but had left several weeks before. They were taking an extraordinary chance, and all of them knew it, but how much more would they be incriminating themselves than they already had?

And so the Wirkuses went off to Marienbad, apprehensive about leaving the Riedes, but ecstatic over their good fortune. By way of sharing their bounty, they telephoned the Jerneitzigs, their landlords, whose dwelling had been demolished, and invited them to use their bedroom while they were gone. The greengrocer had already made plans to be away from Berlin, but Mrs. Jerneitzig gratefully accepted.

The sun had scarcely risen one morning several days after the Wirkuses' departure when the bell at the garden gate rang. Hella, up early, looked out the window and saw two men standing at the gate. She had never seen either of them before. The thought of confronting them filled her with dread, but she was without an alternative. Kurt was upstairs in the bedroom, still asleep. Nor was there any sound of stirring in the Wirkuses' room, where Mrs. Jerneitzig slept with her two children. Ursula, the flirtatious young factory worker who rented the downstairs bedroom, was still asleep as well.

As she walked down the path to the gate Hella could almost feel the blood pumping hard from her heart and priming her muscles for flight. "Yes?" she said.

What happened next did not seem real. The man in front took out an identification and showed it to her and said, "We are from the Gestapo." But he was a nice-looking man in his middle thirties and he was smiling pleasantly at her, and as she passed him and his partner through the gate and led them up the path, wondering if she would make it to the door, it registered on her that in all the times she had imagined how it might happen, she had never envisioned a pleasant smile on the face of her captor.

The pleasant-looking man told his partner to wait outside. Then he took Hella by the arm and led her to the kitchen. "You look a little faint," he said solicitously. "Perhaps you should take some brandy."

"There's a tenant asleep in the next room," Hella said weakly as they entered the kitchen.

He closed the door. "No one need hear our business," he said. Even as he began to speak the words Hella had prayed she would never hear he still smiled pleasantly, almost appreciatively at her.

"Are you the mistress of this house?"

"I am."

"May I see your papers, please?"

Hella fetched her one piece of identity, the pregnancy priority card with her picture and Kadi's name on it. She gave it to the Gestapo agent, who stared at her shaking hand for a moment and then smiled at her again. Then he studied the card and nodded and said, "And where is Herr Wirkus?"

"He is in Marienbad, on convalescent leave, to receive treatments for his elbow." As Hella spoke she put an arm on the table to support herself, and prayed that Kurt would not awaken and call out, "Hella, what's the matter?" Or that Ursula would not come into the kitchen and say, "Guten Tag, Frau Riede." Or that Mrs. Jerneitzig and the children would not begin to make noises upstairs.

"You have been denounced for harboring a Jewish couple," the Gestapo agent said.

"I can't understand that," Hella said. "There are no Jews here." Each word passed through her dry throat like a rasp.

"Have you ever had a couple living here with you?"

"Yes. There was a couple. We met them in a cafe. They told us they had been bombed out of their flat in Berlin. We took them in for several days because we pitied them, but then they left and we haven't seen them since." Hella bit her lip, playing the part. "It was really my idea. I hope this won't get my husband into trouble at his office."

The Gestapo agent smiled again. "How long is it since they were here?"

"A month at least."

"I see," the Gestapo agent said. His smile now was the kind a man gives a woman when he wishes to communicate his interest, and yet when he put his hand on her arm and gave it a gentle squeeze, what he seemed to be communicating more than anything was reassurance. "I want you to tell your story to my partner, so that he can write out a report." He paused and looked into her eyes. "Are you sure you wouldn't like a little brandy?" he said then.

"No. Just let me excuse myself for a moment." She left the kitchen and went to the pump and held onto it for a moment and then let cold water pour over her wrists. When she came back to the kitchen, the agent led her outside and told her to repeat the story. Several times during the narration he prompted her, so that the story became even more emphatic than when she had told it to him. There was no doubt now, the Gestapo agent was helping her. If only Kurt would remain asleep! If only Ursula and the Jerneitzigs would remain in their rooms.

The second agent closed his notebook and put his pen away. The two men started down the path. "Auf Wiedersehen," Hella said.

The first agent turned around and smiled at her in that same warm and solicitous manner. "Better not 'auf Wiedersehen,' " he said. He turned then, and they left.

For a long moment Hella stood, unable to move, not simply

from fright but from astonishment. What the agent had just said made it clear that he knew. He had said in effect, "Let's hope we don't meet again."

In Marienbad several days later Beppo was returning from the baths when the hotel manager rushed up to him. "Your wife fainted a few minutes ago. She's upstairs in bed."

Beppo vaulted the steps to the room. Kadi, her skin chalky, her lips trembling, handed him Kurt's letter, detailing the Gestapo's visit. The letter also informed them that the Riedes had cleared out that day, that they had had to tell Ursula the truth to impress on her that she must stay and feed the chickens, that they had gone to sit in an S-Bahn for several hours, and that finally they had gone in desperation to the hiding place of another illegal Jew, Willy Katz, with whom Kurt had worked at the baron's leather warehouse, and that after Hella had gotten down on her knees and begged, the Katzes had agreed to take them in, but only for a few days.

Now that the charade had ended, the dam that Kadi had erected within herself to hold back her fears gave way, and fright flooded her body. "We've got to get out of here," she said to Beppo. "They'll find us and kill us."

"No. We'll stay," Beppo said. "If the Gestapo is going to get us, they'll get us wherever we are."

33

EVERY DAY of his confinement in Frau Jauch's five-by-six-foot
tool shed Hans Rosenthal had a visitor, some member of one of
the three antifascist families in the neighborhood that knew of
his existence and helped Frau Jauch sustain him. The visitor
would bring a few potatoes or a turnip or a piece of bread, exchange a few whispered words with Hans, and then slip out
through the cottage and the store to the street. And there were
occasional visits from Grandmother Agnes, who brought food,
but because she was there ostensibly to do business with Frau
Jauch, she couldn't linger either. Such news as she had she gave
him in whispers. Once she started to tell him about his cousin
Ruth Thomas, who had also gone underground, but Hans
stopped her. If he was captured and tortured, the less he knew
the better.

So it was that during the fifteen months of his confinement
Hans really had only Frau Jauch to speak to. A less likely soul
mate for a young man of eighteen could scarcely be imagined.
Her contribution to the brief conversation they had each evening in hushed voices had not changed from what it had been at
the outset of his confinement fifteen months before—interpretations of events and prophecies of the future based on her reading
of the Bible. Hans would nod agreeably to whatever statement

she made, but he was scarcely willing to attribute his survival to Scriptural divination.

When he had first come to Frau Jauch's in March of 1943 Hans had expected his confinement to last no more than three or four months. Had he known he would still be in hiding fifteen months later he might not have been able to make it. Frau Jauch must have sensed his claustrophobic restlessness, because, in addition to trying to relieve it with a daily newspaper, she had brought him a primitive radio. At night he could listen to the Berlin broadcasts with the volume at its lowest and his ear pressed against the earphone. And then, early in 1944, she surprised him again with a more powerful and battery-operated model with which he could pick up the BBC in the early morning hours. The signal was very weak and frequently faded away, but each contact injected him with fresh hope.

In her quiet way this frail and tiny woman had managed to sustain him through his unimaginably lonely ordeal. Her existence was so basic to his survival it was as though they were connected by an umbilical cord, through which flowed not just nourishment but the resources by which he could maintain his sanity. Hans did not even want to think about what would happen to him if Frau Jauch were injured or killed in an air raid.

If Frau Jauch herself ever thought about what her presence meant to Hans, she never mentioned it or expressed it in nonverbal ways. Had she had a son, he would have been approximately Hans's age, but she was a spinster, without parental experience, and in spite of everything she had done for him, she had never directly or indirectly asked of him the affection due a mother.

In a way it was just as well. For a Jew in Germany—as Hans knew so well by now—affection was a decided risk. His parents were dead. His brother Gert had been deported to God knew what fate. One uncle had died in Buchenwald, the other at home after two weeks of Gestapo torture. So it was no good to love other people, because you wound up losing the objects of your love.

And then one night in July, Hans learned how effectively he had been fooling himself.

That night Frau Jauch was suddenly seized by violent pains in her lower abdomen. For the second time since he had arrived fifteen months earlier Hans left the vicinity of her house; he raced to the home of a neighbor he knew to be friendly. The neighbor called an ambulance and then accompanied Frau Jauch to the hospital. Twenty-four hours later Frau Jauch was dead of a ruptured hernia.

Hans was devastated. He knew then not only that Frau Jauch had become like a mother to him but that it was even more than a young son's love that he felt. For all this time she had been the sole target of his feelings. Her death, he recognized now, was like the loss of an entire family.

From a practical standpoint it was a calamity. There was no way he could continue to live in her house by himself without revealing his presence. Light, noise, odors—any of these could give him away. Moreover, there was no way he could get provisions. If he did not think of something, Hans concluded, he would simply have to turn himself in to the Gestapo. He had just one possibility, a woman two gardens removed from Frau Jauch's. Her husband was in Russia and her son was in the navy, and she lived in her cottage alone.

Marie Schönebeck had learned a few weeks before that Frau Jauch had a "nephew" living with her, so she was not surprised when Hans appeared. She was, however, astounded by his story, which he revealed to her in full detail. For a moment Hans read her astonishment as disapproval, and he died a little. But then Frau Schönebeck said, as firmly as she could, "You'll stay here." Hans exploded with relief.

Frau Schönebeck passed the word to two trustworthy neighbors that she had taken Hans into hiding. Between those neighbors and Frau Jauch's antifascist friends they managed to collect enough food to feed Hans. But Hans's situation at Frau Schönebeck's was much more exposed, and thus more dangerous, than it had been at Frau Jauch's. During the day he stayed in Frau Schönebeck's bedroom. At night he moved into the living room and slept on the couch. Whenever visitors came he had to hide quickly. And he had to be certain that there were never two plates or two glasses on Frau Schönebeck's table.

For several weeks when the bombs fell Hans remained where he was while everyone else went to the shelters. One evening, however, a friendly neighbor pressed him to join the other neighbors in an air raid shelter they had built nearby, a crude excavation covered with logs, which in turn were covered with earth. Apprehensive, Hans refused. "Come on," the neighbor said, "everyone in there already knows about you."

The neighbor was so insistent that Hans finally succumbed. With trepidation he followed the neighbor to the shelter. When he stepped inside the shelter his fists were clenched. But when his eyes grew accustomed to the light he realized that all the others were smiling at him and nodding agreeably in greeting. They seemed not only willing to share their shelter but exceedingly happy to have him. Before long Hans understood why. The neighbors knew that Hans had been hiding in Frau Jauch's house when that bomb had demolished all the surrounding cottages. As long as the Jew who had saved Frau Jauch's home from destruction was with them, they knew they were safe from the bombs.

34

BEFORE THE DEPARTURE of the Wirkus family for Marienbad, Beppo Wirkus, ever precise, had left the particulars of their return with Kurt and Hella Riede. So when the Wirkuses returned to Berlin late in the evening of a cool June night the Riedes were at the Anhalter railway station to meet them. In spite of the shock he had felt on learning of the Gestapo visit, Beppo was struck once again by how well the Riedes blended into the crowd. Hella, with her blond braids, seemed the most typically German woman on the platform. And Kurt, with his thick glasses, was obviously exempt from military service. Still, Beppo could not help looking up and down the platform for S.S. patrols or Gestapo agents in their unmistakable fedoras.

Kurt quickly brought the Wirkuses up to date. The tiny gardener's house in Birkenwerder in which Willy Katz and his wife lived had proved to be too small. Katz had found them a new hiding place nearby, with a Gentile family. The Wirkuses agreed that they would come to visit the Riedes, provided they found on their return to Wittenau that there had been no further inquiries.

There had not been, Ursula told them. Nor, to Beppo's and Kadi's immense relief, did the Gestapo come for them, as they had feared would happen. Two days later the Wirkuses called on the Riedes. The two couples took a blanket and went to a nearby woods and sat in the shade. There Hella told them the story in detail.

Neither of the Riedes could imagine who had denounced them. They had concluded that a catcher must have spotted Hella, decided she looked suspicious, followed her home and reported her to the Gestapo.

"A 'catcher?' " Kadi said.

And then Hella had to explain how the Gestapo was using Jews to catch other Jews, and how Jews often had an instinctive feeling about who were Jews and who weren't.

Then Hella and Kurt confessed that they were miserable in their new hiding place. Their host and his children were very nice to them, but his wife was hysterical with fear that the Riedes' presence would prove disastrous for her family. She had calmed down a bit a few days after their arrival, but then Hella had been seized with a bad attack of dysentery, and that had made the wife hysterical once more. Moreover, the family was charging them a fortune. The Riedes didn't say it in so many words, but they implied that if it were ever possible they would like to return to Wittenau.

After he had learned of the Gestapo's visit, nothing had been further from Beppo's mind than to invite the Riedes to move back in. But he was furious now with the actions of their hostess, who did everything she could to remind the Riedes how dependent they were on her for their survival. For her part, Kadi could not stand seeing Hella degraded in such fashion. And both of them were bothered by Hella's tears—Hella, who always before had held back her emotions. The result was that they did begin to think seriously about the Riedes returning to Wittenau—as preposterous and dangerous as that might be.

For the next few weeks the Wirkuses inspected every possible place from which a Gestapo agent might be watching their house. By the end of that time they were almost positive that they weren't being observed. But there was another problem. Robert Jerneitzig, their landlord, who had recently been called into the army, had written to tell them that he wanted the Riedes out of the house. His letter was unequivocal. "It's time," he wrote. "It's getting too dangerous."

Jerneitzig's letter swept away the last remnant of Beppo's and Kadi's indecision. "We have said *A,* and now we must say *B,*" Beppo responded. "It was you who brought them to us, and now it is you who want to send them away. Where is the logic in that?"

Beppo waited ten days for a reply. When he received none he decided that Jerneitzig's silence was indication of his acquiescence. As soon as he could, he got in touch with the Riedes and told them to come back. Beppo made them promise, however, as a condition of their tenancy, that they would not leave the house during the day. Since the entrance to the bathroom was outside the house, they were to use a pail to relieve themselves. Kadi would empty the pail after each use.

But the major new safeguard was a hiding place to be used if and when the Gestapo reappeared. It was in the attic, behind a false wall that separated the storage area from a much larger empty space. From the storage area the wall looked sturdy enough, but it could easily be moved aside and then replaced from the other side once the Riedes were behind it.

Beppo had calculated that it would take between seven and ten minutes for either him or Kadi to leave the house, walk down the path to the gate, open it, talk to whoever was there and go back up the path to the house, where, presumably, the ground floor would be searched first. During that time Kurt and Hella would have to gather up all their belongings, go through a blind door to the attic, remove the wall, get themselves and their belongings on the other side and replace the wall. For the first few days after their arrival he insisted that the Riedes practice the evacuation drill until they could accomplish it silently in well under seven minutes. At unannounced times Beppo even went out to the gate and rang the bell and then timed the Riedes. Within a few days the Riedes were able to vanish in less than five minutes.

The two couples would have liked to regain their old esprit, and they tried hard to do so. But a new knowledge hung over them like a massive weight suspended from a thread. Someone out there knew the truth. He had decided to spare them, in all probability, because of a physical response to Hella—a whim as weak as a thread.

IV

DELIVERANCE

35

BY SUMMER'S END it was evident that the war was effectively over. The Russian summer offensives had carried the Red Army all the way to the border of East Prussia. Rumania fell to the Russians, which meant the loss of Germany's only source of natural oil. Paris, four years in enemy hands, was liberated on August 25. What was left of the German armies in France was streaking back to German soil. British and Canadian troops led by Field Marshal Bernard Montgomery liberated Belgium and took Antwerp intact, giving the Allies a fabulous port through which to pour invasion supplies. Five hundred thousand German soldiers, half of them prisoners, were lost to the defense of the Reich. Their equipment was lost as well. Only a maniac would believe that Germany could still win the war. But just such a maniac still ruled the Reich.

Hans and Marushka knew everything, thanks in part to the BBC, but also to their friends. They had learned of the July 20 attempt on Hitler's life within hours after it occurred, and of the prompt execution of the plotters. The attempt, coupled with the defeats, had an unmistakable portent. As the air grew crisp and the city's forests blazed their farewell to the summer season, the lovers could not help but believe that the hostilities must soon end.

The more the city suffered, the more optimistic they became. Inevitably the surge of spirit translated into a desire on Hans's part to get permanently out of his jail. To his astonishment and delight, Marushka agreed. The source of her confidence regarding Hans had nothing to do with the news, however; it had to do with a new piece of identity obtained for Hans through a friend of Werner Keller's. The paper identified Hans as an investigator for the authority in charge of the defense of Berlin. Everyone— the army, the bureaucracy, even the Nazi party—was to assist him in whatever manner he requested.

"Do you think there's any danger?" Hans asked when he first read the paper.

"Not the slightest," Marushka said. "Just be tough. Order people about."

Hans could hardly wait to try out the paper. The chance came even sooner than he had expected. The first chilly weather set Marushka to thinking of a fur coat she had stashed at the home of a friend in the country. There was no way she could absent herself from her duties long enough to get it. "What do you think?" she. asked Hans one evening. "Are you game?"

On the train the following afternoon Hans did not even bother to look up from his copy of the *Völkischer Beobachter* as he handed the controller his paper. The controller read the paper, bowed, clicked his heels and walked on. At the station where he stopped to change trains Hans presented the paper in the restaurant and was immediately served a meal. When he reached his destination he was furnished a car and driver for the ride to the house of Marushka's friend. Back in Berlin, he was once again offered a car to drive him home. No, he said, he wanted to stretch his legs. He took a long, circuitous route until he was certain that he wasn't being followed. Only then did he return triumphantly to the flat.

The flat at this point had a theatrical look about it, almost as though it had been designed as a setting for a stage play about life in wartime Berlin, and specifically about life in an apartment that looked as though it had been hit by a bomb—which, of course, was almost exactly what had happened. The beam that had been installed to prop up the ceiling the previous fall, when a bomb destroyed all of the building with the exception of Marushka's apartment and the one above it, was still in place. Since then a thin sheet of plywood had been slipped in between the top of the pole and the ceiling in order to keep loose bits of material from falling to the floor. Nonetheless little bits of plaster were scattered about each morning, shaken loose by the nightly reverberations of the bombs.

After the direct hit on their building, the building's porter, who had lived in the flat above, had declared it uninhabitable and had found quarters elsewhere. The flat had been taken over by a Polish family that until then had been literally without a roof to sleep under. Having any kind of home in those days was all that mattered, as the incessant bombings destroyed more and more of the city's buildings. Marushka's flat sheltered a continuous stream of itinerants—as well as two new, totally unexpected residents, whose arrival changed Hans's and Marushka's lives.

One day, a nurse who had once looked after the babies of one of Marushka's sisters came calling on Marushka with a special purpose in mind. She was trying to find a home for two Russian girls who had been part of a contingent of children brought from Russia in the aftermath of the German invasion and placed in a children's camp. Now the camp was being broken up because it was no longer possible to maintain it, and the children were being placed with good Nazi families who would be willing to shelter and feed them in exchange for their services. Most of the children had been placed, the nurse reported, but two of them were proving to be a problem. They were sisters, one thirteen, the other seven, and they refused to be separated. The thirteen-year-old could work, but her seven-year-old sister was just another mouth to feed. No one would take them, the nurse told Marushka. Would she?

"I'll have to think about it," Marushka said.

As soon as the nurse left, Hans emerged from the bedroom, where he had been hiding. "For God's sake, let's take them," he said. "They'll be gassed if no one wants them."

It was not so simple. There were forms to be filled out and an approval from the Gestapo to be obtained. Four weeks later the approval came through. Marushka went to a building near the Alexanderplatz that appeared to overflow with children. It was there that she first laid eyes on Tamara and Lucie Geroschewicz.

She had never encountered more suspicious children. Where were they being taken, they demanded to know. They did not wish to lose touch with their friends. And would they remain together? If they were not to remain together now, they simply refused to go. Tamara, small for her age but surprisingly ample, and obviously bright and lively, spoke a little German. She translated for Lucie, the seven-year-old, who looked like a Tatar. It took a little convincing, but after collecting their papers, Marushka finally persuaded the girls to accompany her to the flat.

The smile on Hans's face when the girls walked in the door was almost beatific. "I've made you a pudding," he announced. He had made it of flour and flavored it with orange and saccharin, much too much saccharin as it turned out, but the girls wolfed it down, and when no more could be obtained with a spoon, ran their fingers around the bowls.

"I think I'll heat some water," Marushka said as the girls romped with the dogs. When the water was hot, she and Hans led the girls to the bath, stripped them and put them in the tub. Marushka washed Tamara, and Hans took care of Lucie. The girls hadn't been washed since they had been in the camp. Their brown, curly hair was filled with lice, and their bodies were covered with scabietic bites. "I've never seen anything so dirty," Hans said as he set about scrubbing Lucie. He had to shout to make himself heard over Lucie's screams.

When they were dried, Tamara asked to hear the Russian radio broadcast. "My father is an important member of the party," she boasted. "He is also a general at the front." Hans and Marushka could only wonder if it was true.

The next morning Marushka took both children to her hairdresser, the one who had taught her to cut men's hair. The hairdresser put waves in the children's hair with heat, which killed all the remaining lice.

"What can I pay you?" Marushka said.

"Nothing," the hairdresser replied.

By the time they returned, Hans had another meal prepared. After years of dependence he seemed suddenly filled with purpose. He could not stop smiling, even when he was alone. He already had all sorts of plans in his head about how he would school the children.

But the next morning he lost one of his pupils. At the sight of Marushka leaving, Lucie cried so hard that Marushka finally agreed to take her with her to the animal shelter. It proved to be a providential decision; not only was Lucie mesmerized by the environment but Marushka was able to use her presence to wheedle spare clothing from her clients for her new wards.

Hans and Tamara remained at home. After they had finished cleaning the house, he sat her down for what she confessed was her first lesson in three years. First they worked on German, and then on history. She seemed willing enough, even eager to learn, and yet at the same time distant. Hans didn't know why, but he decided not to press her. He soon had his explanation.

The next morning Marushka gave Tamara instructions to buy bread at the baker's, and gave her money and ration cards. Tamara checked the ration cards. There was one for Marushka, one for Lucie and a third for herself. "Where's his?" she asked, looking at Hans.

"He's got no card," Marushka said softly. In the silence that followed they could hear the pigeons on the ledge outside revving up their wings.

"Is he illegal?" Tamara asked.

Standing there, not knowing what do do, Hans could only wonder where she had picked up the term.

"Yes," Marushka answered.

Tamara was studying Hans now, her eyes narrowed until she too resembled a Tatar. "Political? Or Jewish?" she asked.

At that Hans knelt and took her in his arms. "I'm a Jew, Tamara, just as well hated by the Nazis as you are as a Russian. We have to stick together."

Tamara inspected him carefully. At last she said, "Then you've got nothing to do with Nazis?"

"Nothing," Hans assured her.

There was another moment's hesitation, as if Tamara needed time to digest the knowledge that she had gotten into a house that was against the Nazis. Then suddenly she threw her arms around Hans, and Lucie, not really understanding but knowing it was something good, threw her arms around her sister.

Marushka had watched it all in silence. Now, tears in her eyes, she said, "Tamara, you must never, never say that there's a man in the house. You must teach that to your sister. Because if he's taken, then I'm taken, and if I'm taken, that means death for you."

36

ERIK PERWE, the pastor of the Swedish church in Berlin, smoked cigars when they were available and a pipe when they weren't. Invariably the mouth end of a cigar would look chomped within minutes after he had begun smoking it, and the bits of his pipes had been chewed with such force that they gradually became unserviceable. It was the only noticeable way in which Perwe expressed the tension within him, which by November of 1944 had built to a level that would have been insupportable to a person who had not conditioned himself to contain it.

Since March of 1943, except for brief visits to Sweden, he had been separated from his family, living in a city in which the fearful sounds and shattering impacts of the Allied bombs were a more certain part of daily life than meals or sleep. Even the few hours of each night in which he forced himself to rest were troubled; in his mind were the faces and names and addresses of the Jews he had sequestered in houses around the city. He no longer knew how many Jews, exactly, were being hidden, but he was certain the number was in the hundreds. He knew too that all of them were in ever increasing danger, if only because a few of their number had been caught. No Jew knew where another Jew was living, so exposure of one Jew by another was impossible. But all of the Jews knew that the source of their benefaction had been the Swedish church, and what if that fact were tortured out of one of them?

The Swedish legation had warned the pastor repeatedly that it could be of no help to him if he was caught, but what worried him even more than his own potential jeopardy was what would happen to the Jews, and the Germans who had hidden them, if a member of the church's staff broke down and gave the Gestapo the single clue it needed to uncover the entire network. Would the clue lead to Reuter, the church's inscrutable caretaker, who had found so many of the safe houses? Would Reuter be able to remain silent when tortured, if it came to that? And how would he himself stand up under torture, Perwe wondered.

In a clandestine operation such as he had supervised for more than two years there were now too many ifs. The time had come to reduce them.

In mid-November, Perwe informed the church's staff that he would fly to Sweden within a few weeks for a short visit. His announced purpose was to raise money for Christmas distributions among the needy in Berlin. Vide Ohmann, the church's indefatigable social worker, guessed that his real purpose was to prepare for the reception in Sweden of Jews he would soon be smuggling from Germany. But she did not try to pin him down. He never told you things he didn't need to, and she was used to that by now.

Vide worshipped Perwe. She believed him to be the most astounding man she had ever known. Driving him to the airport early on the morning of November 29 was a precious time for her. He was relaxed, glad to be going home, if only for a spell. He had been scheduled to make the trip early in December, but the head of the Swedish legation in Berlin, Arvid Richert, had offered him his own seat on an earlier flight.

The plane took off at 9:00 A.M. Watching it depart, a nervous mother who had just put her daughter on board said to Vide, "I do hope the flight will go all right."

"Oh, it will," Vide replied, "the Reverence is with the plane."

An hour and twenty-five minutes later the plane, a German passenger craft, was either shot down or blew up over the southernmost tip of Sweden, crashing outside Falsterbo. There were no survivors.

Martha Perwe, who had returned to Sweden with the children the year before, after the church was hit by a bomb, was sitting with them at 1:00 P.M. when she heard the news of the crash on the radio. "How wonderful father wasn't on that plane," she said with relief. "He isn't coming until next Monday." An hour later a messenger from Arvid Richert brought her the truth.

Among the Swedes and Germans who knew of Perwe's efforts there was speculation that the craft had been sabotaged in order to stop him. As carefully as Perwe had worked, his cumulative effort could not escape notice; it was assumed by his friends and colleagues that he knew of the existence of several hundred illegals in Berlin and was planning to "export" as many of them as he could. So real did this assumption become that a number was soon attached to it: Perwe, it was said, was flying to Sweden to arrange for the resettlement of twenty-four Jews within the next few weeks. Supposedly he had data and photographs of these Jews in his briefcase. Among the many prayers expressed in those first hours after the crash was that Perwe's briefcase and its contents had been destroyed.

An assassination that cost the lives of a crew and the loss of a plane did not make any sense, but reason fared poorly in the aftermath of Perwe's death. The news numbed the staff of the church, but their grief was as nothing compared to that of the Jews who had put their lives in his hands. As the story spread by *Mundfunk,* they came to the church, singly and in pairs, asking for confirmation. When it was given, they walked slowly off into corners of the basement to endure their pain alone.

Their grief fell on the shoulders of a young Swedish priest scarcely prepared to bear it. Erik Myrgren would have preferred to be a botanist. So passionate was he about the subject that he had learned the Latin names of 900 different plants. With his slick black hair and handsome heavy face he looked neither Swedish nor priestly, nor had he freely chosen the religious life; his parents, deeply devout farmers from northern Sweden, had prevailed upon him to do so. What they had not been able to repress was the streak of joyousness in him. Erik, ordained in 1942, would still rather play the lute and sing folk songs than preach a sermon. He had gone to Germany in 1943 as pastor for the Swedish seamen who regularly put into the port of Lübeck, across the Baltic Sea from Sweden. On August 17, 1944, the Swedish church in Lübeck was destroyed by a bomb during a raid that took many lives, and Myrgren was called back to Sweden. But then, in November, he returned to Germany to substitute for Perwe during his absence. Until this moment Myrgren had had no contact with Germans, nor was he prepared for the human destruction and demoralization he was now to encounter daily.

One of his first visitors was Herbert Frankenfeld, a gaunt, stooped and visibly frightened man whom Myrgren took to be sixty-five. He was actually in his early forties. Frankenfeld, an attorney before the Nazis came to power, was married to a Gentile woman, who had refused to divorce him despite incessant pressure from the Nazis. He had lived for several years on her ration cards. Perwe had promised to get him to Sweden, he told Myrgren. If that had become impossible, he wanted to take refuge in the church.

"We have no place," Myrgren told him. "Besides, they are not after your wife. You are safest with her."

"I beg you, let me stay," Frankenfeld said.

To mollify him Myrgren told Frankenfeld that he could spend two hours with him that day and the next. Once granted that privilege, Frankenfeld persisted; day after day he would come and sit by Myrgren's side. Finally Myrgren called a halt. The next day he received a call from a man who identified himself as a doctor. He said that he had a sick patient—he would use no names—that the patient had told him about the pastor, and that accepting the patient into the church was a matter of life and death. "I urge you to let him come to you," the doctor said.

"Let him come," Myrgren said.

The "patient" arrived. It was Frankenfeld.

"I must confess," Myrgren said. "I recognized your voice on the phone."

The attorney fell to his knees and crept on the floor to where Myrgren sat. "I beg you! I beg you! Let me stay!"

The sight was so painful that Myrgren had to look away. An old man on his knees, cringing before a youth. In that moment he began to hate the Nazi system.

Frankenfeld remained in the church, joining ten other semi-permanent residents. When he first saw them Myrgren had thought that they were friends of Perwe's who had been bombed out of their residences. Only later did he learn that they were Jews. He responded particularly to the Weissenbergs, Martin and Margot, because they tried hard to be cheerful in spite of the danger and difficulties.

Now the Jews began to appear in large numbers. Their stories were the same: Perwe had promised to smuggle them out of Germany. So were their questions: Could Myrgren fulfill Perwe's promise?

Two years out of divinity school, still in his twenties, Erik Myrgren had become the official in charge of a system that, by its choices, conferred life and death. Each night, whenever he could, the young pastor played his lute and sang his folk songs in order to calm his nerves.

37

WHETHER THE VOLUME of the bombings had increased or whether the anxiety produced by the constant pounding had intensified his perception of the raids, Beppo couldn't tell. All he knew was that by November of 1944 they had become terrifying. At work, he would descend to a subcellar three floors underground when a raid began, listen to the broadcasts telling where the bombs were falling and wonder if the house in Wittenau would still be standing when he got home. Already the bombs had destroyed part of the roof and broken a number of windows. Even if he and Kadi and the baby were spared by their absence at the time of a direct hit, there would be questions about the bodies uncovered in the ruins, which would mean their own death in the end.

Day after day, without reprieve, the Allies attacked their area because of its several important factories. In the house, Kadi tracked the approach of the bombers with the help of an army map. She would listen to the military broadcasts locating the planes on the grids. As soon as it was clear that the planes were coming their way she would grab the boy and run for the shelter. The shelter was near a factory that produced track wheels for tanks—a prime target for the bombers—so Kadi had to be certain that she left in plenty of time to arrive before the bomb-

ers did. One day, as she followed the route of the bombers, she
noted that they had bypassed Berlin. But just as she was about
to return to her household work, the next coordinates indicated
that the bombers had suddenly turned back for a surprise attack
on the city. "Oh, my God!" Kadi cried. She called out for Wilfried, scooped him up and raced from the house. The first
bombs fell before she reached the shelter. They were pelted with
flying dirt. Kadi fell, and the boy with her. She tried to get up,
but she couldn't move. A man ran over to her and tried to help
her, but she was paralyzed with fear and her legs would not respond. Finally he lifted her to a standing position and half
dragged her to the shelter, where they cowered in the crowd of
people, all of whom were as panicked as she was. At last she
looked down at Wilfried. His eyes were wet. He wore a bewil-
dered look that seemed to ask why all this was going on. "I
haven't been bad," he said.

When the bombers had gone, Kadi would return from the
shelter, and Beppo from the office, and, together with the
Riedes, they would marvel that they had survived another day.
Beppo was still struck by the contrast between Kurt and
Hella—Kurt anxious and depressed, Hella calm, almost serene
in her conviction that they would not be hit. Her courage
amazed Beppo. After each heavy bombing she would find out
which areas had been destroyed, then go to those areas and
stand in line for the emergency ration cards being handed out.

But one day Beppo's affection and admiration for Hella received its most severe test. He returned home from work at five
o'clock to discover her parents standing in the kitchen. He recognized them at once, because he had once visited them in
Brandenburg. Beppo liked the Papendicks—Robert, a bald,
broad-shouldered, fat-bellied man with laugh lines in his face,
who had converted to Judaism for the sake of his wife, and who,
for that long-ago act, had been compelled to do forced labor, although he did not have to wear a star; and Figa, a bosomy
woman, with short, dark hair and a round face and spectacles
perched on her nose. But no one had told Beppo that the Pa-

pendicks were coming to live with them, which, he was certain, was the only explanation for their presence. He was right. Robert Papendick had been ordered to join a work group that was building barracks and digging foxholes. As a born Christian, his safety was not in question, but they feared that Figa would be picked up and deported while he was gone.

But Beppo's irritation about being taken for granted, which he tried with only limited success to disguise, was as nothing compared to what he felt on learning that the Papendicks had shipped their belongings to the Wirkuses' address. It was a monumental piece of stupidity, and he had all he could do to refrain from telling them so. He stood, breathing deeply through his nostrils to calm his nerves, knowing that everyone was waiting for his answer. What could he do? He had said *A*. He must now say *B*.

"Where you can hide two people, you can hide four," Beppo said aloud.

Besides, Ursula was gone, transferred to another factory outside Berlin, which meant they would not have to make up a story. And food would not be a problem, thanks to what they had been able to bring from the two family farms. Then too there was the constant supply of eggs produced by the hens. As to lodging, the room Ursula had occupied wasn't large enough for two people, so there was only one solution. The Papendicks would use the little room that Kurt and Hella had been using, and Kurt and Hella would share the larger bedroom with the Wirkuses. In the context of their circumstances, the solution did not seem at all improper; in fact, it gave them all a badly needed laugh.

There remained the matter of the shipped suitcases and the risk that they entailed. But when a week passed and they hadn't arrived, Beppo concluded that someone who knew of the Papendicks' predicament had taken the suitcases, aware that there would be no inquiry. He put the matter out of his mind.

The Papendicks proved to be agreeable guests. They were quiet people, and they took care of themselves. They paid for their share of the food. Because she observed the Jewish dietary laws, Frau Papendick prepared her own meals for the most part, using the Riedes' parboiled potatoes but cooking her portion in chicken rather than pork fat. When the bombs fell, it was immediately evident from whom Hella had inherited her disposition. If anything, Frau Papendick was calmer than her daughter. Faith was her resource. Her words—so reminiscent of Hella's—were like a benediction: "In a house where so much good is done God will not permit something bad to happen."

But it did happen, or almost happened, because of another unbelievable indiscretion on the part of the Papendicks.

On December 23, a Saturday, the gate bell rang, sending tremors through all of them. Kurt and Hella immediately slipped from the room and went upstairs to hide. But there was no place to hide the Papendicks.

Beppo peered outside. An elderly man and woman were standing at the gate. He did not recognize them. Then Figa Papendick took a quick look. She let out an almost mournful sigh. "I know them," she said. "Their name is Zagemann. You mustn't let them in."

"How did they find us?" Beppo whispered.

Figa was so ashamed that she could not look at Beppo. "I gave them your name," she confessed.

Beppo was speechless. It took him a full minute to gain control of himself. Finally he went to the gate. The Zagemanns told him they were looking for the Papendicks.

"The Papendicks aren't here," Beppo said. "We are in danger. Everyone has gone." He could be forgiven a lie, he told himself, if it was to save the five people inside his house.

The Zagemanns explained that they had lost their sanctuary in Brandenburg. They begged him to let them stay.

"But we have no room," Beppo said, holding out his hands. He could not stand the expression on their faces. "Look," he said abruptly, "perhaps I can find you something. Come back in a few hours."

Back in the house, Beppo conferred with Kadi. They decided

to try a devout Catholic couple who lived across the street. The man was middle-aged and worked as a watchman at Beppo's installation. The Catholic couple agreed to take the Zagemanns for two days, no more.

The Zagemanns remained eight days, to the consternation of their hosts, who kept pressing them to leave. They had no space for another couple. They were aware of the penalty to themselves if caught. But the Zagemanns wouldn't leave. They kept insisting to Beppo that the Papendicks were staying in his home. Beppo kept denying it. He felt he had no alternative. If the Zagemanns were caught, they might tell the Gestapo, either because they were tortured or because they might try to bargain for their own lives. Beppo was furious with the Papendicks. Some of his fury escaped, but much of it he held inside, where he could feel it corroding his stomach. The Papendicks, for their part, were aghast at what they had done.

On the eighth day, to everyone's relief, Beppo found the Zagemanns another place to stay. But a few days later the people in the second place of refuge asked Beppo to take the Zagemanns away. Their insistence shortly became an ultimatum. Finally, in a crescendo of emotion, Beppo delivered an ultimatum of his own to the Zagemanns. Either they left Wittenau or he would inform the "Jewish Gestapo." When the Zagemanns finally left, having at last made contact with another family they knew, Beppo cried, and felt so ashamed he would talk to no one for days.

Fritz Croner could only wonder, as he completed his second year of life in the underground, if there was another Jew in Germany in a more anomalous position. He could hardly be accused of living luxuriously, but the truth was that, thanks to his prosperous jewelry trade, he, Marlitt and Lane had all the food they needed in a country where food was now gold. For Lane there was even hot chocolate when she wanted it, and for Fritz, each evening, if he wished, a fine after-dinner cigar. And yet the taste that prevailed in their mouths each day was fear.

The neighbors weren't a problem any longer; they had not forgotten who had put out the fire on the top floor of their building. The real problem was what it had been from the out-set—trading on the black market for the money to buy food, and then for the food itself. Each visitor's arrival, ostensibly to buy or sell jewels, could be a ruse. Each journey by Marlitt into the city could mean the end of their lives together. They had lived illegally for so long now that they were as accomplished at it as anyone in Berlin. And therein lay the risk—that they would take their deftness for granted. That they couldn't afford, because each day they faced a different battle, due to the con-stantly changing situation as Berlin was being methodically de-stroyed. A rendezvous used successfully each day for months might not be there the following morning. A black market con-nection whose reliability had been tested many times might have vanished overnight, picked up by the S.S. or Gestapo, whose paranoia seemed to deepen with each new military de-feat. Every change required adjustments, a fact brought home to them more forcefully than ever as December 1944 arrived.

The Christmas season was upon them. To Fritz and Marlitt that had never meant anything before. But they were living as Gentiles now, and in an apartment building filled with Ger-mans who, if they were anything like their countrymen, would be completely caught up in the season. All of the emotions they brought to the holiday, whether they were practicing Christ-ians or not, were focused on its most prominent symbol, the Christmas tree. A tree with candles was a tradition as old as the German people, and may well have originated with them before spreading to other lands. Whatever their circumstances or diffi-culties, Germans always seemed to find a way to have a tree at Christmas. All this the Croners understood, as well as the prob-lems it could portend.

Lane was three now, able to converse, and the darling of the shelter inhabitants at Bayerische Strasse 5. Fritz and Marlitt did not require much imagination to anticipate the questions the other tenants would ask their daughter when they all gathered in the shelter during the raids. They would want to know if she had a pretty Christmas tree, and what kind of a present she had asked for. To continue their masquerade, the Croners decided, they would have to "celebrate" Christmas.

One day Fritz brought home a tree, which they decorated with candles, in the traditional German way. And Marlitt found a toy for Lane to give to her at Christmas. Considering their circumstances, it did not seem strange at all. But as he lit the candles for the first time, and watched Lane's eyes fill with wonder, Fritz prayed silently for the day when he would be able to light the menorah candles for her in celebration of Chanukah, the Jewish Festival of Lights. He couldn't do that now, any more than he could give her a Chanukah present, for she would surely tell the neighbors.

All through the war Fritz had kept a record of the Jewish calendar so that he could know when to celebrate the Jewish religious holidays. No printed calendar had been available for years, so he had had to make his own calculations, helped by an old calendar he had preserved. If his calculations were correct, the eight-day festival of Chanukah had begun on December 11.

Each night since then Fritz and Marlitt had waited until Lane was asleep and then had stuck little candles into a piece of bread, lit the candles and recalled the miracle of Chanukah, when, 2,100 years before, the forces of Judah Maccabee had routed Syrian invaders from the Holy Land. Back in their temple, which the Syrians had desecrated with a statue of Zeus, the Jews sought to rekindle the Eternal Light, which burns in every temple as a reminder of God's spirit. Although they found only enough oil to keep a flame burning in the cruse for a day, the flame burned for eight days, proof to the Jews of God's presence.

Uncounted times since then the Jews had been driven from their temples; now, 2,100 years later, it had happened again. When they had finished the traditional prayers Fritz and Marlitt added another—for some new Chanukah miracle, some further proof of God's presence.

38

HANS AND MARUSHKA could not get over the maturity of their new Russian wards. They had been afraid that Lucie, the seven-year-old, would reveal to someone in the street, when she played, that a Jew was living inside their house. They need not have worried. Tamara, her thirteen-year-old sister, lectured Lucie on the need to say absolutely nothing about the people she was living with, and from that moment on, Lucie never said a word.

Since coming to Berlin, Tamara and Lucie had been baptized as Catholics. The girls insisted on saying their prayers each night and on going to church on Sunday. After Mass on their first Sunday together Marushka walked the girls over to the Swedish church, where they were given a big meal as well as soap and toothbrushes. Thereafter the girls frequently took their midday meal at the church, which was an easy walk from the flat. They quickly established themselves as favorites among the church personnel, as rare and welcome in the midst of the unending struggle as flowers in December.

It was the same wherever Marushka took them. One day they accompanied her to a nunnery, where Marushka was to inspect a quantity of butchered meat. "I'm sure you must have your hands full," the Mother Superior said to Marushka after she had met the girls. "Why don't you have them bring your laundry over here?" Each time the girls delivered or picked up the laundry the nuns would present them with underwear and rag dolls they had sewn for them.

The girls were as different in manner as they were in appearance. Lucie was a wild child who could not wait to run out and play in the street with the few German children who were left in the neighborhood. Tamara never played at all. After her lessons she wanted most of all to help around the house. Every day she walked the dogs. On the street she was so protective of Lucie that she seemed like a harried mother. Only when they had returned to the flat did Tamara become a child again.

One evening, two weeks after they had arrived, Tamara came up to Hans. "I want to talk to you," she said.

"Of course," Hans said.

"Lucie and I would like you and Marushka to be our mother and father."

Hans was so moved that for a moment he couldn't speak.

Tamara frowned. "Is that not all right?" she asked.

"Oh, yes," Hans said, recovering, "it's very much all right."

From that day on, Tamara and Lucie not only addressed Hans and Marushka as "Father" and "Mother," they referred to them that way in their conversations with each other. "Mother's back," Lucie would cry out. "She's brought something good to eat."

And then Brumm, Marushka's beloved nephew, came home on leave and moved into the flat with Irmelin, his exquisite fiancée At first the girls did not know what to make of him. No assurance that either Hans or Marushka could give them could get around the fact that he wore the uniform of a German soldier. The breakthrough finally came one evening during an air raid as they sat in the cellar shelter.

"Brumm," Tamara said abruptly, "are soldiers frightened in war?"

"Oh, yes," Brumm replied.

"Are you frightened?"

"Of course I'm frightened."

"I'm also frightened," Tamara said. It was obviously an important admission, and just as obviously comforting for her to know that a soldier could be frightened too. Lucie, of course, agreed with Tamara once her sister explained what she had learned.

It was the beginning of a great friendship between Brumm and the girls—and also the beginning of the tales of "The Big Fat Fly Philip."

Hans had listened to the discussion in silence. After the raid he came up from the cellar and said to Marushka, "This just won't do. We can't let the children be frightened." The very next time they went to the shelter he said to the children, "Don't listen to the bombs. Listen to me." And he began to tell them stories about Philip—how he would fly onto Hitler's picture and deposit little black marks on it, how he would fly into the flats of the important Nazis and put little worms in their butter, how he would settle down in the street on a pile of manure and then walk across some Nazi's sandwich. The girls and Brumm would howl with glee and even make up adventures for Philip on their own.

About this time Marushka received word that another of her nephews, Giessbert von Reinersdorf, a lieutenant on the Russian front, had been killed in action. She had not been as close to Giessbert as she was to Brumm, but she had cared for him just the same. Moreover, his death had an added significance because it was the latest in a series of family casualties. Marushka went to her writing desk and searched for a picture of Giessbert, and then sat staring at it, feeling the sorrow lodge in her throat, fighting to hold it there, fearing that if she let it move up it would unplug all of the anguish and grief she had managed to suppress in the past. She shut her eyes, unable to look at Giessbert's image any longer, but the darkness became a theater, and her lids a screen, for the moments in her life that had linked her to her nephew. Then, gradually Marushka became aware that someone was at her side. When she opened her eyes, there was Tamara. "He was my nephew," Marushka said. "He was a soldier, and he was killed."

Tamara looked at the photograph but said nothing. A moment later she walked away. The next morning, however, she approached Marushka with a look that was more appropriate for a funeral. "I know that I should be happy when any German soldier is killed," she said. "But I'm not happy. I thought about your nephew all day and all night, and I believe now that any death is a bad death, whether it's a Russian or a Jew or a German."

Amazed and near tears again, Marushka swept Tamara into her arms.

Just before the New Year, Brumm was called back to his regiment. The girls were not at all happy when the time came to say goodbye. Tamara confessed that she was afraid Brumm would be killed, just like his cousin Giessbert. She wanted his assurance that he wouldn't let that happen. "You see, you're our cousin now, and we can't lose you," she explained.

"I won't be killed," Brumm promised. "Just wait for me. I'll be back one day."

"He's a very good soldier and he'll be very careful," Marushka assured the girls when Brumm was gone. It didn't help very much. They cried for a long time.

The new year did not start well. Two episodes made it clear to Hans and Marushka that, next to the Swedish church, their flat was the best known address in Berlin among Jews in danger. One night, a few weeks after Brumm had left, there was a knock on their door. Hans slipped quickly into the bedroom and got ready to hide in the couch. At the door Marushka found a frantic, distracted young man so out of breath he could scarcely speak. "Let me in, let me in," he begged, trying to push past her and through the door.

"Just a moment. Who are you? And what is it?"

"My name is Hammerschmidt. I've just escaped from the Gestapo."

At that, Marushka all but pulled the young man inside. When he had recovered his breath he told his story. A half Jew, he'd been apprehended by the Gestapo several days before and taken to Oranienburg, a detention center in the north of Berlin. There the Gestapo had offered to barter with him—his freedom for the names of ten Jews. "I have some names in my apartment," Hammerschmidt said.

"What happened then?" Marushka demanded.

"They took me to the flat. I asked to go to the toilet. Then I escaped through the window."

"Let's pray you weren't followed," Marushka said.

"I'm sure I wasn't. I hid for two hours before coming here."

Marushka sighed. "Didn't it occur to you that the Gestapo might have let you escape in order to see where you'd go?"

Hammerschmidt shut his eyes. The idea was not something he could handle. "Come on," Marushka said. As she helped him up she noticed how hot he felt. "You've got a fever," she told him.

The next morning she took his temperature. It was 105. Marushka instructed Hans to keep giving Hammerschmidt liquids, and she gave him a sulfa drug. But when she returned at noon to look in on him, Hammerschmidt was worse.

"I'm not sure this boy is going to make it," Marushka told the others in the living room. "What do we do if he dies?"

"We'll put him in a sack and throw him in the park," Tamara proposed.

"I'm afraid that's not very practical," Marushka said.

That afternoon Marushka called on a doctor who was so old he would have long since retired if there hadn't been a war. The doctor was a friend of a veterinary surgeon with whom she worked. She wasn't positive she could trust him, but she had to take a chance. That evening the doctor examined Hammerschmidt, diagnosed a lung inflammation and prescribed a medication. The next morning Hammerschmidt was better. Within a week he was eating such an alarming amount of food that Marushka searched hard for a place to send him. As soon as she found one, he left.

A few days later there was another visitor, a tall man with dark hair, wearing a messy-looking suit. He'd escaped from Oranienburg, he told Marushka as they faced one another in the living room.

"What gave you the idea to come to my flat?" Marushka asked him. As she spoke she edged her way behind her writing table, hoping to grab her gun through a hole in the drawer.

But the tall man read her mind. "Don't do that," he warned. Then he told her that he had both her address and the church's. When the church couldn't help him, he had come to her flat.

"Well, if you're staying here, I'd better get you something to eat," Marushka said. She summoned Tamara and instructed her to go to the church and, in addition to getting some food, find out if the man had been there.

While Tamara was gone the man explained his escape. He'd been detailed to clean up a batch of S.S. uniforms, had stolen one and walked out of the camp. Then Tamara returned with word that a man had been to the church that day who fitted this man's description. As the man ate his food Marushka begged him to leave. "You're in deadly danger here," she said. "The Gestapo patrols this street every half hour. If you're caught in here, it doesn't mean just your death but mine and everyone else's." He agreed to leave if he could have some food to take with him. Later that night Marushka led him through a series of connecting cellars to an exit down the street. "For God's sake," she exploded when she returned, "from now on we don't open that door to anyone we don't know."

But the next person to come through the door was a good friend, Werner Keller, the former pilot, who now worked for Albert Speer, and what he brought with him was infinitely more upsetting than the presence of the most difficult stranger. It was word that the Maltzan family estate in Silesia had been taken by the Russians. This time Marushka could not restrain her emotions; she threw herself on the couch and cried until it did not seem possible that her body could manufacture more tears. Despite her estrangement from her brother and difficulties with her sisters, she had always felt rooted to that expanse of Silesian soil. That was where she had walked as a child with her father, examining the chestnut trees he had planted on the birth of each of his children. She had known every tree, every culvert, every brook; she had been nurtured, she believed, not so much by her mother as by the earth of this estate. Now it was gone forever.

The children watched in silence, not really understanding how or why their own Russians had caused Marushka so much grief. Hans could understand it, but he was not able to do much about it. He was certain it would do no good to point out that she had always known it would happen; this was not an event that submitted to any rational analysis.

At last Marushka stopped crying. But then she began to pace back and forth in the small living room, the Scotch terriers pacing behind her. For more than an hour she paced, the dogs always at her heel, until Hans said at last, "Please sit down." Words unspoken were conveyed in that remark: that this was land lost, after all, not lives; that there were more significant losses to mourn; that she, at least, had not had a mother exterminated by the Nazis. Marushka knew exactly what was implied, but she had neither the heart nor the strength to reply.

The next day a friend, Gregor Zivier, did it for her. He had come to console her after learning the news. It would have been evident even to a stranger that Hans and Marushka were at odds, but Zivier knew them so well he could also divine the problem. "Hans," he said, "it's not only the Jews. The Germans are suffering too. People are at the front who didn't want this war. Their families are being bombed. You can't suppose that one side is suffering and the other side has a lovely life.

Marushka has lost family too. You're not well, but look at her. She looks like death."

They sat in silence then, unable to continue, knowing that this was an argument without a winning side.

39

THE THREE MONTHS since Erik Perwe's death had been a time of almost unbearable pain and strain for Erik Myrgren as he awakened to the realities of Nazi genocide and his own responsibilities to oppose it. Even the stories told him by the distraught Jews who had stolen into the church through back alleys or during the air raids or under cover of darkness had scarcely prepared him for what he was subsequently to learn about the church's involvement in the labyrinth of clandestine work.

The young pastor of the Swedish church in Berlin had not come by the knowledge automatically. Only Erik Wesslen, the church's go-between with helpful Gestapo contacts, knew the entire story, and Wesslen's first response to Myrgren had not been open at all. He liked the young folk-singing priest well enough as a lively addition to the staff, but taking him on as a partner in the game of life and death he played each day was another matter. In Perwe, Wesslen had had a tested ally with the commitment, poise and experience to carry off his masquerade. In Myrgren he sensed a youthful, joyous spirit that had not yet been tempered by the realities of Nazi Germany, a mind that despite the accumulating evidence, still resisted the idea that such bestiality could exist in modern times. His capacity for discretion, his stamina and resources, his reserves of courage, his commitment to helping others, even his abilities and intelligence—all of these were unknowns. More than that, his knowledge of the operation was nil. Small wonder that in the days after Perwe's death Wesslen was upset and wary, and reluctant to impart secret knowledge to his successor.

And yet he would have to do it. Erik Myrgren, scarcely out of the seminary, was now the titular head of the parish, through whose authority—and only through whose authority—the operation could continue, because he controlled the supplies on which the operation existed. Those supplies were the coin of Wesslen's barter with his contacts in the Gestapo; they could not be dispensed without the parish priest's approval.

Wesslen watched Myrgren closely in those first bewildering days after news of the crash had reached them, and was, perversely, encouraged by what he saw. Myrgren's flashing smile almost vanished. The sparkle dimmed in his eyes. As he shouldered the sorrows of more and more Jews, he seemed, like a weight lifter, to gain muscle under those added burdens.

Personal factors too worked to gain Wesslen's trust. Myrgren was much closer to Wesslen's age than Perwe had been; for both young Swedes the responsibility that fell to them seemed more awesome and intoxicating than it might for older, more seasoned men. Then too their memories of Sweden were those of contemporaries. And they shared a mutual passion for botany which they indulged when they could—Myrgren, the frustrated naturalist, Wesslen, the would-be landscape architect, whose studies had initially brought him to Berlin. Together they marveled at the innate grace and natural beauty of the city that somehow survived the bombings, the lakes and parks and forests with their thick stands of birch trees so reminiscent of home. Such comparisons would catch them off guard, provoking sighs and silence and far-off looks.

But talk of home and plant life and the problems of young men was reserved—once Myrgren had gained Wesslen's trust—

for their rare, precious moments of repose. What they spoke about at their meetings in the church each morning was far more serious—the art of exchanging goods for lives.

Wesslen taught Myrgren everything that Erik Perwe had known. The young pastor learned how to swap liquor and money—both of which the church seemed to have in abundance for this work—for such provisions as gas and coal, which were needed if the church was to continue to operate. He learned how to obtain ration cards and false documents for the illegals. Using the records of Swedes born of Swedish parents in Berlin, Myrgren could literally create a past for an illegal. A Jewish woman of thirty-five came to him one day in the second month of his tenure, clearly exhausted from hiding herself for almost two years, and with no place to hide any longer. "Can't you counterfeit some kind of identity for me?" she begged.

"Oh, yes," Myrgren replied. He searched the church's baptismal records for a girl born of Swedish parents thirty-five years before. Then he made certain that neither the child nor her parents were still in Berlin. Finally he wrote out an attestation, using all the details of the former residents' histories. The woman promptly took the attestation to a district in which all records had been destroyed and received a new identity card.

Part of Myrgren's education was in learning to determine which of the persons coming to him for help were Jews and which were Gestapo plants. As a student of the Old Testament he knew an enormous amount not only about the history of the Jews but about Jewish religious practices. He was able to use this knowledge to excellent advantage. First he would ask the petitioners routine questions, such as where they were born, what their parents' names had been, and whether they practiced Judaism. Then he would ease into some simple questions about Jewish history.

One day Myrgren received a visit from a tall light-haired man who said he was an underground Jew but whom Myrgren immediately suspected of being a Gestapo agent. For fifteen minutes the pastor questioned the visitor. It was obvious from his answers that he wasn't a Jew.

"Why are you here?" the pastor asked at last.

The visitor said he had come looking for a friend; the name he gave was one Myrgren had never heard before. "I don't know him," he said.

"May I stay a while? Perhaps he'll appear."

"No, he won't. And you may not."

Much of Myrgren's knowledge of Hitler's Germany was acquired through his contact with its suffering victims. But the most graphic lesson of all came one evening at Christmas time and was delivered by a German visitor.

He came in late and unannounced, a man of fifty, with a matter-of-fact manner. He said that he had been a friend of Erik Perwe's. He owned a factory that manufactured brushes. He had many Jews working in the factory under false identities, he confided. All of them were blind. Then he came to the purpose of his visit. He told the young pastor that he had been asked to bid on a contract to provide brushes for a number of concentration camps. Not being familiar with the needs of the camps, he had asked the authorities for permission to visit them. The permission was granted, but when he got to the camps he had to content himself with interviews with the people in charge. He was never permitted to inspect the facilities. Finally at one camp he became acquainted with a garrulous sergeant, who told him what was happening. Jews were being gassed to death. Their teeth were then extracted and heated to melt out the gold. Their bones were ground for fertilizer, and their fat was converted to soap. The factory processing the bodies used up more than two hundred Jews a day, the sergeant said.

For several minutes after he had told his story the brush manufacturer sat in silence with the Swedish minister.

"Why are you telling me? What do you want me to do?" Myrgren said at last.

"I would like you to spread the word that this is happening," the brush manufacturer said. "I would like you to get word to

Sweden. Perhaps if you can tell someone, the facts will be publicized." He paused for a moment. "For whatever you can do, I thank you," he said. The he rose and left.

Myrgren did not get up. He was not certain that he could. He felt pressed against his chair by an enormous weight. He knew that a part of his life had just ended.

Half an hour passed before he forced himself from the chair. Time to start, he thought. He went into the hall to look for Wesslen. He would tell Wesslen the story. And then, between them, they would have to come up with a way to move more Jews to Sweden.

For months now, persons with any claim to Swedish identity had been petitioning the Swedish legation for evacuation to Sweden. Few of them had the necessary papers, but members of the legation staff were more than willing to give them the benefit of the doubt. They began to issue emergency passports without the legation minister's knowledge. It was only one step further to issue provisional passports to German Jews—some known personally to them, others vouched for by Erik Myrgren and Erik Wesslen—and to send these Jews, one by one, along with the Swedish-Germans, to Lübeck, where, if all went well, they would board a ship for Sweden. But the risk of discovery was great; the Nazis made random checks on the passports, and the process was maddeningly slow. Myrgren, with Wesslen's help, kept searching for opportunities to send a group of Jews out at once.

A possibility appeared in February 1945, when Count Folke Bernadotte, vice-president of the Swedish Red Cross, arrived in Berlin on a complex mission. Bernadotte hoped to persuade the Germans to let the Red Cross evacuate all Scandinavians held in concentration camps. He proposed to do this with a fleet of buses and trucks that would be shipped from Sweden to Germany. Bernadotte had a secondary objective, which was to evacuate, as well, many hundreds of German citizens of Swedish origin, most of them the wives and children of German men who had been killed or were missing in action. Some Swedish-born Germans had already succeeded in getting out, and the stories they told on their arrival in Stockholm—of air-pressure bombs that could kill people in shelters even without a direct hit; of Germans, their shoes torn away by the blasts, wrapping their feet in newspapers; of young men strung from lampposts by the S.S., with signs around their necks saying "He didn't fight hard enough," or "He left too soon"—as well as the sapped and frightened and disheveled look of the refugees themselves, had created strong public sentiment for a bolder evacuation program.

Bernadotte was a man well suited to his mission. He had the bearing and cultivation of an aristocrat, but he was at heart an unpretentious man with enormous compassion and inexhaustible patience. He was also a keen observer and, most important, an optimist who believed in human decency. He would need all of those qualities, for he would be dealing with Heinrich Himmler, the chief of the S.S. and Gestapo as well as the German police system, Minister of the Interior, Commander in Chief of the Home Army and commander of the regular German armies fighting the Russians on the Oder River front—"the man who," Bernadotte would later observe in his memoirs, *The Curtain Falls* (1945), "by means of his terror system had stained politics with crime in a manner hitherto unknown and who, by means of this very system, had up to now held the tottering Third Reich upright." Small, ascetic, with a receding chin and an enigmatic smile, Himmler was mindful of his reputation as history's most productive executioner, a fact borne out by his conversational references as well as two classical psychological signs of guilt—chronic stomach cramps and a handwashing compulsion. The second most powerful man in the Reich, Himmler was devoted to Hitler and his objective, particularly to the perpetuation of the "master race," although he himself was the physical antithesis of the model "Aryan."

Himmler's initial reactions to Bernadotte's proposals were negative. He became particularly heated when Bernadotte suggested that the Norwegians and Danes in the camps be moved to Sweden and placed under custody there. "If I were to agree to your proposal," he said, "the Swedish papers would announce with big headlines that the war criminal Himmler, in terror of punishment for his crimes, is trying to buy his freedom." He was less emotional but no less hostile in regard to Bernadotte's second proposal. "I don't feel inclined to send German children to Sweden. There they will be brought up to hate their country, and spat at by their playmates because their fathers were German." When Bernadotte pointed out that German fathers would be comforted to know that their children were safe in Sweden, Himmler replied, "Their fathers would no doubt much rather see them grow up in a shack in Germany than have them given refuge in a castle in a country which is so hostile to Germany as Sweden is."

But Himmler soon changed his mind, possibly because the idea for a negotiated peace with the West had already taken root in his mind and he saw Bernadotte as the logical go-between. In any case, he sent word to Bernadotte that Swedish women were to receive exit visas. If any of these women had been in trouble with the police and might as a consequence not receive their visas, he would personally review the matter.

Bernadotte returned to Sweden to prepare his expedition. Within a few weeks he was back again with buses, troop carriers, mobile field kitchens, ambulances and 250 volunteers. Their principal work was to move Norwegian and Danish prisoners to a camp near Hamburg, as a preliminary to evacuation, but by mid-March they were also assisting in the evacuation of the Swedish-born women and their children. In Berlin the assembly point for the operation was the Swedish church on the Landhausstrasse. In the crush of people one morning the figure of Officer Mattek was scarcely noticeable. Slowly he made his way to the church, where he found Erik Myrgren, and led him to a corner. "There's no Gestapo control today," he said softly. "If you want to send some Jews out on the buses, do it."

Quickly the pastor went to the cellar and spoke to half a

dozen Jews, one of whom, Erik Jacob, had lived in the church for a year. When the buses rolled out an hour later the six Jews were on them.

In the basement later that day Myrgren saw his friends the Weissenbergs. They had lived in the church now for nearly two years. They would have liked to be on a bus, but they were unwilling to risk the trip without papers. They did not want Myrgren to see their depression, but they weren't very good actors.

"Don't worry," the pastor said, "you'll be next. We've got a plan for you."

In mid-March the younger son of Robert Jerneitzig, the greengrocer who had befriended the Riedes two years before, contracted diphtheria. A fortnight later he was dead. Jerneitzig received a leave of absence from his unit to return to Berlin for the funeral. After the funeral he brought his wife and second son to Wittenau and informed the Wirkuses and Riedes that he was deserting.

That night Beppo and Jerneitzig burned the grocer's uniform and papers, then buried the charred remnants in a compost heap in the garden. The next day, after a restless night in the overcrowded house, Jerneitzig went to stay with a friend in Helmstedt. But two days later he was back for good.

So now Beppo and Kadi were harboring four Jews—Kurt and Hella Riede and Hella's parents, the Papendicks—and a deserter. It never occurred to either of them that there was anything else to do. They tried their best to arrange comfortable sleeping annexes in the cellar and the corridor.

March 30 was Good Friday. That morning Erik Wesslen received a telephone call from the Gestapo directing him to appear for questioning by the end of the day. He said he would come. Then he put the phone down slowly and carefully and stared at it for a long time.

He'd been expecting the call for months. Considering the

work he'd done to save Jews and others from the Nazis, it was a miracle that it hadn't come before this. He'd hoped that if and when the call did come, he wouldn't lose control. Too many people were dependent on him for him to be able to indulge his emotions. He tried now to think of his problem as systematically as he had thought through all of his rescue efforts and black market arrangements and bribing of the right people in the Gestapo and S.S. But in spite of his efforts to maintain control, he had the distinct feeling that a linchpin had been pulled from his body and it would disassemble into a thousand parts if he so much as moved.

He was still at his desk twenty minutes later when Myrgren found him. The pastor, who had just finished the regular 11:00 A.M. service, was wearing his Swedish clergyman's dress, a black gown that reached to his feet and a stiff white collar with two linen tabs hanging beneath his chin. That morning he had preached on the passion and death of Christ, citing the suffering and disasters that the wickedness of men had inflicted on all mankind. The sight of the pastor, whose work in the last four months had removed all his initial doubts, served now to release all of Wesslen's blocked emotions. Quickly he blurted his story.

Myrgren sat down heavily and stared at Wesslen. "It must be Okhardt," he said at last.

Okhardt was a young German connected with the resistance who had been sent to the church by Countess von Maltzan. Myrgren and Wesslen had found a safe house for him with the help of Reuter, the church's caretaker.

Now the two men regarded each other in silence, both of them with the same thought: What would happen if the Gestapo tortured Wesslen in an effort to make him talk? Would he? Would the church and its allies such as the countess and all of the Jews and other refugees sequestered in homes around Berlin be exposed so late in the game, when it was almost won? Four months earlier it had been the pastor's courage that Wesslen had questioned. Now it was his own. Suddenly he was shaking. "I'm finished," he said softly.

Myrgren shook his head. "You have no reason to be afraid," he said. "The war will be over soon. The Gestapo's too busy. They'll never get around to you. Just don't go."

40

DEATH WAS EVERYWHERE NOW. Bodies lay in doorways after every raid, dragged there by survivors. Hours later burial details would appear to cart the bodies off, not to graves but to funeral pyres. There were too many dead for graves.

Each day there were stories of more deaths in the newspapers, but Hans and Marushka read the stories with the same sense of resignation with which they might read of an increase in the price of bread. They had passed the point of feeling—or so they thought, at least—until word reached them that Irmelin, Brumm's fiancée, had been killed in an air raid.

She had stood the war so much better than all of them that her death seemed particularly unjust. She had never complained of discomfort, never broadcast her fears. She'd been the one they'd always counted on to walk the dogs or run the countless errands that neither one of them could do—Hans because he was hiding and Marushka because she was working. All she had asked in exchange was to be part of the household when Brumm was in Berlin. Now they could not imagine Brumm's presence without his exquisite fiancée, so wise beyond her years. Seeing their love had measurably strengthened their own belief that a future existed for them all. Now that belief had been assailed and—for days after they heard the news—all but destroyed.

Once, after their baby had died, Marushka had argued to Hans that every life, no matter how brief, had a purpose. As senseless as Irmelin's death seemed, it did soon fill Marushka with a sense of purpose. Brumm had been wounded again—a piece of shrapnel had lodged in his hand—and evacuated to an overcrowded military hospital near Berlin. Marushka was determined that her nephew would never fight again. She went to the hospital and looked up the chief medical officer. "I have a proposition to put to you," she told him. "Let me take my nephew back to my flat. I'll tend to his wound, and you'll have a free bed." The doctor was delighted. As soon as Brumm was in the flat Marushka infected the wound with a culture from a diseased animal. Then she carefully rebound the bandage. Within two days Brumm's hand was so swollen that he could not have possibly handled a weapon; it would be weeks before he would be fit for duty again, and by then, presumably, the war would be over.

Certainly the final scene of the tragedy seemed about to be performed. The Yalta Conference had just ended. It was no secret in Berlin that Roosevelt, Churchill and Stalin had pledged a final coordinated attack on Germany from all sides. In the east the Russians had already penetrated the Reich. In the west the Americans and British had launched their massive assault on the Rhine. There was no doubt whatever about the outcome of the tragedy. It was evident from everything that had gone before that Hitler would fight to the end, regardless of the cost. Berlin would be defended, and Berlin would be destroyed.

For the thousands of helpless Berliners the one overriding task was to avoid being destroyed with their city.

Her success in keeping her nephew out of further combat emboldened Marushka to try to help a number of acquaintances who, for one reason or another, had avoided the draft but were now being called up for the defense of Berlin. In her practice she had frequently used a somewhat unorthodox treatment for restoring the paralyzed limbs of animals. The animals were deliberately injected with a serum designed to produce jaundice. The jaundice produced a high fever, which spread through the body; that, in turn, caused blood to flow to the fevered parts. It was the flow of blood that restored the limb, and once that happened the jaundice could be cured. Why not induce jaundice in her friends, Marushka asked herself. A number of them agreed to the plan. For good measure she gave them a second injection to induce diarrhea and vomiting.

Some days later a doctor she knew stopped Marushka on the street. "There's the damndest bug running around," he told her. "High fever, symptoms of jaundice—God knows where that came from—accompanied by diarrhea and vomiting. We're seeing it only in men—and two days after we've cured them they're sick again."

"Odd," Marushka said,

And then one day a small and sickly-looking German in his thirties came to see her at the flat. He had a heart condition that had kept him out of the service, he explained, but now he was being conscripted along with everyone else. He'd heard about the injections she'd been giving. He was afraid to take those because of his heart condition, but could she possibly break his arm?

"I'd really prefer not to do that," Marushka said.

"I want you to do it," he insisted.

Marushka sighed. "As you wish," she said. She drew a chair next to the stove, sat him down and tied him so that he wouldn't fall. Then she put him out with a dose of ether. Next she placed two bricks on the stove, and then placed his left arm so that his elbow rested on one brick and his wrist on the other. Then she took an axe and hit his forearm with the dull end. Nothing happened. She swung again, and again nothing happened. She knew what was wrong; she wasn't swinging hard enough; she couldn't bring herself to inflict that kind of pain on a human being.

Out came Hans, wearing his dressing gown and pajamas.

"Here, let me do it," he said. He picked up the axe and raised it over his head.

Marushka screamed. "Not with the blade, you idiot."

Startled, Hans checked his swing. He looked first at Marushka, then at the axe, then back at Marushka, a sheepish look on his face.

Marushka put a hand to her heart. Then suddenly she laughed. In a moment they were both laughing so hard that they had to lean against the wall.

At last Hans gave the man's arm a whack with the dull end of the head. "I think you've cracked it," Marushka said. When he awakened he thought so too. He couldn't have been happier.

There was a small farewell party in the cellar of the Swedish church on the night of April 10. The guests of honor were Martin and Margot Weissenberg, who, after hiding in the church for two years and one month, were to fly to Stockholm the next day as Martin and Margot Berg, citizens of Sweden—provided their passports passed the controls at the airport. The Weissenbergs were jumpy, which was why Erik Myrgren had organized the party. He played his lute and sang songs, hoping to calm them down. It helped, but not enough. It was obvious from the faraway look in their eyes that their minds were on the following morning, when they would be putting their lives on the line.

The lives of those who had conspired to make the journey possible were equally at risk. It was Erik Wesslen who had begun the arrangements in mid-March, when it became easier to get passports from the Swedish legation. The affair had been handled through a junior member of the legation, supposedly without the minister's knowledge. Yet even Wesslen wasn't certain whether the minister knew. The passports had come through the week before. There remained the problem of travel permits. They'd asked Officer Mattek from the police station across the street if he could help. "I'll try," he said. A few days later he appeared with the permits. He'd gotten them from "a friend," he said with a little smile. He wouldn't say more.

Myrgren played and sang late into the night. Finally he put his lute aside and, motioning the Weissenbergs closer, he said softly, "Look, I'm positive it will succeed. Things are much easier now. We have good contacts at the airport."

In spite of Myrgren's efforts, the Weissenbergs did not sleep well that night. Early the next morning Myrgren, Wesslen and the Weissenbergs drove to the Tempelhof airfield in the church's car, a DKW. It was the first time the Weissenbergs had been outside the church in more than a year. The daily Allied bombings had been as much a part of their lives as anyone else's, but there was no way they could have imagined the devastation that had been wrought. As they drove the four kilometers through Schöneberg to the Tempelhof airfield, passing street after street of gutted buildings, Martin Weissenberg could only say, over and over again, "My God! My God!"

There was almost no traffic, but their pace was maddeningly slow nonetheless because the streets were clotted with fallen trees, rubble and wrecked cars. Twenty minutes passed before they reached the field. Inside the terminal they found Helje Klintborn, the twenty-eight-year-old Berlin representative of ABA, the Swedish airline. Without a word Martin Weissenberg handed their documents to Klintborn, who took them to the police. Then the two Jews and two Swedes went off to the center of the big terminal building and waited, trying without much success to make small talk. Erik Myrgren smoked one cigarette after another.

Ten cigarette butts were lying at his feet when Klintborn emerged from the control office. He smiled lightly and waved the documents at them. Somehow they all managed to hold back their tears. But when the flight was called, they all embraced. Then Klintborn took the Weissenbergs on board.

After the takeoff the Swedes waited in the airport until they could no longer see the plane.

•   •   •

At sundown on April 16 Fritz and Marlitt Croner stood before a table on which stood a single glass of wine and a plate of boiled potatoes. There was no parsley or lamb bone or bitter herbs or any of the other symbolic foods used by the Jews for the last three thousand years to celebrate the Passover. Nor, for the first time, did they have any matzoh, the unleavened bread that the Jews had carried with them into the desert in their hurried flight from Egypt; the supply that the Croners had retrieved from their apartment on Christmas Eve of 1942 had been finished the previous year.

It didn't matter. Both Fritz and Marlitt felt a closer kinship than they ever had before with the ancestors who had struck out against such odds in search of the Promised Land. As Fritz opened the haggadah and began to read the prayers, each word somehow seemed to be telling not only the story of the Exodus but of their own flight to freedom as well—a flight that had begun in December of 1942 and was now in its twenty-ninth month, a flight in which, like the Jews fleeing Egypt, they had been pursued not only by the enemy but by their own paralyzing doubts. Now, believing that their deliverance was imminent, they prayed:

> *Blessed art Thou, Lord our God, Ruler of the universe, that Thou hast given us life and sustenance, and brought us to this season.*

41

FOR NEARLY TWO YEARS Ruth Thomas had been accepted as an "Aryan." At a client's house on April 20, 1944, as she was fitting a dress, she'd even been offered some wine and asked to join the others in a birthday toast to the Führer. But since the day she had fled her catcher she had never walked the streets without searching the crowd for his face—or for any eyes directed at her, for that matter, eyes that might belong to other Jewish turncoats. Now, in mid-April 1945, the prospect of exposure as a Jew, forbidding as it was, paled before the new crisis that confronted Ruth and Mother.

They were running out of food.

For weeks they had been rationing their remaining supplies, eating so little that they both felt weak and dizzy. Try as she might, Ruth could not keep herself from thinking about food and plotting ways to get it. Each day that the jaws of the Allied vise closed in on Berlin, the center of Ruth's universe, her stomach, seemed to constrict as well. Their supply of food could not last another two days. And even if they were miraculously to find food for sale in Berlin, they were without money to buy it. All of the valuables they had carried away with them the night they went into hiding were gone, sold long ago to raise money for the purchase of black market food. To the east, the Russians had reached the Oder River, thirty miles from Berlin. To the west, the Americans were approaching the Elbe River, fifty miles from the city. At the rate the Allied armies had been advancing, they could be at the outskirts of Berlin within a week. But so far as Ruth knew, the city itself was a fortress. It could be another two months before the war would end. After all they had surmounted—thirty months of hiding in the very stronghold of their enemies—how ironic to die of starvation.

There was only one recourse: to go to the farm owned by the parents of Hilde Hohn, the S.S. officer's wife who had taken her in when she'd first gone underground. It was a recourse, however, fraught with danger. The farm was near the Elbe, at the other end of a no-man's-land blasted daily by bombs.

Hilde refused to go. She was petrified by the bombs. The raids on Berlin were bad enough, but at least there she could go to a shelter before the bombs began to fall. If she made the trip, she would have no certain shelter and no advance warning of the raids.

But someone would have to go or all of them would starve. Hilde looked at Ruth. "Will you do it?" she said. "If you'll do it, I'll get the tickets."

"I'll do it," Ruth said.

Herr Barsch, Hilde's father, didn't want Ruth to go alone. He could not conceive of a woman making that trip by herself—a Jewish woman least of all. The police frequently boarded trains to look for deserters and underground Jews. Herr Barsch offered to accompany Ruth. They agreed to meet at the Bahnhof Zoo.

That day the British came over and dropped hundreds of bombs. A Luftwaffe officer Hilde knew took Ruth to his shelter. Hilde arrived with the tickets, some money and a special request that she nervously confided to Ruth. She had no way of knowing for certain, she whispered, but she had a premonition that her husband would be turning up soon in Berlin. If he did, his S.S. officer's uniform meant certain death. His only chance to survive was by passing as a civilian. Would Ruth bring back a business suit of her husband's as well as some old civilian identity papers?

What an irony—helping to save an S.S. officer's life! But Ruth said nothing to Hilde, because she herself would not be alive if Hilde hadn't helped her.

As soon as the all clear sounded, the officer took Ruth to the Bahnhof Zoo. She wasn't surprised when Herr Barsch didn't appear. She decided to go alone.

Bedlam awaited Ruth in Stendal, the first stop on her journey. The town had just been hit hard by the bombers. The waiting room of the station was so jammed with people trying to get out of town that Ruth could scarcely move. The power lines were down and there was no electricity. The room was lighted by candles, which cast a drab light over the people and made them seem like ghosts. A soldier standing next to Ruth asked her if she was hungry. When she said that she was, he gave her an apple and some bread. At last she found a space to rest next to some exhausted children. Lying there, munching her food, watching the ghostlike people, Ruth thought of how God had caused the waters of the Red Sea to close over the Egyptians after he had parted them for the Jews. Throughout her ordeal she hadn't prayed, but a line from Exodus now leaped to her mind: "The horse and his rider hath He thrown into the sea."

Then another fleet of bombers came over the town and began to drop its cargo. The station emptied swiftly. Ruth left with the others, not so much because she feared the bombs but because she was less likely to be detected as long as she stayed with the crowd. Besides, she was sure there would be no train going from Stendal that night.

She walked to the main road and waved down an army truck. The driver took her a few miles along the road. Then she hitched a ride on a horse-drawn cart. It had been hours since she'd had anything to eat. She went to the restaurant in the next town and told the manager that she had money but no ration cards. The manager served her some soup.

Finally the train for Werben came. She boarded, and the train set out. But they were scarcely out of town when the bombing started again. The train braked so abruptly that the passengers were thrown violently forward. They fled to the woods, Ruth with them. As the planes made their bombing runs Ruth prayed, "Dear God, don't let them hit the locomotive."

She was not in the least worried about herself. The bombs didn't bother her, and never had. Had she not been practically forced to go into a shelter during air raids, she would have gone for walks. "These bombs are not meant for us," she and Mother always told each other. It was a horrible kind of positivism, but it worked.

Once again her prayers were answered. She boarded the train, and was soon in Werben. From there she walked the rest of the way to the farm.

Frau Hohn, Hilde's mother-in-law, was overjoyed to see Ruth. She said she'd been praying to her saint for Ruth's safety. She put Ruth, now clearly exhausted, to bed. When Ruth awakened, Herr Barsch was there. He'd caught the same train from the Bahnhof Zoo but had been unable to find her. His own journey had been as hazardous as Ruth's, and he was visibly upset.

All that day, as Ruth rested for the return journey, Frau Hohn argued strenuously against the trip. The Americans would reach them any day, she pointed out, and when that happened, the war would be over for them, regardless of what happened in Berlin. The battle for Berlin would be the worst one of the war, she was certain. If Ruth returned, she could be killed in the fighting or by the bombs. If neither of those things happened, she might eventually starve to death. At the very least, she would be raped by the Russians. "The Russians won't let even a mouse out of Berlin alive. Wait for the Americans," Frau Hohn counseled.

Her advice gave Ruth no comfort. For weeks the *Völkischer Beobachter* had been filled with headlines about the savage treatment of German women by Russian troops. A seventy-year-old woman raped. A nun ravished twenty-four times. Ruth had no illusions about those headlines; she was sure they were fabrications. Still, the subject had been raised frequently among the women in whose homes she sewed. The specific word "rape" was never used; the women always referred to "it." Surely "it" had happened to German women along the conqueror's path. Surely these conquerors had in mind the treatment accorded their women during the invasion of Russia by the German Army. And even assuming she could successfully avoid "it," how was she to survive? There was another rumor abroad in Berlin: when the Russians arrived they would seize all available food and starve the Berliners for two months.

But even if the rumors were true, even if Frau Hohn's advice made infinite sense, Ruth couldn't accept it. She could not let her mother starve or face the Russians alone. "We've made it this far together," she said. "If we have to die, we'll do that together too."

That night there was no train for Berlin, so Ruth and Herr Barsch were forced to wait another day. They left the following night, with bags of food strapped to their backs and bundles in their arms. They had mutton, chicken, bacon, eggs, potatoes, onions and flour—the kind of food that hadn't been seen in Berlin for months. The flour was full of sand from the grinding stones, but it would more than do.

They took the train to Goldbeck, where they were told it would not go any farther. They walked to the road and stopped an S.S. truck loaded with hay. Herr Barsch sat on the hay. Ruth sat with the driver. Aircraft flew above them shooting tracers, but Ruth had no idea whose they were. Suddenly what she thought was lightning flashed across the sky. She turned around and saw more lightning. "Is that a thunderstorm?" she asked.

"No," the driver said. "Those are the Americans."

So they were that close. It was true. All she had to do was wait and she would be in an American-occupied zone. Thousands of Germans were on the road, walking west, toward the Americans.

By the time the truck arrived in Stendal the town was nearly empty. There was no train. Soldiers advised Ruth and Herr Barsch to flee to the west. Herr Barsch turned to Ruth. "What are you going to do?" he asked.

"Go to Berlin."

Barsch shook his head. "I'm staying. The Americans will be here soon. Then the war will be over for me."

They said goodbye. Ruth walked out to the road and tried to hitchhike. But no vehicles stopped. Finally she stepped into the path of an oncoming truck. "If you hadn't been good-looking I wouldn't have stopped," the driver said when she got in.

The truck was carrying munitions. It stopped at an armaments depot just outside Berlin. Ruth hailed another truck, which took her to Charlottenburg. As she got down from it she spotted a pay telephone. Why not, she thought. I've been lucky this far. Perhaps the phone will work. It did. Any doubts she might have had about her decision to return to Berlin vanished the moment she heard the joy in her mother's voice.

It took her two hours to reach Pankow. She could not believe the devastation. Buildings crumbled. Trees uprooted, lying across the streets. The streets strewn with brick and pocked with craters. People moving slowly, their hair gray from the dust of crumbled brick and plaster, their bodies sagging, their faces drained by fatigue.

It was growing dark. Ruth had no idea where she would find Hilde at this hour. She would try in the morning. There was something she had to do first. Throughout the return journey she had been sustained by the thought of what she would fix to eat as soon as she returned home. She'd decided on dumplings cooked with bacon and onions. And that was exactly what she began to prepare within two minutes after she stepped in the door.

But just as Ruth finished cooking, the air was filled with a terrible sound. Hissing and howling, Russian artillery shells rent the air overhead and hit their targets with such force that neighboring buildings shook. From the streets came the terrified screams of pedestrians caught in the sudden bombardment.

Her mother's eyes grew so wide they seemed to fill half her face. "Come to the basement," she cried.

"No!" Ruth said.

Her mother looked at her in astonishment.

"I'm going to eat my dumpling," Ruth said. "I've spent two days and three nights going for this food, and now I'm going to eat it."

For a second Mother regarded Ruth as though she were seeing a madwoman. Then, without another word, she rushed out of the apartment and down the stairs. Ruth took her plate to the window and ate her dumplings as she watched the flashes from the guns in the distance and the shells explode on Pankow.

42

THE RUSSIANS had advanced to the outskirts of Berlin, but the center of the city—technically, at least—was still in German hands. During the daylight hours, however, Russian air attacks made movement impossible. Berliners driven by hunger to stand in line for food were mowed down by strafing aircraft that flew too low and moved too fast for the civilians to take cover. Whatever needed doing could be done only at night, and even then the hazards were enormous. One evening late in April, Marushka and Brumm left the flat to forage for food. All about them the city seemed to be exploding, as though a well placed shell had set off a chain reaction in a great munitions dump. Shells screamed and whistled through the sky, so filled with crisscrossing patterns of light that they could have read a newspaper. The air was so thick with smoke and the acrid smell of explosives that they could taste it, so hot from the fires that it singed their nostrils and parched their throats. An elderly woman, her dark hair turned white by plaster and dust, walked by them, as oblivious of where she was as of the blood running down her face. On the wall of a building was a splattered poster warning that those who surrendered would be shot or hanged.

Suddenly, as they approached a horse-drawn ammunition

truck, Brumm tackled Marushka chest-high and crashed with her through a door and down a flight of cellar steps. An instant later there was a deafening roar as a Russian shell hit the truck, and truck, horses and driver were blasted into small pieces.

Almost all military supplies were moved about the city by horse-drawn vehicles now because there was no longer any gas. The streets were littered with dead horses. At night many Berliners crept from their shelters, knives in hand, to cut up the horses for food. Everyone was possessed by the same idea—to stash away a supply of food in anticipation of the Russians. Once they arrived, everyone was convinced, there would be no food for some time.

Marushka did her share of butchering these days. Even with a mob about her fighting over a horse, she was at a distinct advantage. Their knives were sharp, but hers was a veterinary knife, suited to the purpose. Moreover, she knew exactly which portion of the horse she wanted, the flesh between the shoulder and the leg. One day, coming upon a group of Berliners shoving one another about, she shouted, "Don't behave like idiots. Stand quietly and let me divide the horse, and everyone will get a part."

Brumm was still in uniform. Without it he would have been dead. The S.S. patrolled the streets for deserters, shooting anyone on the spot whose papers seemed the least bit suspicious. Hans remained hidden in the house with the girls. Marushka refused to let them out; she didn't want them to see the carnage in the streets—an arm here, a leg there, heads without faces, bodies without heads.

The big task was to get ready for the Russians; to hide their valuables—Marushka put her jewelry and a gold dinnerware set into the couch, her money in ceramic pots which she then filled with grease—and to heal Brumm's hand, find him civilian clothes and get him some civilian papers so that he wouldn't be taken prisoner.

It was Tamara who came up with the great idea. "You must say he has consumption," she announced. "Russians are frightened to death of consumption. When the Russians come I will tell them that he is your nephew and that he has got consumption." Then Tamara was told to round up some handkerchiefs and spot them with eosin, a red-colored substance that looked like blood, especially when it dried.

Beppo Wirkus no longer went to work. He spent his days in the cellar of the house with the others. If a bomb dropped close to the house, he would rush upstairs to check for fires. One night four phosphorus bombs fell next to the house. He put them out as quickly as he could, praying as he worked that his silhouette would not invite some rifleman's fire. He had no idea where the Russians were, but he was sure they must be close.

The cellar wasn't large. It extended only under the kitchen and hallway. The space was so cramped that it was next to impossible for all of them to lie down at once. Most of the time they sat or reclined in camp chairs. The noise of battle above them, as well as their tension and excitement—for they all knew that the end was near—made sleeping extremely difficult. Soon all of them were punchy. Even Hella and Frau Papendick were feeling claustrophobic. The air didn't help; there wasn't enough of it to support so many people for so long a time, and it soon became rank with the smell of unwashed bodies. To add to everyone's discomfort, stomachs and bowels protested the adversity by going out of order.

And then one morning the shooting stopped.

They waited for several minutes, almost unwilling to express the joy that lay compressed in their hearts. Then Beppo led the others upstairs, and while they waited, he peered outside. Russians were walking down some nearby railroad tracks. "We're free," he cried. The others rushed outside. But their joy was premature. Polish and Ukrainian forced laborers had also been freed, and now they rushed into the town and began to plunder the stores. Beppo and Kurt looked at each other as the same thought crossed their minds. "Come on," Kurt said. They raced to the store of a man who had befriended them even though they were sure he suspected the Riedes' identity. "Leave this store alone," Beppo cried out on an impulse. "The man who owns it is a Jew."

The laborers backed off then, but instead of being grateful, the grocer rushed at Beppo. "Are you trying to get me killed?" he cried. "What if the Germans counterattack?"

"Don't worry, they won't," Beppo said.

"You're dead if they do," the grocer raged.

An hour later they did. As soon as they saw the Russians falling back, the Wirkuses, Riedes, Papendicks, and Jerneitzigs hurriedly packed a bag apiece and fled on foot in the direction of Hampstedt, six kilometers distant. None of them even tried to count the number of bodies the S.S. had strung from lampposts and trees.

After eating her dumplings Ruth Thomas had finally gone to the basement shelter. But she had been unable to sleep there and had returned to their apartment. Just before nodding off she had told her mother, "In the morning there will be no more shooting, and the war will be over."

Now it was morning, and her mother was leaning over her and shaking her awake, her eyes like two clear pools, a crazy smile on her face. "Listen!" she said.

Ruth listened to the silence. Then she leaped from bed and threw her arms around her mother. Together they hugged and danced about the room. "We made it! Mother, we made it!" Ruth cried over and over again.

Then they heard voices. Together they crept to the windows that no longer had glass in them, only shutters to cover them, and they peeked through the cracks and saw Russian soldiers standing in their back yard.

One of the strategies the women of Berlin had discussed in regard to "it"—the prospect of rape by Russian soldiers—was to make themselves appear as unkempt and old-looking as they could. But for Ruth this was no time to take such precautions. Her soul rejoiced. She ran to her dresser and took her nicest scarf from the drawer and wrapped it around her head. Then she took a white handkerchief and, waving it, danced down the stairs.

"Be careful," her mother called.

Two Russian soldiers met her at the foot of the stairs. One was fair, the other dark. Their appearance stunned her. They were tall and broad through the shoulders and chest, with thick necks supporting heavy big-boned faces. Their uniforms not only fitted them well, they seemed surprisingly clean and well kept, as though they had never been worn in battle.

In crude German the Russians demanded to know if German soldiers were hiding upstairs.

"No soldiers," Ruth said, shaking her head for good measure.

The soldiers then indicated with signs that they wanted to inspect the upstairs, and they insisted that Ruth lead the way.

Ruth's mother, watching from the landing, shouted, "Don't let them come up! Don't let them come up!" But even if she had wanted to, Ruth could not have stopped them, and, besides, as happy as she was feeling, she didn't see the harm.

In the kitchen of their apartment the fair-haired soldier pointed to his wristwatch. "Uri! Uri!" he demanded. Ruth assumed that he was asking if she had a wristwatch. She indicated that she didn't.

Suddenly the blond soldier pushed Ruth's mother into the hall and slammed the door behind her. Then the dark-haired soldier seized Ruth. "No! Not me! I'm Jewish!" Ruth shouted. She struggled free of the soldier, then scooped up the seam of her gray flannel skirt and ripped it open. Inside were her real identity papers, which she shoved at the Russian.

"Jewreka?" he asked.

"Yes."

The soldier grinned now. "Mama Jewreka," he said. She could not understand what he said next, but she sensed his message. Since his mother was Jewish, that made them part of the same family—and so it was all right if he took Ruth. Again he tried to pin her down, but Ruth fought so hard that he finally let her go.

Ruth ran into the hall. Her mother wasn't there. Then she ran to the basement. She wasn't there either, and no one knew where she was.

When even the German radio stations were acknowledging that there was fighting within Berlin, there could be only one conclusion in the mind of Willy Glaser. His first sight of a Russian soldier only confirmed the fact. Here and there pockets of resistance still kept up the fight, but Willy didn't let that stop him. He walked from one side of the shattered city to the other, certain that if God had guided him this far through the danger he would not forsake him now. The closer Willy got to Ruth Gomma's house the faster he walked, and by the time he reached her block he was running. He raced up the stairs and burst into the room without bothering to knock. He swept the startled Ruth into his arms and cried, "The Russians are here! The war is over! My name is Wilhelm Glaser!"

For weeks now Hans Rosenthal had been waiting restlessly in Frau Schönebeck's house for his long ordeal to end. For three years he had eluded the Gestapo. For twenty-seven months of that time he had lived in virtual solitude. He could scarcely contain his desire to run into the streets and embrace his liberators.

When he had removed his Star of David early in 1943 at the suggestion of Alfred Hanne, the manufacturer of canned heat, Hans had carefully hidden it among his few belongings in anticipation of this day. The night before, with shaking fingers, he had sewn the star back onto his coat. In the morning he heard tanks on the asphalt roads. He crept from his house, crawled to the street and looked through the bushes, only to find himself staring into the cannon barrel of a Russian tank. "Don't fire!" he shouted. He pulled a white handkerchief from his pocket and waved it frantically. Then he stood and raised his hands and watched the Russian soldiers come forward. It was the longest moment of his life. Only in that interminable moment did he realize that, although he had made it to the end of the war alive, he could be killed by Russians.

"*Jude! Jude!*" he shouted. "*Ich bin Jude!*" He was sweating and trembling.

The Russian soldiers apparently understood that much German. But they shook their heads and trained their guns on him.

Just then a Russian officer rode up on a bicycle. "What's the trouble?" he demanded. He listened to the troops, all the while staring at Hans's star. At last he approached. "You're a Jew?" he said in German.

"Yes!" Hans said.

"Say the *Sh'ma.*"

A gasp of relief escaped from Hans. "*Sh'ma Yisroel adonoy elohenu adonoy echod,*" he recited as forcefully as he could.

The major turned to the troops. "He's a Jew," he announced.

The soldiers smiled. They nodded. Then they shouldered their rifles.

The Russian officer, a major, turned back to Hans. "These soldiers are from a division that found many S.S. who had sewn on Jewish stars. They had orders to shoot them all."

Later that morning Officer Mattek decided that he had better have a look into the church to see how his friends were doing. As he was crossing the street from the police station to the church a grenade exploded at his feet and tore his legs off. He died before anyone could reach him.

By evening the Russians had reoccupied Wittenau. The four couples and two children returned to the Jerneitzig house. When Beppo went into the kitchen the following morning he saw a Russian in the garden with a sack over his shoulder. When the Russian saw Beppo he made signs for him to open the gate. Beppo did and the Russian left. When Beppo turned around he realized that the hens were gone.

He could not be bitter. Let him have them, he thought, as he savored the first silence he had heard in months.

An hour later the bell rang. "I'll go," Herr Papendick said. He had learned Russian as a soldier during World War I. He walked to the gate now and spoke to the Russian soldiers there.

"Are there any German soldiers hiding in this house?" one of them demanded.

"No. We are Jews here. The Germans in this house hid us."

The soldiers raised their eyebrows and looked at one another. Then, apparently willing to believe someone who spoke their language, they waved goodbye and moved on.

Later that day the Russians set up a field kitchen, from which they distributed soup with meat in it to the German civilians. Seeing this, Kadi and Hella set out to get their allotment. On the way back they spoke with a Russian officer whose German was flawless. He told them that the red flag was flying from the Brandenburg Tor. He said there was a rumor that Hitler had burned to death in his bunker. He had been to the bunker, the Russian said, and had seen the bodies of the Goebbels family. Frau Goebbels and the children looked very peaceful, as though they were asleep. It was very sad, the Russian said.

In one inconceivably calamitous moment the most joyous of days had been transformed into a nightmare. Her mother was suddenly, inexplicably lost. Ruth Thomas could feel the waves of hysteria cresting, then crashing in her body.

The basement was filled with Russians—sturdy and well nourished to a man, wearing starched and clean uniforms, orderly, businesslike, paying Ruth scant attention. She moved among them asking for someone who spoke German. At last she found an officer who did. "I've lost my mother," she cried. "Can you help me find her? For the love of God, can you help me find her?" The officer shrugged and shook his head. He explained that the Germans still held the other side of the building. He guessed that Mother must have inadvertently gotten onto the German side.

The apartment building, built on a slim triangle of land, was shaped like a ship, its narrow bow at the point where two diagonal streets converged. The two wings of the building fanned out from that point. In the basement the wings were separated by a thick wall. The Germans were holed up on the other side, and would have to be blasted out, the officer explained. He shook his head once more. "I don't think you'll see your mother again," he said.

"Oh, my God!" Ruth cried. She reached out to the officer to keep from falling. Then she saw some neighbors. "My mother! Have you seen my mother?"

A woman told her she had heard someone yelling on the other side of the wall. "It could have been your mother," she said.

For Ruth the next hour was the longest of the war. She waited, helpless, while the Russians blasted the Germans from the other side of the basement. She had never been this close to fighting or gunfire in her life. The noise shook her bones. Her teeth chattered. Her body was clammy with sweat. The roof of her mouth was dry. Every explosion reverberated in her head and sent stabs of pain down her back. But the physical response was as nothing compared to the fear that her mother was on the other side of that wall, meeting the same fate as the Germans. When the fighting stopped, Ruth clambered over the rubble and, heart hammering, searched among the bodies. Mother wasn't there.

As the Russians moved on, Ruth moved with them, believing that her only chance to survive a battle that had suddenly begun to ebb and flow was to remain with the side she was sure would eventually win. Then suddenly it was quiet. Ruth left the last building in which she'd taken refuge and began to walk the streets. She could not begin to count the bodies.

She had lost all sense of time. She did not know what day it was, let alone the hour. Nor did she know where she was, or how to get back to her apartment. Even if she had known, she would not have attempted to get there. The situation was still too fluid, and, besides, what was the point of returning? Her mother was lost. What a ghastly joke! Twelve years of escalating horror, thirty months of illegality—all of this she had pulled Mother through, only to lose her on the verge of liberation.

A chill wind was blowing through the streets, pushing along swirls of brick and plaster dust. Petals from the blooming fruit trees were mixed incongruously with the dust, and the perfume from the blooms lent a fragrance to the smell of the fires, a fragrance obliterated from time to time by the smell of death.

The war seemed to have passed Ruth by. In the distance she could hear the booming of the big guns, the *pat pat pat* of strafing and the popping of flak, but the area in which she was walking was calm, for the moment at least. Some of the Russians were setting up their bivouacs in abandoned yards, under the blooming fruit trees. She could hear their voices and their clanging mess kits and, far in the distance, a melody from an accordion.

Exhausted, Ruth crept into an abandoned house and hid under a bed, where she promptly fell asleep. When she awakened she had no idea how long she'd been there. She felt faint from hunger. When she could stand it no longer she ventured into the street.

Several miles away, the city was on fire. She thought it must be the center of the city, where Hitler's bunker was located. The city center was southwest of Pankow, she knew, so now she had a better idea of where she was. Some Russian soldiers gave her some food. When she had finished eating she returned to the house and hid again, making certain that no one saw her enter.

In the morning it was so quiet that Ruth could hear a water pump handle squeaking somewhere nearby. She peeked out a window. The street was filled with people, all of them with white bandages and handkerchiefs wrapped around their arms. They looked gray and wrinkled and tired beyond remedy.

Ruth left the house and began walking in the direction of the fire she had seen the night before, which still cast a pink glow against the grayness of the sky. Her slow gait did not even quicken when the surroundings began to look familiar.

At last she reached her apartment building. It took her several minutes to mount the five flights of stairs. Beaten, defeated, she opened the door and walked inside.

There sat her mother.

A sob escaped Ruth's lips. She rushed to her and embraced her and let her tears cascade. When at last she quieted, her mother explained: She'd gotten lost, but had returned to the apartment the moment the battle ended, and had been waiting there ever since.

In the distance they could hear the fighting, but for Ruth and her mother the war was finally over.

They all heard the clumping boots at the same time. Some soldiers, two at least, had entered the courtyard, and now they were mounting the stairs. Hans rose at once and was about to speak when Marushka put a finger to her lips. She went to the drawer of her writing desk and got her pistol, the one given her by Borker, the racist army major. Hans came over. "Let me go," he whispered.

Marushka shook her head.

"Then wait until Brumm gets back," Hans insisted.

Again Marushka shook her head. Brumm had gone out two hours before to look for food. By the time he returned—if he returned—the soldiers upstairs might have gotten them all killed. "I'll get the Polish boy," Marushka whispered.

She crept up the stairs to the bombed-out flat in which the Polish family had taken shelter and found the boy. He was not more than sixteen, but he was big and strong and not at all afraid. She motioned for him to follow her.

They found the soldiers in a corner of the building, setting up a machine gun post. With all the firing going on, their own footsteps could not be heard. When they were two feet from the soldiers Marushka shouted, "Throw up your hands." The soldiers were too startled to do anything but that. "Now turn around," she ordered. They did. They were S.S. men, both of them in their early twenties, with blond hair and nice features. "I'm not going to have this house shot up. I'm just not going to have it," she told them. "I'll give you your choice. You can give me your weapons and your uniforms and stay with us, or you can be shot right here and now. Which will it be?"

"You can't give up!" one of them shouted back. "You can't win the war if you give up!" The other nodded his agreement.

"You stupid idiots, the war is lost. Now come on and make up your minds."

For another moment the soldiers struggled with themselves. Then simultaneously their bodies seemed to be drained of adrenaline and their faces to show relief, as though someone had forced them to a decision they had wanted to make but had been incapable of making alone. Marushka and the Polish boy marched them to the cellar, took their uniforms from them and locked them up. The Polish boy took the uniforms to the courtyard and burned them.

An hour later the first Russian came walking up the street. He was carrying a light-colored sun umbrella. A moment later another soldier appeared, and then the armored vehicles. All of them—including Brumm, who had sneaked back into the house with some bread he had managed to find—stood at the boarded-over window and looked through the cracks.

"Let me go out," Tamara said. "I'll talk to them."

"I'll go with you," Marushka volunteered.

In the street Tamara strolled up to one of the tanks. "Hello," she called out in Russian. "I'm a Russian child." Heads popped from the tanks. "I'm staying with good German people. They're against Hitler."

One of the Russians called back to a comrade, who turned and called to another. "They're getting an officer," Tamara explained. He came forward in a moment, a tall man in his early thirties, an incredulous look on his face. Tamara repeated her story. The officer said something to the soldiers. Several of them dismounted with cans of food in their hands.

There was nothing for Marushka to do but invite them in. "This is my adopted father," Tamara explained as Hans came forward. "He is a Jew."

And then Brumm came in from the bedroom. At the sight of him the soldiers stirred. "And this is the nephew of my mother," Tamara said quickly. "He's got consumption." As if on cue, Brumm began to cough into a spotted handkerchief. To a man, the Russian soldiers all drew back. "My mother was frightened that if she sent her nephew to a sanitarium, the Nazis would kill him. So she kept him home," Tamara added quickly.

The Russians seemed satisfied with that explanation and turned their attention to their breakfast. Besides the meat they had brought loaves of black bread. While Marushka made tea a Russian excused himself and returned a few minutes later with a bottle of brandy. The Russians refused to drink. Marushka drank a tumbler straight.

Fifteen minutes later the Russians left. The girls ran to Brumm and danced him around the room and then out into the kitchen. Hans and Marushka stood alone in the living room. For a moment neither of them spoke.

"It's over," Hans said at last.

"Come on," Marushka said, "let's go out on the street." She hesitated. "But first shave off that horrible beard."

Laughing, Hans went off to the bathroom.

For twelve days Fritz Croner had hidden in the cellar storage room of the flat at Bayerische Strasse 5, carefully rationing out the bottles of boiled water he had put up for this period, quietly sneaking into the garden each night to relieve himself. Not once had he gone to his flat, or even to the basement shelter used by Marlitt, Lane and the other tenants, for fear he might be caught by the military patrols looking for deserters, or by his eventual liberators, who, despite his protests, might shoot him as a Nazi.

Nor did these possibilities represent the only danger. The focus of the fighting was the Olivaer Platz, not fifty meters from their building. The explosions of bombs and shells rocked the building. Snipers were everywhere, shooting at any form or movement suddenly visible through any window.

Fritz spent the days sitting or lying on a mattress he had dragged into the cellar storage space two weeks earlier. He existed on canned food and the boiled water he had put up in fifty bottles. At night he crept into the small garden in the back of the building, where, in other times, the women of the building had hung their laundry to dry. One night he found twelve dead Germans lying on the grass.

And then, one morning at last, Fritz was awakened by silence. For almost an hour he waited, not trusting his senses. Finally he crept up the cellar steps and, scarcely daring to breathe, went cautiously outside and stood on the steps of the building. There were Russians in the streets. Without taking his eyes from the soldiers he silently said a prayer. Then a Russian, obviously an officer, approached. "Soldiers?" he said in German, pointing into the building.

"No," Fritz said. "Only an old man." He did not know if he was understood, but he went on. "I am a Jew. I want to thank you." The Russian shook his head and shrugged; he obviously didn't understand. So Fritz repeated the words he had found in a Russian-German dictionary in anticipation of this moment. "I am a Jew," he said in German.

The officer shook his head, and now he spoke in broken German. "No. Jews. Germany. Dead."

Carefully Fritz raised a hand to his shirt and unbuttoned it. Then, slowly, he reached beneath the shirt and pulled out his undershirt, to which he had pinned his Jewish identity card— once again, in anticipation of this moment.

The officer looked at the card incredulously. "You're really a Jew?" he said suddenly in Yiddish.

"I told you so," Fritz said when he had recovered from his astonishment.

The Russian grinned at him. He reached into his pocket and pulled out several watches. "Here," he said, handing a gold one to Fritz, "have a watch."

Then Fritz turned and walked swiftly back into the building and down to the shelter. "The Russians are here," he announced to the other tenants.

Fritz took Marlitt and Lane immediately to the flat. They hid there for several hours, hoping that if the Russians came looking for women, they would find what they wanted in the cellars and not bother looking in the flats. But there were no longer any Russians in the streets when Fritz finally peered outside, only dead and dying German soldiers and dead and dying horses.

At last Fritz opened the window. A warm and fragrant breeze immediately flowed into the room. Lane came over to the window. "Oh, Uncle Fritz, it's so nice outside," she said.

Fritz put his hands on Lane's shoulders and turned her to him. "I'm not your Uncle Fritz," he said, his voice breaking with emotion. "I'm your father. From now on you can call me Papa."

Lane thought for a moment, and then she nodded. She did not seem in the least surprised.

They waited for another hour, watching the sunny street. There was no movement and no sound, except for an occasional low moan from a dying man or horse. At last Fritz said to Marlitt, "Let's go. I want to show people that we're living. I want to tell myself that we're free."

They walked from the building and into the street and then down the street, stepping around the bodies, Fritz on the right, Marlitt on the left, and Lane between them, holding onto their hands.

AFTERWORD

ON LIBERATION DAY, Fritz Croner made a pilgrimage to the apartment of Frau Kosimer, his "Catholic" benefactress, to thank her once again for hiding him and his family the night they went underground, only to learn that she herself was a Jew who had lived on false papers throughout the war.

On May 4, 1945, two days after the fighting had stopped in Berlin, Russian troops set fire to the Swedish church on the Landhausstrasse. Erik Myrgren, Erik Wesslen, Vide Ohmann and other members of the church staff spent the next several weeks in the Swedish legation alongside the Tiergarten and were then evacuated to Sweden via Russia.

In mid-May several Russian soldiers seized Tamara Geroschewicz, the thirteen-year-old Russian ward of Hans Hirschel and Countess Maria von Maltzan, dragged her to a bombed-out flat above the countess' apartment, and raped her. Alerted by Lucie Geroschewicz, Tamara's younger sister, the countess summoned a passing Russian officer, who accosted the soldiers as they emerged from the building. The soldiers were quickly arrested, tried and executed by a firing squad.

Within the month Makarow, the white Russian who had befriended Fritz Croner throughout the war, was arrested by the Russians and deported to the Soviet Union. He was never heard from again. Nor were other persons whose deportations were related in this account: Fritz Croner's parents and uncle; Hans Hirschel's mother; Ruth Thomas' husband; Kurt Riede's mother and stepfather; Wilhelm Glaser's mother; and Hans Rosenthal's nine-year-old brother.

Soon after the war ended, Wilhelm Glaser and Ruth Gomma were married, as were Hans Hirschel and Countess von Maltzan. The latter couple were divorced some years later, only to remarry each other a few years before Hirschel's death in 1975.

All of the other principals in this narrative were still alive in December 1980, and all but Joseph and Leokadia Wirkus were still living in Berlin. Hans Rosenthal, married and the father of two children, is West Germany's best known television personality, the chief of entertainment for RIAS Berlin, master of ceremonies of numerous quiz shows, and the president of a soccer team. Fritz Croner has prospered as a jeweler and devotes much of his time to lecturing to youth groups about his own experiences and those of other Jews during the Hitler era. Ruth Thomas has pursued a wide range of interests since the war, including music and design. Wilhelm Glaser is retired, following many years as a merchant. Kurt Riede, also retired, lives in Frohnau, on the northern fringe of Berlin, with his wife, Hella. They have frequent reunions with the Wirkuses, who live in Düsseldorf, where Wirkus is a civil servant. Countess von Maltzan practices veterinary medicine in a ground-floor apartment a block from the Kurfürstendamm.

One other party to this account continued to live in Berlin following the war—Stella Kübler, the "blond ghost," whose work for the Gestapo accounted for the capture of hundreds of underground Jews. In 1946 Kübler appealed to the Jewish community of Berlin for help, on the grounds that she had been a victim of the Nazis. Recognized by a number of Jewish survivors, she was arrested by the Russians, tried and sentenced to ten years of forced labor. On her release in 1956 Kübler went to West Berlin, where she was again recognized, arrested, tried and sentenced to ten years of forced labor. But the sentence was overturned on the grounds of double jeopardy. Kübler, who reportedly still lives in Berlin, maintained throughout that she had been mistaken for another catcher.

Exactly how many underground Jews were still alive in Berlin when the war ended is a matter of conjecture. In June of 1945 the Jewish community of Berlin placed the number at 1,123. But others suggest that the survivors could not have exceeded a few hundred.

Whatever the correct number, it is tempting to ask how these few—less than one percent of the number of Jews in Berlin before Adolf Hitler took power—survived when so many others did not. What special qualities linked Fritz and Marlitt Croner, Hans Hirschel, Ruth Thomas and her mother, Anna Rosenthal, Wilhelm Glaser, Kurt and Hella Riede, and Hans Rosenthal? The answer is as obscure as the question is obvious. Certainly all of them wanted desperately to survive, but so, presumably, did all the Jews who perished. And certainly all of them had faith that they would somehow prevail in spite of the inhuman struggle that confronted them—but they were not the only Jews to have such faith. "Those who survived said they believed they would, and this belief undoubtedly sustained them," Hans Rosenthal reflected in Berlin in 1978. "But how many of those who perished also believed they would survive?"

There are, however, two questions that can be asked more profitably. The first is why the principals in this story did not leave Germany before it became impossible to do so. The second is why they elected to remain in Germany after the horror had ended. The questions are not unrelated.

The decision to leave Germany after the advent of Hitler would seem an easy and obvious one now, but the prospect of abandoning one's traditions, relationships and possessions for the hazards of a foreign land and tongue, with little or no capital to begin life anew, could not have seemed attractive at the time. So there were compelling reasons for the Jews in Germany to deny reality—either refusing to believe that the Nazis represented an enduring menace or that they themselves were vulnerable. Somehow they would be spared, many Jews believed, either because they had good contacts or simply as a consequence of luck. By the time reality had overpowered even these considerations, it was too late. The Germans would no longer let them leave.

Was there some other element influencing those who remained? After four years with this material I am unable to dismiss the thought that it was desperately important to these survivors to affirm that they were something more than Jews. In Nazi Germany that was an impossibility from the first day of the Third Reich, but the need to be German in spite of everything has resonances in every Diaspora Jew. Acceptance as Germans—or Americans or Frenchmen or Englishmen—implies acceptance as Jews. For most Jews this is life's preoccupying struggle.

The Jew is loyal to his country in a way that is perhaps incomprehensible to non-Jews. He needs to belong, not so much for the privileges of membership as for the assurance that as a legitimate citizen of his country of birth or choice he is free at last to be a Jew as well.

ACKNOWLEDGMENTS

No previous book of mine has involved so many people or such generous donations of time.

I would like, first, to thank all the major figures in the narrative for their willingness to bring such a painful past back to life: Fritz Croner, Ruth Gomma Glaser, Wilhelm Glaser, Countess Maria von Maltzan, Hella Riede, Kurt Riede, Hans Rosenthal, Ruth Thomas, Joseph Wirkus and Leokadia Wirkus.

I am grateful as well to those who helped me reconstruct the involvement of the Church of Sweden in clandestine efforts to save Jews and other oppressed persons from the Nazis. The trail led from Berlin to Sweden, where I found Erik Myrgren, the pastor of the church during the closing months of the war, Vide Ohmann and Meri Siocrona, who had worked as aides of the church, and Martha Perwe, Erik Perwe's widow, who, in addition to relating the story of her husband's work, gave me his diary to use. Göte Hedenqvist, one of the pioneers of this extraordinary human salvage operation, confirmed details of the Church of Sweden's historic role. A three-part series in *Expressen,* Sweden's leading evening newspaper, in June 1945, helped to flesh out the story. One part was devoted to an interview with Martin Weissenberg less than two months after he and his wife escaped from Berlin with the church's help, when his recall of the events was fresh and keen. All of the sources connected with the Swedish church in Berlin had vivid memories of the work of Countess von Maltzan and the assistance she furnished the Jews, both on her own and in conjunction with the church.

In Stockholm, I had the additional help of Staffan Hedblom and Kjell Holm, of the Swedish Foreign Office, and of two good friends, Sven Broman, the editor-in-chief of *Året Runt,* and Trent Eglin, a young American who makes his home in Sweden. Another good friend, Gunilla Nilars, of Swedish Television, and her associate, Inger Söderman pointed me in the right directions.

In Berlin, Ilan Goldman, a talented young journalist, demonstrated incredible resourcefulness and initiative in checking through the past, and he also served as translator at all my interviews. His mounting excitement as the many stories developed reinforced my own. I am also grateful to Christa Maerker, friend and fellow journalist, to the author James P. O'Donnell for sharing so much of his knowledge of Berlin and World War II, and to Gisela Weissner, of the protocol office of the city of Berlin.

I would like to thank the staffs of the Jewish Community House in Berlin, the Wiener Library in London and Tel Aviv, and Yad Vashem in Jerusalem for their assistance and guidance. Doctor Dov Kulka, of the Department of Jewish History at the Hebrew University of Jerusalem, and his assistant, Esriel Hildesheimer, resolved many conflicts that could not be settled elsewhere.

While several dozen texts and innumerable survivors' accounts deepened my understanding of this event, one extraordinarily rich and comprehensive book was my companion throughout: *The Twelve-Year Reich: A Social History of Nazi Germany 1933–1945,* by Richard Grunberger (Holt, Rinehart and Winston, 1971).

Many times after my return from Europe I felt the need to consult with an old friend and former colleague, Tom Tugend, who is now an information officer at UCLA but whose early years of life were passed in Berlin.

I am grateful to Eric Lasher for urging me to take on a project that meant so much to him, and to my agent, Sterling Lord, for acting as our go-between. And while most writers are lucky to have the wise counsel of a single editor, it was my good fortune to benefit from the wisdom of three: Nan Talese, Tom Wallace and Catherine Shaw. The manuscript of this book also received a close and loving copy editing from Louise Lindemann.

Most acknowledgments include a traditional thank you to the author's family for their patience and understanding. In my case, I am thanking two coworkers: my wife, Jacquelyn, who helped me throughout an intensive research trip to Germany; and my son Jeff, whose gift for languages and degree in history were put to heavy use in Sweden, Israel and the United States.

L.G.